# UNITED!

## About the Author

The secretive and pseudonymous Richard Kurt is thirty-one and has been writing mainly about Manchester United since 1992; he started going to Old Trafford in 1975.

A former history and politics teacher, he dabbled in academia and the pop business in Manchester before becoming a full-time author in 1994. He also writes voluminously and monthly without fail for the top fanzine *Red Issue* but has shied away from all offers to become a 'proper' journalist, freelancing for other publications only occasionally.

A founder of the Independent Man United Supporters Association with the 'Dirty Dozen' in 1995, he has also co-produced and performed on football/pop crossover recordings for Exotica, scripted and co-produced a United video documentary and appeared as a so-called expert on dozens of national TV and radio programmes, usually bizarrely disguised.

When portrayed by some as a shadowy Mandelsonian figure in the world of Man United activists, he might smirk off the record but he is also quick to point out that he lives with young Emma, has never been to Brazil and hates Judy Garland.

He is currently spending a lot of time in Provence writing a novel and thinks that this collection of despatches might prove to be his last United-related book.

# united!

## despatches from old trafford

richard kurt

EDINBURGH AND LONDON

First published in Great Britain in 1999 by
MAINSTREAM PUBLISHING COMPANY (EDINBURGH) LTD
7 Albany Street
Edinburgh EH1 3UG

ISBN 1 84018 202 4



A catalogue record for this book is available from the British Library

Typeset in Garamond
Printed and bound in Finland by WSOY

*This collection is dedicated to the memory of the late David Hewitt, legendary bon viveur and good mate, who got me started back in '92.*

# Contents

## 1995–96



## 1996–97

# Acknowledgements

Writing about United for the best part of a decade has incurred a great deal of indebtedness to others. Once again I'd like to thank the following for umpteen varieties of help, work, wisdom, comradeship, etc. etc. Without them, I'd have ground to a halt somewhere back in 1993. Apologies if I've inadvertently missed anyone . . .

Chris Robinson, John Daniels, Andy Pollard, Andy Walsh, Peter Boyle and the K-Standers featuring 'Southy', Jim Phelan, Phil Lyon, 'Deep Throat', Pat Crerand, Bill Campbell and co., Graham Beech and co., 'Drastic', Bert Foulds, Ray Ford, 'Joolz', Tony Jordan, Mike Brennan, Dave Taylor, Carl Jordan, Tony Veys, Steve Doyle, 'Lance', Barney Chilton, Phil Holt, 'Coco', Colin Blaney, Dave Strachan, 'Red Attitude', Jamie Smith, Jason Davies, the other 'Captain' Jason Davies, *Les Mousquetaires* (Bernard Morlino, Eric Cantona, Claude Boli), Alex Ferguson, Chris Hutton, Helen Gummer and co., Julian Alexander, Andy Spinoza, Arthur Albiston, Bob Stephenson and co., Michael Crick, Richard Williams, Nick Hornby, Hunter Davies, Johnny Cigarettes, Mike Sweeney, G. Dykes, The UWS Crew (Andy Mitten, Steve Black, Joyce Woolridge, Jim White, Tony Graham), Dave Kirkwood, Andy Edwards, Alan Godwin, Adam Brown, Angelo, the staff at Central Library Local Studies Unit, Andrew Goodfellow, Ian Marshall and co., Richard Milner, Luc Zentar, CP Cheah, Paul Simpson, Richard Jones, Scott Morgan, Dave Hannighan, Paul Collier, Eamonn Roane, Jim Dickenson, 'Brownie', James Grieve, Kev Abram, Michael Nicholas, Michael Coughlan, Robbie Jones, those who wrote in to contribute to *United We Stood* and *The Red Army Years* and, of course, my family, especially *Maman* and Emma.

## Author's Note

This collection greatly expands, improves upon and definitively replaces the author's previous anthological book *Despatches from Old Trafford 1993–96* (published by Sigma Press, Wilmslow, 1995), which was mainly circulated in north-west England, is now out of print and will never be reissued.

Most of the material in this anthology has previously appeared in the following newspapers, magazines and volumes, whose publishers and editors the author duly thanks:

*Red Issue, Red News, The Independent* (London), the *Sunday Tribune* (Dublin), *FourFourTwo, Total Football, The Game, Zeitgeist, United We Stood, As the Reds Go Marching On* and *Cantona.*

Other work by the author has also appeared in the *Daily Telegraph*, the *Manchester Evening News, United We Stand* and various web-zines, as well as in the author's books listed below:

*United We Stood* (Sigma, Wilmslow, 1994)

*As the Reds Go Marching On* (Mainstream, Edinburgh, 1995)

*Cantona* (Pan/Macmillan, London, 1996)

*The Red Army Years* with Chris Nickeas (Headline, London, h/b 1997, p/b 1998)

*Don't Look Back in Anger* with Chris Hutton (Simon & Schuster, London, h/b 1997, p/b 1998)

*Red Devils* (Prion, London, 1998)

All these books are in print and should be quite easily available: you can write direct to the author c/o any of the publishers listed above or c/o *Red Issue* if you have any trouble, or if you have any other queries. Please enclose an s.a.e. Web-surfers should find up-to-date stuff at the Richard Kurt site; any engine will get you there.

# Introduction

There is a decentish justification for the publication of this anthology – apart, that is, from the need to pay off Hector for another year and thus get my prison-free sequence up to seven years. My first publishers Sigma Press and I tried something like it back in 1995 when, in authorial terms, I was barely out of short pants. It was called *Despatches from Old Trafford 1993–96* and I hadn't written enough to fill it myself, necessitating emergency transfusions of articles and cartoons from generous and accommodating colleagues and cronies. None complained about my imposition, nor that they were poorly, if at all, rewarded for their hasty endeavours. That gives you some idea of the degree to which I was your typical Young Shit In A Hurry as the footie publishing business took off with me clinging to its tail, and also some idea of the remarkably decent nature of the lads around the fanzine scene at Old Trafford.

The original collection came out in the autumn of '95. Sigma being a small (but perfectly formed) outfit, the print run was modest and distribution mainly within Greater Manchester, Lancashire and Cheshire. In any event, it was largely swamped by the attention given to my Mainstream book about the 1994–95 season which came out virtually simultaneously, got well reviewed and duly took up all the available space in many a Red Christmas stocking, leaving no room for *Despatches*. Which was largely how it should have been – that original *Despatches* didn't quite work as a publication. The fanzines were very supportive, as they always are of well-intentioned efforts by fans, and the *Total Football* reviewer gave it a four-star rave, stunning in its enthusiasm for the 'king of the zoo terracing', as it embarrassingly called me. (Lads in the pub, in mock-genuflection, made monkey noises at me for weeks afterwards.) But later I realised Scott Morgan in *FourFourTwo* had been right when he wrote that 'although the quality of much of the writing will stand the test of time, it's a bit too early for the Greatest Hits'. With only one book behind me, and barely two years into my *Red Issue* contributions, it was indeed premature. I didn't have enough gear to draw on and, as a scribbler, I was still very much in the learning stage. The book quietly sold out its print run and I filed Scott's review away in the reminder pile: I'd have another go one day when the time was right. Which, as a presumption clearly inviting a slapdown from reviewer or reader, I've decided is now.

Why? Well, millennial round-ups will be all the rage when this thing appears, I guess; I've built up a stack of books, *Red Issue* articles and other odds 'n' sods upon which to draw; the club being up for sale, whether to Murdoch or A.N. Other, marks the end of an era for us traditional fans; and I've realised, looking over all the acres I've scrawled, not only that I have developed since 1995's callow days, but that, horrendously, I don't think I'm going to develop much further as a 'football writer'. What I call 'maturity' will still strike some as being woefully childish, but there you go – if you don't like it, fuck off. (Giggle snigger.) An open goal to a critic here – 'If this is as good as he gets, then he needn't have bothered starting' – yet the small but loyal band of East Stand readers seems to have enjoyed the ride and that'll do for me. Now that I've progressed as far as I can go on this rather specialised track and written all the books I wanted to write on the subject, I'm going to follow my only true hero and quit while I'm ahead. (Possibly returning for the odd Munich memorial volume . . .) Thus Scott Morgan will surely agree with me that this is now *precisely* the correct moment for a so-called Greatest Hits.

We've concentrated here on the best of the equivalent of 'singles' rather than 'albums'; I have tried not to include more than the odd smattering of material from my other books and instead have gone mainly for very contemporary-feel *Red Issue* pieces and other periodical or newspaper articles. Even where stuff has appeared in a book, it will often have been in *Red Issue* first. Certain types of piece recur and get their own subheading: pisstakes masquerading as spoof tabloid articles, ads and announcements are a *Red Issue* staple and here form part of the mythical *Daily Spurt*, 'pages' of which are interspersed throughout; the natural fascination for the two most intriguing United personalities – Fergie and Eric – drew us repeatedly to them and means they have their own 'Gaffer Tapes' and 'King Chronicles' strands; and although *Red Issue* tends otherwise to keep away from the strait-laced 'personality profiles', believing most football people to be essentially boring and certainly less fun than the fans themselves, some nonetheless slip through to make up the 'Redheads' series. As for the provenance of the pieces, they're my *Red Issue* originals unless otherwise stated. With a bit of tarting up here or there.

Which brings me back to where we came in and the lads who dug me out on *Despatches* Mark One. The main reason for compiling both this and the original *Despatches* was to transmit to a different, more 'innocent' audience a feel of the fanzine *Red Issue* – or at least those bits for which I'm personally responsible, in the case of this particular edition. I'd been reading the top-selling United fanzine for a couple of years before I plucked up the courage to send in my first contributions in 1992 and had thus *objectively* already concluded that it was not only the most essential work a Red could read but also one of the best-realised publications in the country, hitting its targets and pleasing its readers just as well as, say, *The Spectator*, *The Sun* (ugh) or the *NME*.

Normally, a writer who also does his own books is proudest of his work as an *author*; his paper or mag is merely the rent-payer. But I would always prefer to be associated with the name *Red Issue* than with any of my books. I mean, I do think that my books are generally good – or, at least, that they largely fulfil the aims I set out for them and which my readers expect from them – otherwise I wouldn't keep inflicting them on the people in the stands around me and expecting them to cough up the excessive asking prices. I wanted to write mildly amusing, literate, post-Hornby tracts for the committed and aware hardcore Red and that's what I think I did – and the reviewers and buyers seemed, on the whole, to agree. But somehow it's not an *honour* to write books – it's too selfish and obsessive an endeavour, I suppose – whereas I *do* feel honoured to have been in the *Red Issue* first team all these years. Not just because of the quality lads who work on it – brilliantly talented and consistently hilarious cartoonists; witty, clued-up, truthful writers; an editor who doesn't realise he's part-genius – but also because of its quality core readership. You can't put one past them or teach them anything about football they don't know; they spot bullshit or posing a mile off; they won't begrudge you fulsome credit when you do well; and they'll pan you, but mercifully, when you cock up. The readers and writers understand each other in a way few publications can emulate: when *we're* on form, and *they're* up for it, the results are unbeatable. *Red Issue* at that point becomes a community, not a magazine – and for an entrance fee of just a quid. Best of all, this is almost a closed community because it's still *ours*: non-attenders would struggle to find it outside Old Trafford's environs; the hack-pack have been too lazy or too stupid to discover what would be a rich source of both stories and enlightenment to them; the sleazy, corporate ad-pound is frankly unwelcome. *Red Issue* is one of the last bits of the Old Trafford body still unconsumed by the '90s necrotitis of modernising commercialism. As such – and, admittedly, I say so from a position of *parti pris* – the continuing successful well-being of the dozen or so lads in the *Red Issue* team matters as much to me as that of the dozen in Red shirts. I believe the mag's relationship to the true spirit of the club is like the ravens at the Tower of London: if it ever goes west, you can be sure the rest will follow. But as long as there are enough of the kind of people who contribute to or buy *Red Issue* still going to Old Trafford, that'll mean there's still hope and fight left in us yet.

## *A Note about the Contents*

These days I generally write around 8,000 words a month for *Red Issue*, more if there's a big story running that gives me an excuse to indulge in three pages of frenzied speculation or slagging. I do a lot of ultra-topical stuff, especially anything involving money, politics or scandal, the epitome of which is the infamous 'Backbeat' gossip column. Little of that features herein, given its inbuilt obsolescence. I'm also responsible for a couple of running features and usually come up with some so-called comedy pieces too, plus the odd set-piece article when we get an unusual day out somewhere.

Anyway, I've selected bits of this material together with stuff I've done for magazines, newspapers and so on. I'm not saying it's all the best writing I've ever done – I suspect that a slight majority of that is in my books – but they're all pieces I still like or would be pleased to see preserved between harder covers. I've tried to choose what still reads well today and to string it all up so that it takes you through the story of United from '93 onwards, albeit in a haphazard and impressionistic fashion. This isn't supposed to be a rigid blow-by-blow account of our ups and downs, more a series of temperature checks and flashpoints. I hope that by dipping in at some random point, you'll get a sense of how we were feeling and thinking at the time – or, at least, of how I interpreted it. You might notice that my own style – ebullient, flowery and flagwaving at the immature start – gets more world-weary, cynical and maturely critical as it goes on, notwithstanding the wisecracks. No apologies for that: it reflects the journey made over the decade by every traditional Red I know. No apologies either for the fact that so much of this concerns subjects other than the actual football played by United on the park: if being a fan consisted of nothing but talking about that, the boredom would have killed the game long ago. Bitter Blues, Scouse scum and Fartin' Martin guest-star heavily, and so they should.

Enough self-indulgent rambling. If you like the book, check out the others or, better still, get yourself a sub to *Red Issue.*

RICHARD KURT
MANCHESTER, JULY 1999

# 1993–95

### *King Chronicles: Divine Intervention*

(from *United We Stood*)

As we sit back this summer basking in the glory of May, we can now recognise at precisely what moment Fate changed course and sent us forward to claim the title. Leeds had phoned Martin Edwards to enquire about Denis Irwin, amusing in itself since the Sheep had had him on their books and dumped him. After Edwards had finished laughing, Alex prompted him to ask about Eric Cantona. 'OK, then, he's yours,' says Sgt Wilko and the deal is done in a trice. A fairly ridiculous scenario to set up the most epochal transfer since Robbo's arrival over a decade before.

JFK's shooting had nothing on this. Where were you when you heard the news? Everyone can recall the shock, the joy and the pure *schadenfreude* of that moment. Manc phone lines burned hot as the news spread, whilst our Yorkie friends were paralysed by the trauma. Let us be honest: few of us had any real idea of what Eric was going to bring us; we may even have had nervous doubts. But what was undeniable and utterly delightful was the knowledge that all Leeds would be devastated beyond endurance. The savage outbreak of recrimination, despair and anger in Sheep City was wondrous to behold. This was worse than Revie's death, worse than the '73 cup final, worse than your favourite ewe giving you an STD: all that could be heard from the east was the desolate howling of the betrayed lover.

I'd seen Eric play in France and had long been convinced that he was a Gallic George Best. When he came to England, I longed for him to come to OT but knew that Alex would never countenance such a presence in the dressing-room. I despaired when he settled in Leeds and fully understood the rapture of Elland Road as he unveiled his unparalleled majesty. Leeds fans, for so long the epitome of xenophobic macho-men, became homosexual Francophiles overnight. In a way this was not that surprising. Here was a player of thrilling flair, excitement and glitter-drenched individualism who thus, as such, was totally alien to Leeds fans; it was akin to showing primitive man fire for the first time. The Sheep duly warmed their genitalia on his incandescence on the pitch, and me . . . I felt as bitter as the most acerbic of Blues.

But as it turned out, there was no marriage between Leeds and Eric, just the briefest of affairs that left the Sheep impotent and frustrated. The spotty, shaven-headed Tyke fan had been granted a few nights with Kim Basinger and had fallen hopelessly in love, only to watch in horror as she went off hand in hand with the hunk from down the road. Back to the local wildlife for Leeds; the start of a beautiful relationship for the Reds.

Why Eric left Leeds is a question shrouded in mystery and speculation. At the time, unsavoury rumours abounded which tended to refer darkly to 'off-the-field behaviour' – what *Private Eye* would term 'Ugandan discussions'. Certainly such stories kept *Red Issue* in jokes about donkeys, sex and housewives for months. When Eric's book came out, he accused Wilko of driving him out with his contradictory comments which left Eric bemused and uncertain of his standing. Wilko struck back in *The Sun*, claiming Eric had forced him to sell, and for a while legal action seemed possible. This wasn't even handbags at ten paces, more pouting at thirty miles. Frankly, who cares? The French Genius, a supposed *enfant terrible*, became Eric the Red, King of Old Trafford, and history was made. Leeds were left with piles of Cantona Christmas presents; United were left with a superstar, a title and a glorious future.

Perhaps the key to this is understanding that Eric is typically French. Anyone who's studied history knows that glory – *la gloire* – is all to the French. Just winning is not enough; it must be done with style, panache and passion. Why did the French turn out to support Napoleon in such huge numbers when he came back from exile in Elba? Because they wanted glory, even if that meant glorious defeat. How could Leeds ever hope to fulfil this genetic need of Cantona? A club whose greatest moments are only remembered by the rest of the country for their cynicism, negativity and 'efficiency'? A club whose recent title was won by default from a team they haven't beaten since 1981? A club so unused to flair or style that they left Eric on the bench more often than not? The Sheep were dreaming to think they could hold him there: Elland Road is the last place on earth for a true artist.

Of course Eric came to us – who else in Britain can claim to have elevated true glory to the highest principle of living? Where else could Eric's existential vision be realised? Eric, an Albert Camus fan, would dismiss any notion of destiny, but for those who believe in such things, how obvious it was that Eric should've ended up at the Theatre of Dreams.

*(Surely life couldn't get any better for Reds than it was in that glorious summer of '93? Erm, yes, actually. We gawped and marvelled as United put all to the sword in '93–'94, playing the best football most of us had ever seen. The soi-disant expert can analyse all the footballing reasons why we became so dominant but, in a moment of humility, one should also recognise that extra magic ingredient for which no manager can legislate – luck.)*

## ***Touched by the Hand of God***

Well, I can't think of any other explanation for something totally fundamental which has changed at United. I hesitate to say it explicitly in case whatever magic has been woven vanishes upon its discovery, but the United of '93–'94 have, at last, been blessed by Divine Luck. And the sod of it is that although the results of this heavenly intervention have made me orgasmically ecstatic over this last year, somewhere deep down I miss the old masochist angst that misfortune can bring. What a headcase.

As I write this, the past week has witnessed the following. We won an away match after a crucial pass was played to Giggsy by a corner flag. In a cup draw full of difficult potential ties, we draw the walkovers at home. Out of the blue, UEFA decide to fix the Euro Cup for the future in such a way that benefits us more than any other team. Then, best of all, for the first time in living memory English fans emerge from a bout of foreign aggro to be hailed as heroes and saints instead of Visigoths and vandals. All this in one week? How it befits the anniversary of Eric's arrival, for it was November 1992 when, as we can now appreciate, God became a United fan.

For as long as I can remember, United were always spectacularly unlucky; the Fates seemed to conspire against us in the cruellest ways. In fact, it amazes me that we ever managed to win anything even in the Busby years, so determinedly did the Almighty try to screw it up for us. In the old days, we would be allowed to charge gloriously to a dozen semi-finals of FA and Euro Cups before cocking up horrendously; a speciality was beating the best like

Benfica before being humiliated by nobodies from Belgrade or chucking away three-goal leads from home legs. That era was capped in an almost beautifully miserable way when grinning Destiny allowed City to help relegate us at Old Trafford via Denis Law's heel – how immeasurably wretched to be buried by your own King. How typically United.

I started supporting the Reds the day after that match. It seemed to me with my warped childhood mentality that any team that managed to win anything in such a cosmically hostile environment would truly be champions; the presence of a devil in the club crest struck me as being hugely apt and frankly asking for trouble since God was clearly a Scouser. As Nick Hornby points out in his classic *Fever Pitch*, there is an immense, grim satisfaction to be gained from feeling that the world is not only against your team but seems to conspire to cause you disaster at every turn. It binds your own kind together; suffering, not success, is what makes the true Red.

I can't write anything about Wembley '76 or '79 because dwelling on those losing goals makes me regress instantly to that greatest teenage trauma; no girl could break a heart like Alan Sunderland or Bobby Stokes did. But the '80s offered sufficient proof that United were a cursed club to such an extent that every other bugger in the country began to notice. How could they fail to do so when our bad luck gleefully manifested itself in every aspect of our life? Hot new signings would instantly freeze under the baleful glare of the OT lights. We would go top on a Saturday; by Wednesday the hospitals would be full of long-term injuries. The FA automatically allotted our crucial cup ties to blind officials – and TV would helpfully beam these catastrophic events live to a nation that delighted in the rank injustice of it all. 1991–92 was quintessential United; we stuff the Sheep twice, convince everyone we are the best team in the country, and yet Fate still contrives to rob us. How outrageously unlucky to lose our best player to meningitis, of all things – surely a sign that forces beyond football were at work. How statistically unlikely that four players should contract flu on the eve of the QPR game with such morale-shagging consequences. When a few months later Dion Dublin was carted off within weeks of his arrival, I honestly thought that only some sort of Faustian pact with Satan himself would give United the power to overcome this ridiculous quarter-century of cosmic piss-taking. When Eric arrived, my paranoia was such that I considered the possibility of him being a Leeds agent sent to destroy us from within. There was surely no way that he could actually turn out to be a bargain, for I knew it had been decreed many aeons ago that all other clubs set secret 'United prices' for all their players of treble their worth in an attempt to bankrupt us. Of course, I didn't realise that Eric was not as other men and that in fact he had been sent by heaven to remove the curse and to bless us with Divine Luck.

Since then we have all had our moments of revelation; mine was when he made that cracker for Irwin when his foot virtually kissed the ball to Denis – it's football, Jim, but not as we know it. The Prince of Light had arrived to illuminate our way to the Holy Grail.

And so it has come to pass that in the twelve months since his coming, the Force has been with us. The few minor reverses we have had were caused by us, not by Fate. Everything goes our way. Hated opponents disintegrate with lovely regularity. Our stars remain undimmed and uninjured. Classic goals stand unmolested by pedantic offside decisions. Our free kicks rocket home; their penalties are superbly saved. Instead of struggling to succeed against the odds, we are odds-on for the double. Amidst all this, we cling to Eric for the saviour that he is; the greatest nomad since Moses responds by nailing his future to the United banner. Could life be any more perfect?

Well, maybe . . . I have heard the first whispers of 'Lucky United' growled in Scouse and Tyke accents in the way we used to moan 'Lucky Arsenal'. It's not a label to be welcomed. Perversely I begin to yearn for that feeling of being up against it, of being persecuted, of extracting improbable triumphs from the jaws of seemingly inevitable defeat. A bit of bad luck wouldn't go amiss – as long as we still win in the end, of course. As Hornby remarks, one of the best feelings in football is to go a goal down – preferably from a blatant offside position – when the team are playing well; the sense of injustice and anticipation of an avenging fightback is fire to the soul. So of course I still want us to clinch the double at Wembley in May but I'd rather luck played no part. Let us concede two dodgy penalties and be down to ten men before we win 3–2 in injury time after fighting savagely for every yard. Now *that's* what I call United.

*(As it happened, the author's desire for a bit of ill-fated adversity was fulfilled, if a touch prematurely. The Ides of March and the first serious signs of unhinged Gallicisms threatened to derail us entirely until a becalmed Eric returned to pull it all out of the flames. By the time we got to Wembley with a second title in the bag, Lady Luck was back on*

*her knees in front of us, and keeping Peacock's first-half volleys out of the net too. Not that we had everything our way, of course. Villa prevented a treble at Wembley in March but far more aggravating had been the termination of our European Cup challenge. Galatasaray away was an unmitigated disaster all round and not an event that did much to correct the world's 'Midnight Express' view of the Turks. The serious coverage in the fanzines was excellent and a reminder of their importance at key moments; within a couple of months, in typically Mancunian style, we felt more able to take a more black-humoured view of the Ottoman onanists.)*

## Turkey-Shoot

Yes, yes, I know it was some time ago and we've all been studiously trying to forget what happened, but every time I see a Champions' League table with that dreaded name 'Galatasaray' in it, I still feel intensely aggrieved. Admittedly, on the basis of what actually happened on the pitch, they deserved to be there, but one only has to watch the pre-second-leg footage from the United video to see that the lack of proper civilisation in Turkey created such angst in the United team that what followed was scarcely sport as we know it. What they did to our fans alone merited their exclusion from the cup as a nation unfit to receive visitors.

In any case, what are Turkish teams doing in the *European* Cup anyway? Technically a small percentage of the country is in our continent, but basically Turkey is a huge Middle Eastern slavering beast that has one of its buttocks accidentally draped over the intercontinental fence. Politically and spiritually, they're nothing to do with Europe. It seems to me that they're trying to wheedle their way into Europe and the EU so they can spend the next century living off Euro subsidies whilst continuing to behave like some tinpot Third World dictatorship. United fans are not the only ones to get treated like infidel barbarians over there – witness the persecution of the Kurdish minority over the years. The rules of law, human rights and the Olympian ideal that sport should never be treated as an extension of warfare didn't appear to carry much favour in Istanbul, did they?

History should have told us to expect this sort of thing. Who did the Turks pick to play alongside in the championships of 1914–18 and 1939–45? The Germans. To err once like that is forgivable; twice demonstrates that you are an arse. What happened when our own Lawrence of Arabia went over there to play for Arabs United against the Turkish Ottomans in 1917? They reacted to a thumping defeat by putting him in a cell and rogering him senseless all night long. Not very sporting. Eric may have been unhappy about being hit by a police truncheon but at least he didn't find a Turkish pink torpedo up his bottom. More recently, a dispute on Cyprus in 1974 about whether Galatasaray or AEK Athens were the better team ended nastily when the Turkish Army in true Bitter fashion invaded the pitch and they have been there ever since.

No, it can't be allowed to continue. Individual Turks are great – those blokes in the city centre who run kebab houses draped with United flags are a case in point – but as a nation they're a menace to European standards of fair play. United know better than most what it's like to play in a hostile atmosphere and our fans have had their fair share of police harassment, but we have got to draw the line at being expected to perform in a war zone. Unless they apologise and give our lads full compensation, the club should give notice now that we will refuse to play in Istanbul again and challenge UEFA to get it sorted.

That Turkish Delight always did make me spew . . .

*(Meanwhile, the prolonged 'Swales Out' campaign at Maine Road kept us all amused for several months during the season as Bluenose hordes actually kept us off the back pages once or twice by virtue of their increasingly desperate agitprop activities. Our* Red Issue *mole leaked to us the following top-secret Spartist bulletin.)*

## 'For Blue Eyes Only'

KINGS OF THE KIPPAX DIRECT ACTION WING: SUMMARY FOR JAN '94

### Dec 28: At home to Southampton

We had asked for chants of 'Swales Out, Franny In' for thirty seconds every five minutes throughout the first half. Unfortunately too many of our lads can't afford watches or even tell the time, so this was not a total success. The post-match demo was cancelled after our placards were nicked by the local Doddies to make roaches.

### Jan 3: At home to Ipswich

Match abandoned after thirty-nine minutes by southern bastard referee. Obviously a United fan as he doesn't come from Manchester. Demo organised spontaneously to protest against the victimisation of City by the, er, winter weather. We note that this never happens at Old Trafford and must be a result of the Rag-loving media's conspiracy against us.

**Jan 8: FA Cup weekend**

Protest against the failure to win the cup for twenty-five years. We know this is a result of draw-fixing by the FA who want to see United at Wembley and us out, which is why they make us play at the toughest of grounds, like The Shay and Gay Meadow . . . er . . . our direct-action cells will be organised to invade the pitch at the first sign of impending defeats, thus forcing replays until we finally get through to the next round. NB: Will volunteers please wear United scarves during these excursions so that we can spread conspiracy theories for weeks in our fanzines.

**Next Sky Live Match:**

Prevent City game being shown by dropping keks and mooning at cameras. We never win Sky games, presumably because the lads can't handle the thought of being watched by more than 20,000 people. United forced this Sky deal on the rest of us for this very reason.

**Next Wednesday:**

Pre-match demo and march on Town Hall to protest against expected 2p rise in price of Turkish Delight which collectively will cost us a fortune at the next derby game. Future demos to be organised about media portrayal of Moss Side, United always being on *Match of the Day* and the lack of City star pictures in *Shoot!*.

**Finally:**

It has been suggested that we are devaluing the fan protest as a weapon by having one every bloody week for whatever reason takes our fancy; critics say it's a pathetic attempt to appear important and take some attention away from Stretford United because aggro is the only way to get City on the telly. Nothing could be further from the truth, nor is it the case that we are total paranoid obsessives about United, desperate to get the glamorous Reds to pay some attention to us – of that there can be no doubt.

PS: Members shouldn't miss the joint workshop in Bootle with the

Liverpool Action Group entitled 'How to Win Public Support by Continual Self-Pitying Whinging'. Don't bring your cars, however.

COMMUNIQUE ENDS

*(Remarkably, the Bluenose hordes succeeded in their goal and the arrival of supposed plutocrat Francis Lee gave us Reds a few seconds of concern. Hindsight hoots with laughter. Now they're in the third division, one wonders if the following fears will ever be expressed again?)*

## Forward with Franny?

Come on. Be honest. Deep, deep down inside, underneath the jokey exterior that makes cracks about bog rolls and gleefully sings 'nineteen years . . .', there lurks a fear that the Franny hype is true. That a new era has begun. That wads of dosh will roll into Maine Road. That on a wave of relief and celebration, the Bittermen will emerge from their Greater Moss Side shacks to watch a team that might start playing football and even attracting decent players. What if, horror of horrors, City become . . . *a good team*?

If you're a teenager, none of this might strike a chord since you've never known the Blues to be anything but a complete and utter joke. You might think that the club's only reason for existence is to provide something for us Reds to piss ourselves laughing at and even feel pity for; for approaching two decades, City have been the beggars in the footballing street.

However, if you're an old bastard like me, heading towards the abyss of thirty, you'll understand this deep fear. You'll remember that for most of the '70s, City could legitimately claim to be the best team in Manchester. Ha! Look at those words! Have you ever seen 'City' and 'best' in the same sentence before? But it was true. Even in 1976, when we managed to finish higher than City for once, they still found the time to hammer us 4–0, a result that scarred me for years. I had no time to loathe the Scousers or the Sheepmen; I was too busy trying to survive in a playground full of mini-Bittermen.

So I take the threat of a resurgent Franny-led City very, very seriously indeed; I have no wish to return to childhood trauma, ta very much. Of course, it is more than likely that all this hype will explode in the Blues' faces, showering Manchester with pustules of Bitterness. Can any Blue have confidence that City will know how to spend the bog roll millions, if they eventually materialise, at all effectively? Can we look forward to a procession of Steve Daleys marching into Moss Side and becoming as shite as the current side? Perhaps Lee will prove to be such an incorrigible businessman-type that he'll be as tight-fisted as Alan Sugar or even end up seeing City as his personal cash cow (like someone we all know, hey kids?).

Anyway, all I want to make clear is that one shouldn't be ashamed to admit to feeling just a tinge apprehensive, to fearing that we might not be able to sing 'twenty-five years and won fuck all' one day. Maybe it would be a good thing if both City and Liverpool got their act together; trophies are more fun when whipped from under the noses of deadly rivals. It's hard to feel hostile about bloody Norwich farmers or Brummie Villans, as we were expected to do in '93, isn't it? So I can handle a new, improved City, but only as long as United remain one step ahead at all times. Alex, I'm relying on you. I don't want to go back to feeling eight years old again. I'd look daft on a mini-Chopper.

*(Another wonderful summer, 1994's: a double in the bag, and a World Cup to enjoy without bloody England and all the attendant nationalistic guff to spoil it. You will perhaps note, in the following piece, that there were no mondial previews of the kung-fu kick. The author's debut book,* United We Stood, *was published later that summer and work began preparing a new volume for the publishers of this book about the season to come. Little did anyone anticipate what traumas would await . . .)*

## USA '94 – UK '95?

World Cups always set off fashionable little trends in footie around the globe, usually of the silliest sort; after Italia 90 and Roger Milla, no self-respecting forward could let a goal pass without carrying out some sort of porno-flick lambada by the corner flag, for example. So what about USA '94's legacy?

Poor Escobar, shot dead in Medellín after his own goal put Colombia out, gives us a promising precedent. Pampered footballers get bonuses for every conceivable reason – winning, scoring, league points, even attracting good attendances. But do they ever get done when they cock it up? Of course not. How about a sliding scale of physical punishments for crap displays? I could quite happily have put a couple of bullets through Waddle's shit haircut for his 1990 miss in Turin. Obviously execution should be reserved for particularly serious foul-ups, but that still leaves plenty of scope for personally tailored punishment. Clayton Blackmore's nightmare in the New Year's Day massacre of '92 could have been dealt with by injecting him with a dose of the pox, forcing him out of bedroom action for a few weeks in the hope that his football might have improved. Neil Webb, lumbering around that season at his fattest, should clearly have been banged up in Strangeways for a fortnight and starved until his body began to resemble that of an athlete once more. Any more fumbling errors from Schmeichel should see him despatched to spend a night naked in a Turkish bath with some randy lads from the Kurdish Liberation Front – that would certainly sharpen up his concentration in future.

Actually, Medellín sounds a familiar sort of place – full of drug cartels, gun-toting kids and filthy, violent peasants. It's the South American Moss Side, isn't it? If I were a City striker, I'd make sure I didn't miss any derby-day penalties next season or 'El Loco' Leroy might be waiting around the corner with redundant betting slips and an Uzi 9 millimetre . . .

The other feature of USA '94 that would amuse the Premiership was the obscene celebration style of Nigeria. After one particular goal, the scorer ran over to the corner, got down on all fours and cocked a leg to feign urination. (Honest, it was on BBC1.) What a brilliant move! And he didn't get booked either. Apparently, as long as the celebrant doesn't gesture obscenely at the fans, such bawdy behaviour must be acceptable to FIFA. Perhaps we can expect Sharpe to peel away after scoring, frantically simulating masturbation? Or Keano to stand astride a beaten goalie and pretend to drop a steaming turd on his face? Such antics would certainly liven up *Match of the Day* – 'Well, Alan, nice goal wasn't it? And a great doggy-sex impression from that big number nine . . .'

What we *don't* want to see is anything like the feyness exhibited by Brazil, holding hands as they come out of the tunnel; with the slightest encouragement, players of a particular (litigious) club we cannot specify might be all too keen to take the field in a daisy-chain formation with their dicks shoved up each other's nether regions.

One trend we shouldn't expect the rest of the Premiership to pick up on is that of playing skilful, attacking football. That will, of course, continue to be the sole preserve of Man United. Eat our shorts, suckers.

*(And for most of the autumn and early winter, that was the case. For the Premiership, anyway: we learnt about the exceptions in the Nou Camp.*

*And how thoughtful of the team to provide us with something special to wash away the taste of Catalan crustaceans . . .)*

## 'One, Two – One, Two, Three – One, Two, Three, Four – Five-nil!!'

(From *As the Reds Go Marching On*)

Like many other Red pessimists, I'm prone to bricking it before a Manchester derby. However well we're playing and however appallingly City are flailing about, we seem to prepare for the worst and pray for the best. In retrospect, it should've been obvious that this game was only ever going to go one way – although no one could have foreseen quite how spectacularly. All the traditional indicators of victory were in place: United under pressure to bounce back from some disaster at home or abroad; City players both past and present mouthing off in the press a week in advance; Sky cameras ready to capture yet another Blue humiliation, et cetera, et cetera. This year's Terry Phelan Award for Premature Vocal Ejaculation went to Mike Summerbee, the Fat Smugness himself, who whilst squatting behind the Sky Sports desk predicted that his son would lead the Bluenoses to certain triumph. His utter post-thrashing dejection on camera was indeed a picture to savour. When will the Bitters learn that pre-match bullshitting is the occupation of the terminally classless? As usual, Reds kept their heads down and concentrated on letting their feet do the talking on the night itself. Mouthy Magoos were left struggling to extract their size ten club feet from their gobs. Ha, ha, ha.

If, in tabloid terminology, the Barca defeat was 'a mauling, a thrashing, a humiliation', then what was this? A wholesale genocidal massacre, perhaps? As the fifth rifled home, heads filled with happy visions of Bluenoses impaled on spears, pleading for mercy as Sparky and Ince took turns to mangle City genitals with their hobnailed boots. To say that this was a historic derby win is to damn it with faint praise; this was a once-in-a-century, life-affirming orgasm-fest of almost unparalleled proportions. If City ever recover from this virtual execution, it will be to live on as useless vegetables, to be forever pitied – so no change there, then. Those poor, under-privileged Bluenoses had had barely a week to celebrate their impromptu twinning with the Catalans before they were given a sudden, devastating taste of what we had felt like the previous week

– only much, much worse. This was repaying their premature *schadenfreude* with maximum high-street-banks' compound interest. After all, at least we didn't have real Barca fans around us to take the piss for the next six months. But the Bitterman can rest assured that be he at work, rest or play, the diligent Red will never let him forget this night, until such a time as the result might be avenged. Computer projections suggest that this might occur sometime in the 2090s. Welcome to the hell that is the rest of your life, my Blue-hued friends.

History matters. As a former history teacher, I would say that, but this is a city that has a proper pride and respect for its past; moreover, most footie fans have an encyclopaedic knowledge and understanding of their clubs' histories that would impress A.J.P. Taylor. During those eighteen minutes when the score stood tantalisingly at 4–0, 43,000 heads contained but one thought. We didn't chant 'We want five' for reasons of greed or ritual – we sought the exorcising of demons from the soul.

Let me inject a personal note. I don't want to come over all Nick Hornby (it would mess up his nice shiny head) but one of my greatest childhood traumas was the 4–0 defeat in the League Cup at City back in November '75. I was only eight but I can still recall word-for-word the vivid description my father brought home after being out in town that night; he described the howling desolation he had seen in men's faces, the atmosphere of grisly doom in Stretford, and how even the cars of returning Reds crawling through Manc at hearse pace seemed to transmit the depression of their occupants. To me, it was as if the club itself had been mortally wounded, and all of us with it. I skived two days off school but still suffered the consequences from the mini-Bitters for months afterwards.

September 1989: you're older, you 'understand', and as an adult you can handle your grief a little more maturely (though not much). The deficit is four goals again but this time the inclusion of the number five in the scoreline makes it even worse. For the next five years, you face the witty Bitter T-shirts commemorating the fluke result; never mind that this was their one victory in the last twenty attempts, the sheer dominance of that score provided the Blues with their lifeline. However brilliant we were, however many times we stuffed them, however many trophies we won, the Bluenose could always resort to his lifetime maxim – '5–1'. And you know what? Even though I wrote in *United We Stood* that Bertie Magoo's addiction to this Maine Road mantra was the most telling indictment possible of Blue inferiority, every time I heard or saw the numbers '5' and '1' together, I felt a little stabbing pain inside – it was either my soul or, possibly, my bile duct. Whatever, now I can admit it, and so can you: five years down the road, it still grated the edges of the Red heart.

So, if you are a neutral reading this, can you now understand why Old Trafford abandoned its customary reserve and grabbed each other by the pork sword that night, so to speak? In the stroke of a Kanchelskis instep, the unfulfilled desire of many a lifetime had at last been delivered to us. Yes, yes, we'd had three-nils and three-ones in which we'd played them off the park and planet; yes, we'd knocked them out of cups, robbed them of title-winning points and helped get them relegated; and yes, the timing, manner and importance of last year's double victories will probably never be surpassed. But the fact remains that most of us had never seen City properly slaughtered with a scoreline to reflect it in our lives; instead, since our promotion, we'd had to endure two four-goal stuffings and live with years of the resultant taunts. You would think that the hatful of derby victories would amply compensate, but it didn't quite, did it? As in *The Princess and the Pea*, Reds in the bed could still feel that 5–1 or 4–0 niggling, even under the layers of subsequent derby wins. Now, thanks to the inspiration of Eric, Incey and Andrei, we regal Reds, the Kings of Manchester in perpetuity, had got our fairytale ending – for a 5–0 win demolishes all that went before it. A generation of Bitter Blues will now be haunted by the memory of the demolition derby; Moss Side urchins, when they reach puberty and finally learn to count to ten, will still stay in remedial classes because they can't bring themselves to utter the word 'five'; and TV directors worried about offending family viewers will be heartened to see Red crowds at derbies giving up the two-fingered salute in favour of the five-digit wave. Mmmm . . . '5–0'. It has a lovely ring to it, doesn't it? With Zen-like simplicity, it perfectly encapsulates the imbalance of forces in Mancunian football. As the West Stand Boys would have it, 'City – you're so shit it's unbelievable.'

*(And, occasionally, United were so shit it was unbelievable too. Gothenberg away, and yet another European campaign savagely curtailed, springs to the forefront of the mind from its resting place in the lobe-zone marked 'Fuckin' Huge Disasters'. The roasting by Blomqvist capped a wretched spell for Rovers-reject May, on whom the fanzines*

*now declared open season – although, in fairness, Ferguson's pig-headed insistence on playing the poor sap at right-back was the true cause of our common misery.)*

## Daily Spurt Video Offer

You've seen *Giggsy's Soccer Skills*; now enjoy . . .

. . . *Play the May Way*
– with new boy, David.

*The offside trap*
'I've been trying out my new secret method of playing the offside trap which always seems to get the fans going. As soon as Brucey shouts, the other three lads step up smartly but I leg back towards the corner flag as quick as poss and try to hide from the linesman. Then, if the attackers beat the trap, I can suddenly materialise from nowhere and make the saving tackle! Er . . . or not, as the case may be. Obviously, we're still ironing out a few flaws here; I might have to dye my hair cos Mr Linesman always seems to spot my bright ginge-minge barnet. But the lads seem to appreciate it in their special-sense-of-humour way – Brucey always shouts over a cheery "May, you wanker!".'

*Tackling wingers*
'With these new FIFA laws, you've really got to watch yourself, haven't you? What I advise all young players is to follow my example: when a winger comes up to you with the ball, don't go in there feet flying. In fact, it's better not to go in at all. Sort of jump about from left to right, hold him up for a few seconds, just long enough for all his colleagues to arrive in the box, then let him go. Brucey and Pally will deal with the cross, won't they? No need to make rash challenges and get booked – a good pro doesn't need to get suspended and miss those win bonuses, does he? I think Peter appreciates all the extra handling practice this tactic gives him – he always shouts a merry "You ginger twat", which I think is a Danish pregnant goldfish. Crazy guy!'

*Covering your colleagues*
'It's essential to support your central defensive team-mates when play pulls them out of position, so I'm always ready to get across and

stand in for Pally or Brucey at a second's notice. Funnily enough, I find myself needing to do this more and more, drifting cleverly into the box for up to 90% of the game. The lads are always pleased to see me help out in the thick of things and they certainly don't think I've forgotten I'm supposed to be at full-back. Pally's Geordie humour is such a laugh – he always greets me in the box with a hearty "Get out of the way, you dick!".'

*Overlapping up the wing*
'This is the easiest thing I've had to adjust to at Old Trafford. Mr Ferguson just told me to watch Paul Parker play, do whatever he does, and I'll make a good full-back yet. So when I get the ball on the wing, I leg forward, look up meaningfully several times, then hoof it either to the opposing goalie or into the stands. The tactical purpose of this escapes me but I always do what I'm told. Keano loves it when I do this – he always rushes over and spits in my face. I think this is a quaint Irish sign of appreciation for the best players, like that bloke Kubilay.'

*Handling the media*
'Obviously this is so important at such a big club. I always try to be cleverly humorous in my interviews. So when I was on TV with Brucey next to me, I said, "Why don't you pack your bags and leave, Stevey?" It was so funny! Brucey didn't know what to say but he gave me a playful kick in the Achilles tendon later to show we were mates. Actually, it was a bit hard, come to think of it. Likewise, when *Man U Mag* asked me to name my fantasy footie team, I called it Man City! Hilarious or what? This is what my new intellectual friend Choccy called "irony". A United fan who saw me the next day shouted "Bluenose knobhead" at me, which proved he'd got the joke and wasn't bad at this irony game either! It's a laugh a minute here, you know.'

This great video is now available in a series along with *Corner-taking with Giggsy* and *Controlling Your Rage the Keano Way*, priced £37.99, with a limited edition (20,000) 'Fred the Red' gonk thrown in for free.

*(Without doubt the single most tedious running story in the media is the synthetic outrage explosion every six months when United rotate a kit. Reds tapped by hacks spin various versions of the following every time,*

*yet still the press come back for more. And people wonder why football fans try and beat up football journalists from time to time . . .)*

## Kits out for the Lads

There are three unavoidables in life: death, taxes and media outcries when United release a new kit. You would think that people would grow tired of whinging every year about the latest Umbro abortion but it seems the appetite for counterfeit outrage is still unsatisfied. The latest Tesco-bag sartorial disaster has, of course, topped the lot in the cynicism stakes. Not only was it released after Christmas, when many would have received 'obsolete' kits as pressies, but its design bears only the most tangential relationship to United's history. So when an *Independent on Sunday* journo phoned me up for my opinion on this and other merchandising matters, he was no doubt expecting to hear me parrot the usual anti-Edwards/Freeman diatribe.

'So, what's your view on this cynical exploitation then?' he asks.

'Brilliant stuff,' I reply.

He gasps in horror at the other end of the line.

'Surely you're not condoning this rip-off?' he exclaims frantically.

'Yes. I'd like to see a lot more of it too,' I tell him.

As I went on to explain to the hapless hack, I couldn't give a toss about the entire merchandising operation anymore. If you're going to rely on the Superstore and Megastore game as a major source of income, you might as well do it properly and screw every penny out of the saddos who spend three hours at a time in there. Of course, it's grossly cynical to bring the kit out after Christmas – but it will probably double the amount of kit cash United will make this financial quarter. On a pro-rata calculation, merchandising money contributed at least £2.5 million to the Cole fee; if it means we as a club have more money to spend maintaining our status as the best team, who cares if the souvenir groupies are the ones who are financing it by spending so much on tacky crap?

Of course, I've never worn a club shirt or been inside the Megastore, nor do I have children whining about the new kit's desirability, so this is an easy attitude to take. It's also true that the entire merchandising operation in general is embarrassingly naff and a source of shame; it might even be true, as the last *Red Issue* suggested, that merchandising considerations will affect team decisions especially where Giggs and Sharpe are concerned. But, overall, I feel a warm glow every time I hear some marvellously nasty piece of MUFC product has been a success with the masses. I think of day-trippers shelling out £100,000 in three hours in the Megastore or of out-of-town non-attenders getting fully kitted up in their local emporium and feel misanthropically content. Thousands of sad bastards are spending all they've got spare to subsidise our team, at no cost, beyond embarrassment, to us (by 'us' I mean the merchandise-subsidised hardcore who keep their money for fanzines, fags and Fosters).

At the end of the day, Brian, how can you have any sympathy for anyone who falls into one of the following categories of the 'exploited'?

1) Parents who are so enslaved by their brats that they can't say 'no' to demands for a new kit
2) Anyone tasteless enough to buy *and wear in public* the new kit
3) Anyone so ignorant as to not know that a new kit was coming in January and who went out and bought an obsolete kit for Christmas
4) Oh, sod it – anyone who goes inside the Megastore, full stop

Funnily enough, the *Indie* journo mentioned that he was having trouble finding a United-supporting parent to go on the record and complain about the kit 'scandal'. That doesn't surprise me. The only people out there complaining are the media and other clubs' fans. Most of us just couldn't care less anymore. We live with the embarrassment, of course, which will endure as long as a man so apparently tasteless as Edwards remains in charge. He, as CO, is responsible for the glitz-shlock bad taste typical of the lower-middle-class, minor-public-schoolboy type; this is a man who apparently thinks titles like 'Europa Suite' and 'Premier Lounge' are 'classy', a man who seemingly believes introducing 'Fred the Red' the day after we retained the title was tasteful timing. So, if we're always going to be blushing about the latest exploits of the commercial department, at least let's have the consolation of knowing that we're making a packet out of it. Let's face it: anyone paying £40 for that new shirt and wearing it *deserves* to have their wallet bled dry.

*(The New Year of 1995 – and it's easy to forget that for a few days between Bramall Lane and Selhurst Park, life seemed so sweet . . .)*

## Andy Cole – An Apology

It has been brought to our attention that many observers may have got entirely the wrong impression of our attitude to Mr Andrew

Cole. Due to, er, typographical errors and general media distortion, Reds in the past have appeared to view young Andy as any of the following: a one-season wonder; a talentless goal-hanger; a gun-toting wideboy; a poor man's Chris Eubank; a general Geordie-loving arrogant twat of the first order.

Naturally, none of this was ever true and we would like to assure everyone that our opinion of Mr Cole has always been consistent, namely that he is a fine, upstanding young man of supreme athletic talent, one of our favourite and most-admired players of recent years and a credit to his ethnicity and family. When, for example, we sang 'You'll never play for England' at him up at St James' Park, all we meant to express was our view that he was too good for Venables's outfit and instead deserved to play for Brazil.

Anyway, we hope we have clarified our position on this and cleared up any misunderstandings. Incidentally, in the spirit of friendship, may we direct traumatised Toons to seek solace from fellow north-eastern sheep-shaggers at Elland Road, whom we understand to have had some experience of this sort: how painful it must be to have Fergie plunge his hand into your chest and rip out your heart, tee-hee . . .

*(And then it all kicked off. Literally. Two days after Cantona's kung fu, the author grabbed the chance to defend our God in* The Independent *as Reds began to rescue the agenda from those who sought to crucify Eric. Paddy Crerand had led the way and the rest followed, swords and pens aloft . . .)*

## King Chronicles: The Ties that Bind the Devoted and Their Idol

(From *The Independent*)

Buried in *The Sun* faxline column the day after the Selhurst Cantona Catastrophe was this glimpse into the secret heart of the Red hardcore: 'Leave Eric alone. The supporter deserved it for wearing appalling clothes; Cantona should've hit him harder.' Sarah from Hertfordshire, despite your sex and location, you are indeed one of us.

Who's 'us'? The thousands of Old Trafford zealots, the home-and-away brigade to whom Eric is known simply as *Dieu.* Some of us are old enough to remember when Bruce Lee impressions and worse were a predictable feature of every terraced afternoon. We were the shameless proles bellowing 'Ooh-ah Cantona' for a solid ten minutes after the Frenchman's supposedly disgraceful exit last Wednesday. We are not, however, the alleged United fans whom the media hauled out of the Megastore on Thursday to parrot routine condemnations of the Blessed One. Nor are we much loved by Manchester United plc – or by anyone else, for that matter. We are the Old Trafford Underclass: no one likes us and we don't care, as Millwallians once sang.

What we like, however, is simple enough: thrills, passion and fight. All three values are encapsulated in and personified by the talismanic being of Eric Cantona. And if the rest of the world is allowed to continue worshipping their God, despite His two-footed challenges of earthquake, pestilence and famine, then we too can still smother Eric in adulation, forgiving his own temporary bouts of madness that hurt us all.

I must have spoken to nearly a hundred true Reds over the past forty-eight hours; to a man they stand squarely behind their King. Their sole desire is to see him back in the Red shirt; all other considerations remain secondary. To us, he is like the elder brother we look up to who's simply got into a spot of bother with the law; however much we disapprove of the offence, he is family and as such receives the automatic support that blood ties engender.

Yes, we publicly accept the essential indefensibility of his actions, but we will enter every possible plea of mitigation we can think of on his behalf to every debate, hearing or court appearance to come; the defence campaigns have already begun. Some outsiders appear to find our refusal to cut Cantona adrift astonishing or even disgusting, but then how can an outsider comprehend the bonds that bind the devoted and their idol together? Remember that the greatest losers in this affair are the match-going United fans – our season is virtually destroyed, our icon's career on the edge of ruin and our dreams of the European Holy Grail banished. Yet still we love him. Woe betide any who would seek to divorce the lovers from the loved; 10,000 enraged Reds waving broken bottles outside your front door is not a prospect to be welcomed, I would have thought.

Above all, spare us the sanctimonious waffle paid by the yard that is spouted by the monstrous legion of ex-pros and soi-disant experts. Eric has not traumatised millions of children or brought the game to the brink of the precipice. Football needs the Cantonas as much as it needs the Linekers – the Establishment might not admit it, but this is an entertainment industry that thrives as much on horrendous controversy and appalling ill deeds as it does on good play and clean living. Brawls, bungs, drugs and karate – we love 'em all. Save your family values for the tennis club; 'Keep Football Filthy' is our slogan for the post-PC '90s.

*('Think of the children! For mercy's sake, won't someone think of the children?' shrieks the gossiping harridan minister's wife in* The Simpsons *at regular intervals. Britain was full of mewling Helen Lovejoys that week, more often than not fat, drunk, lecherous tabloid desk-editors whose usual occupation is to place naked women on kids' breakfast tables every morning. As another Simpson, Bart, remarks, 'We need another Vietnam to thin out their ranks . . .' The author was prompted to place this online with the much-missed 'Zeitgeist' Net salon.)*

## King Chronicles: The Kids Are All Right

(From *Zeitgeist*)

I'll be honest with you. Like many Reds I spoke to during the Selhurst Shellshock aftermath, I couldn't give a toss about such concerns as 'setting a bad example to children' or 'bringing disrepute to the game'. Whenever I hear sanctimonious waffle on such subjects, I do as Goebbels and reach for the revolver. Disrepute is the lifeblood of the soap opera that is British football. Imagine a Premiership peopled by those of the purest Lineker mentality; the game would be dead in three years, bored to tears by relentless godliness. As for the kiddies, I would suggest that football already kowtows to family values quite enough as it is, thank you; besides, any parent who either a) seeks to make a bleedin' *footballer* their child's role model or b) seeks to shield the little chap from all life's nasties hardly deserves much sympathy.

However, if we must pretend to be sensible, serious and – ugh – responsible, then we can still find cause to say 'bollox' to the sanctimony-peddlers. Just what example did Eric set, after all? Surely it was an object lesson in what can befall the miscreant? Misbehave on the field and look what happens to you, kiddies – crucifixion and a six-month ban. From the bad example, you can teach the good lesson, as every pedagogue knows. On *Granada Upfront*, some lynch-mob lemming reckoned that kids all over the country would now be attempting to execute Bruce Lee drop-kicks on innocent spectators. Even if such a moronic prophecy were to come true, what of it? If every footballer were held responsible for the imitative actions of every braindead teenager in the land, what absurdities would result? Here's a story from *90 Minutes*: fourteen-year-old Graham Evans tried to copy Jürgen Klinsmann's diving celebration but got stuck in the mud doing so, breaking his ankle. Hugely amusing, of course, doubly so for him being Scottish, but should Klinsmann be hauled before an FA tribunal for setting such a potentially dangerous example to kids? Or be held responsible for the negligent antics of a stranger? Get real.

Having mentioned the Tottenham Teuton, it reminds me of a perfect illustration of what truly constitutes 'bringing the game into disrepute'. I once met a relative of the Milan defender Costacurta on an Adriatic beach. As is natural between two male strangers, football became the main topic of conversation within sixty seconds and he proceeded to tell me how devastated the player had been to miss the European Cup final. Not only would history record him as missing from the honour role of the greatest club display of this generation, he had also suffered unbearable torments during the semi-final, when he feared that his sending-off was going to cost his mates and their legions of fans the final place they'd spent two years trying to achieve.

Now remember who put him in that position: Jürgen Klinsmann. It was his wanton, deliberate impression of an assassinated President when there had in fact been no contact whatsoever that set off that catastrophic chain of events for the young Italian. Fortunately, Monaco still lost the game, but Klinsmann emerged unscathed and unpunished, able to ply his trade for the loathsome, cynical German team in USA '94 and then at that temple of cheating disgrace, White Hart Lane. As I write this, Klinsmann is on *Sportsnight*, being lionised by an orgasmic Motson and subtly portrayed as a 'decent foreigner' in contrast to the despicable Cantona. Vomit-inducing is too mild an epithet. If you're looking for bad examples to children, if you're seeking events that bring the game into disrepute, if you're looking for genuinely dastardly foreign villains, then I suggest to you that Eric would have had to have sliced someone's testicles off to come anywhere near the crime perpetrated by Klinsmann that night. The 'victim' at Selhurst Park was a repulsive creature who had brought the assault upon himself and who deserved, and received, no sympathy at all. The Klinsmann victim was just a decent player, robbed of his just rewards. Now Cantona is banned and disgraced;

Klinsmann has become the 'good German', loved by all. Pass the bucket.

*(The March Wednesday we beat Arsenal 3–0, a posse of us piled into a van afterwards and drove all night to London in order to witness, we trusted, a victorious day out for the Cantona brigade . . .)*

## *King Chronicles: Lessons at the Court of King Eric*

It was supposed to be an enjoyable enough wheeze: fifteen of us down in London to appear with Boylie on *The Big Breakfast*, promoting 'Eric the King', headed off to Croydon Magistrates' Court for an Eric-supporting singsong. After all, it was going to be a formality, right? The only debate would be how big a fine Eric would get; no harm in us entertaining the media hounds while the world waited for a decision. Ha. By midday, we were left reflecting not on a successful day's record-PR but on our witnessing first-hand one of the most shocking episodes of this increasingly seismic season.

Turning the corner onto the road where the court was just after ten, we marvelled at the sight outside the entrance: a camera-rich sprawl of over four hundred hacks, technicians and curious onlookers, but with scarcely a Red to be seen. The media vultures were spread across the pavement, along the central reservation and on top of every available roof. As we legged across the road, roaring 'Eric the King', every telephoto lens and video camera swung towards us, capturing Boylie's Boys and the K-Stand placards in their full glory. As we dished out press releases and gave interviews, convincing the most sceptical of hacks that *all* Reds are behind Eric, we gleaned that the media were mostly bored. They didn't expect a real news story to emerge here, just an anticlimactic fine; this was merely a circus of visual images, capturing pix of media scrums and harassed celebs. The guys with the notebooks assumed they'd be in for an underworked afternoon and had nothing better to do than talk to the likes of us, busy reciting lyrics and badmouthing Simmons. They were, at least, grateful that Eric had typically eschewed the limo and walked the three minutes from hotel to court, seemingly none the worse for his night of champagne, clubbing and gig by The Artist Formerly Known As Talented. At least that guaranteed them the celeb-surrounded-by-paparazzi pictures that papers rather tediously demand these days.

So there we all stood for the best part of two hours, the world's eyes and ears patiently waiting for news from the lucky recipients of Press Pool passes inside. As we sweated gently under the London sun, Pete Boyle clambered up some vacant ladders to lead us through a few terrace classics to the bemusement of assembled hackery; a few shy London Reds turned up to swell our numbers, whilst the half-dozen Palace fans knocking around kept very, very quiet indeed. The Anti-Nazi League, there to make the most of the anti-racist opportunity, pointed these creatures out to us: 'South London scum,' remarked one succinctly. Later, with us Reds long gone, these vermin suddenly found their tongues when Eric finally emerged. Typical standards of Palace bravery, making a stand only when there's no chance of a comeback. No doubt Simmons had thought himself similarly secure when he stepped forward that fateful night . . .

Getting inside to see how the King was doing – Incey's committal being an early formality – was harder than getting a face-value away ticket. Southy successfully found a way of making repeated ten-minute trips to the court bogs without being promptly ejected, thus being able to emerge to tell us how cool Eric was looking, mixing his customary swagger with some required elements of humble penitence. Amidst the steady stream of exiting local crims, bemoaning their latest drug-dealing fines on mobile phones, came Red-friendly journos whom we corralled behind our pen to pump for info. Jim White of *The Independent* seemed cautiously happy: 'poor prosecution performance' and 'Eric's behaving himself' gave us heart. Then the BBC North correspondent, attracted by our chorus of 'One Charlie Lambert!', told us about the reading of Simmons's uncensored statement and that two of the bench were women. By 11.30, any lingering worries we'd had were dispelled. Eric's brief had been excellent, whereas theirs had been lacklustre; Eric had said all the right things and pushed all the right emotional buttons; a female-dominated bench, knowing what your typical prim, twinset bench-woman is like, would surely be in thrall to Eric's brooding charm and appalled by Simmons's language. The verdict would be at any moment, then it'd be down the pub with the hacks for some Boylie buffoonery on table-tops with lager-tops.

But the bench weren't straight back at all. As the delay stretched on past twenty minutes and hacks jostled impatiently for shot positions, my own alcohol pangs were replaced by well-founded concern. What could be taking so long to discuss? I turned to a K-Stander and remarked that they must be debating more than the mere size of a fine; this was sounding like one JP arguing for a fine, one undecided and one pressing for something much worse. Having once been in Eric's position myself, I knew the warning signs only too well.

Even so, when the news broke, the supposed thrill of being there at the centre of a media explosion was memorable only for the sense of horrified shock. Southy and Peter Peet ran out, white-faced, to tell us the worst; for a moment, we guffawed at their attempted kidology, only for the sentence to be confirmed by the racing hacks behind them. Journalists are not, by their nature, easily taken aback, but today those correspondents around us were genuinely appalled. For about three minutes, chaos reigned as journos tried to piece together the facts, before animated debates about legal processes broke out everywhere. Was Eric going straight down? Could you actually get time for common assault as a first-time offender? Could you appeal against a sentence like that? 'What the fuck happens now?' screamed a quality journo. 'Someone please tell me, now!' For about sixty seconds my head was in pieces, like the rest of the lads'; I recovered sufficiently to dredge up old criminal process lessons and tell the hack that, whatever happened, a judge-in-chambers had to be found immediately to give Eric bail pending appeal. (Such is British justice – our magistrates cannot be allowed to operate unless tended by a fireman-judge, ready to rush in to correct patent miscarriages like this.) Thankfully, Maurice Watkins did find one, down the road at the Crown Court, who did the necessary. We, of course, wouldn't have left the scene unless we'd known Eric's freedom was secured.

Suddenly, the massed media snapped back into gear, looking for someone, anyone, who would go on the record to provide confirmation of what the journos clearly felt – that a judicial outrage had just been perpetrated. With evident relief, they remembered they had some genuine Reds from Manchester on hand. The pack descended on us, pulling us all over the pavement to speak to camera, mike and dictaphone. Lads who'd never spoken to the media in their life ended up doing half a dozen interviews, to the nationals, radio and TV; how surreal to see Southy, the most down-to-earth, unmetropolitan lad imaginable, going straight from *The Times* to French TV's main news crew . . .

Our duty done, we withdrew from the battleground, staying just long enough to salute the Guv'nor when he finally emerged. Some of us had been up for thirty-six hours already and Mancunian beds were calling. On the journey home, we listened dumbfounded as the media explosion ran its course on every radio station in Christendom, several bulletins opening with comments by Pete and the boys, intermingled with us singing 'Eric the King' outside the court. Some of us realised that, for once, *we* – not the media or superstore part-timers – had set the agenda. This wasn't like the original kung-fu aftermath, when true Reds had to struggle to rescue the news agenda after sad twats had condemned our King on air whilst we were all still stuck on coaches returning from Selhurst. We had got on first, and spoken in the most cutting, condemnatory way possible about the crass misjudgement. In doing so, we challenged any naysayers to go against the prevailing orthodoxy, always a difficult task on a running news story once the initial die is cast. Besides, once BBC radio stations had broadcast us saying that 'the magistrates deserve a good karate-kicking', anyone else going on to defend Eric would sound quite moderate and reasonable in comparison . . .

Now this is sounding a bit self-congratulatory, which was not the intention. It may well be that our presence and contributions made no difference, that the press and media would have taken such a pro-Eric line in any event, purely on the case's merits. Maybe so, but who can be sure? Apart from writing this to let those who couldn't be there know what it was like, there is a point to this. It has been argued in the past that Reds should not discuss anything with the media, that we will be used by journos, who are scumbags anyway, and that those who engage in these activities run the risk of being seen as self-promoting media groupies. That day at Eric's court has convinced me that this argument, though appealing, is nevertheless to be rejected. Two particular remarks that day led me to conclude that committed Reds should take every opportunity offered to air their views publicly. A very famous journo remarked to me that the world divides into two: agenda-setters and agenda-followers. Power, of course, lies with the former. 'Get in early, seize the initiative and repeat what you're saying to everyone at every opportunity,' he advised, 'and you'll find the media and the authorities will follow.' Later, a radio analysis featured a summary of the day's expert comments; the presenter noted that all the legal-eagles had talked of the media influence on the magistrates and that the relentlessly anti-Eric nature of much of it must have convinced the court that the public would allow them to 'get away with' imposing such a draconian sentence.

So, at the risk of being branded a media slag, let me put this to you. Our justice system – and all quasi-legal authorities like the FA – do not, as they are supposed to do, operate independently of mob opinion. In fact, in a mass-media-dominated age, authority increasingly kowtows cravenly to public opinion as selected, distorted and presented by the media and, in particular, the press. Forget rules of evidence, codes of punishment and the like; authorities of any kind now act on the basis of what the lynch mob, as represented by the tabloid, will allow. If you want to make the world's powers treat United, our players and us in the best, most favourable fashion possible, you have one target you can influence – the media.

And because they have, essentially, an open agenda, you *can* make a difference. Control the media and you control the world. Party politics apart, papers have no fixed principles of any sort. They will go with whatever sells, whatever will run and whatever doesn't offend their core readership or advertisers. The consumer is king and that man is you. What is more, MUFC supporters have a potential power to influence the media, and therefore the powers that create our football-supporting conditions, that no one else can rival. Not only is our club the most newsworthy in itself, but we are also the most numerous consumers by a mile. We didn't get our act together in the past, or did so too late or too half-heartedly; whilst we were discussing whom we'd allow to talk to us about Eric, the media and the authorities were already way ahead of us, building a gallows. We have so much power but never use it – do you think *The Sun* and its trio of cretinous football writers would still be allowed to maintain their anti-United, anti-Eric vendettas if we'd boycotted the bastard paper? Look what Liverpool fans achieved with their boycott – they turned *The Sun* pro-Liverpool within the year. We have treble 'Pool's fans, so what could we achieve? Anything, mate. I'll put it crudely: the media follow what they think the public wants; the authorities, in turn, follow the media. If you did absolutely nothing to protest against Eric's treatment beyond arguing about him in the pub with Bluenoses, then you haven't really been much of a help, have you? The media – and therefore the authorities – will follow the lead given by whoever makes the most noise. So write angry letters, get onto phone-ins, use faxlines, hassle TV programmes and generally get yourself involved with the media whenever there is a cause to be fought, because otherwise your power as a Red is lost to us. And if you get the chance to put the true Red view on radio or on TV, do it. It may well be purer, ideologically sounder and cooler to say 'fuck off', but it doesn't help build a more Red-friendly world.

*(Both Andy Walsh and the author had been busy helping Boylie run this campaign and both realised that the lessons outlined in the latter half of this piece applied across the board. When Chris Robinson and Johnny Flacks decided to launch the United Independent Supporters Association soon after, Walsh and Kurt rushed to join the Dirty Dozen founders and took this mindset in with them. IMUSA is today the most media-savvy pressure group in sport; of all the by-products of the kung fu, IMUSA was perhaps the most unexpected and most welcome.)*

## Daily Spurt News: 24 March 1995

STRING 'ER UP!

OUTRAGE AT BONKERS BEAK

The magistrate who sentenced Eric Cantona to two weeks' pokey, Mrs Jean Pearch, is at the centre of a tabloid storm, with her sentence being replayed time and time again by a slavering media.

PUNISHMENT

'What sort of example is she setting the children?' asked one despairing onlooker. 'I try to teach my kids to respect the law and authority, but when they see her going over the top like that they just won't listen to me.'

'She's in big trouble now,' warned one legal-eagle. 'When a judge gets hold of that sentence, he's going to come down on her like a ton of bricks. I wouldn't be surprised if she got suspended from the Croydon Mags first team, for a start.'

UNDERSTANDABLE

But there were some there to defend her. A Miss Patricia Crerand, respected ex-magistrate, said she could understand Pearch's actions. 'You know what it's like up there, with all those people having a go at you, with all the media attention and the pressure to perform; sometimes you get a rush of blood, you overreact and then, bang, you've gone in two-footed with a two-weeker. It could happen to anyone.'

INEVITABLE

Mrs Pearch already had a reputation as a hard-line disciplinarian, having promised to the *Croydon Advertiser* that she'd be cracking down on offenders; many predicted that with her track record of going in hard, something like this was inevitable. *The Sun* have claimed that it's all part of her genetic make-up – 'a Christian mother from Norbury, what do you expect?' – but whatever the reason for her moment of madness, she would now be ill-advised to go anywhere near Manchester.

TRAUMA

Meanwhile, the after-effects are plain to see. 'My kid was terrified when he heard that sentence,' said one father. 'It could have traumatised him for life, hearing that.' And in Manchester schoolyards, the hot new game is called 'Croydon Magistrates', with eight-year-olds being sentenced to Chinese burns or beatings for late five-a-side tackles. Mrs Pearch was unavailable for comment and is also an old bag.

*(As if Eric's eventual nine-month ban wasn't burden enough to carry, our shoulders began creaking even more ominously when Inter Milan turned up waving billion-lira contracts in Eric's face. We prepared for the worst and made our desperate last appeals, the author getting a front-page chance to plead directly to God with an open 'Dear Eric . . .' letter in* The Independent. *Months later, Fergie himself was still quoting lines from this piece and praised it in one of his books thus: 'Fabulous – it was a great article by the boy Kurt.' Which the boy Kurt much appreciated.)*

## King Chronicles: 'Dear Eric . . .'

(From *The Independent*)

'Rumour has it that the Milanese piranhas have sensed your blood is in the water after that nasty Pearch attack and are coming in to snap you up. As another semi-hinged magician once said, you cannot be serious. Inter Milan of *tangentopoli*? Didn't you have your fill of gangsters at Marseilles? Martin Edwards may be sharp but at least his violin case contains a musical instrument, if you get my drift. Let me appeal to your Bonapartist sense of honour and tradition. Could you really exchange the Red of United, the symbol of glory, flair and self-expression, for the dull stripes of Inter, the club who gave us *catenaccio*, Euro Cup bungs and a succession of psychotic international full-backs? And what of your burning ambition, to be crowned the King of the European Champions? Inter are the Manchester City of Italian football; they will never become the best team in their city, let alone country or continent. As a good existentialist, you have no truck with facile notions of destiny but you have spoken of your mission to lead us back to the Elysian Fields on which we last gambolled in '68. Abandon this admittedly Herculean, mould-breaking task now and you will forever regret it: you will have become the David Owen of football. Stick with us and prepare for government.

Are you still not convinced? Then be threatened by brutal honesty. You are one of the great egoists of the age, on a par with Jim Morrison and Mick Jagger, radiating the arrogance of one who has much about which to be arrogant. You hog centre-stage and hug the limelight, revelling in your supremacy over the mere mortals of opposition. How will such a Lion King fare in Italy's Serie A, though? Clogging, donkey centre-halves are in short supply there, *mon roi*, where you will discover the number five and six shirts conceal the lithe torsos of deadly assassins. The space and freedom you exploit here will be replaced by confinement and the oppression of man-marking. Serie A clubs are stuffed full of luminous talents, players who are the best their countries have produced: no longer will you be the only pole star in the constellation. Forget the individualist liberty you exalt at Old Trafford; in Italy, the collective is all. You will be forced to conform or join the rest of the libero-spirited, languishing in Serie A Reserves. Besides, the Italians cannot stand to be out-poseured, especially not by the French. You are a challenge to their preening sense of virility, *un vrai homme* amidst a nation of mamma's boys. Just ask Dennis Bergkamp.

Above all, in true Geminian fashion, you need to be loved. Could anyone adore you like we do? You're not even on the pitch yet we sing for you like we do for no other. We wear your name with pride wherever we go, we champion your cause at every opportunity, we bow every night to your picture that has replaced the Pope's by our bedside. You have become more than a mere star or hero or leader; in crowning you the King of Old Trafford, the first to reign since Law, you have become an icon of religious scale. The number seven shirts we wear bear the simple legend *Dieu.* How much more homo-erotic can you expect us manly Mancs to be in order to convince you of our eternal fidelity? You once called United your 'perfect wife' – what grounds have we given you for divorce? As Macmillan would say, 'these little local difficulties' will soon pass and the forty weeks in the wilderness will be over. Return to the bosom of your forgiving family at OT and let us bellow 'Eric the King' for you once more.

*(Hey, it worked [snigger]. There would be more scares, of course, but we were always on the edge with Eric, weren't we? For now, we'd just have to dig in and wait for Red October. Oh, and try to win another double in the meantime. The story of our strangely glorious failure is fully recounted in the author's book* As the Reds Go Marching On.*)*

*(At the end of the '94–'95 season,* FourFourTwo *ran a series of player profiles under the title 'The Boy's a Bit of a Disappointment' and there was little surprise that United's resident City fan David May headed the list. The author tried his hardest to resist breaking the rule that you don't criticise your own in public but just couldn't stop himself. Forty thousand fellow sufferers may well sympathise.)*

## Redheads: David May

(From *FourFourTwo*)

My girlfriend, who has a weird female way of prejudging players, took one look at David May on his arrival and pronounced, 'Ginger, curly hair and freckles – he's no good.' If only Fergie could pick up some of this feminine-intuition malarkey, for, as we all now know, Davey boy is not exactly this year's number one Megastore poster. Indeed, as his harsher *Red Issue* critics would contend, the points we lost due to his nightmare showings at full-back have been as instrumental as King Eric's absence in our losing the title. The chant we had prepared for him of 'Ooh-Ay, David May' has sadly been heard in only the most ironic of tones.

Back in those carefree days of August '94, when King Eric roamed free, Paul Parker was fit and Rovers were beaten at Wembley, life was so much sweeter. How we revelled in capturing May from the enemy camp, outwadding Blackburn's sugar daddy for once and leaving a dirty great hole in the Rovers defence. How delightful too that Rovers fans should be so hugely miffed at the blow to their pride; even as late as January they were still bellowing 'Judas' at him on the Old Trafford touchline, bunging thirty silver five-pence pieces towards him for good measure. As usual, the alarmingly inbred Lancastrians were rather slow on the uptake – many of us had already decided May was clearly a Dalglishean agent sent to destroy us from within.

He made a terrible start and from then it was all downhill. Revealing that he had been a City fan as a teenager was bad enough, without him going on to name his fantasy football team MCFC. We can safely assume that had May not become a footballer, a career in public relations would not have been his next choice. Bluenoses at United are supposed to repent of their sins upon signing for us, not continue shamelessly to flaunt them. All in all, it was a bad omen: City fans at United usually come to a grim end, as Mark Robins once discovered.

Still, we could have forgiven him this unfortunate accident of Blue birth had he not proceeded to offer definitive proof that your standard English centre-half is about as adaptable as a three-pin plug and about as much use in Europe too. Now admittedly, even demi-gods like Pally and Bruce would struggle at full-back, but at least they'd be able to keep their heads above water. Poor David simply drowned, all at sea when more than ten yards away from his comfy centre-half home. On those occasions when he was actually in position on the flanks instead of loitering without intent in the box, he succeeded in making every trundling journeyman wide player look like a dazzling, dashing winger in the Giggs and Best mould. Within weeks he had become the Skoda of English defenders: everything else can overtake it with ease, no one else wants to own one and it's the butt of every bar-room joke going. At times, he resembled a demented owl, his head swivelling wildly as if through 360 degrees as he tried to locate the ball and opponent. As teams started to cash in by playing two or three left-wingers against him, unchallenged crosses whizzed over from his corner with depressing regularity. Only the domineering presence of Pallister saved us from further ignominy.

Not that it was all Davey's fault. Ferguson, typically, refused to concede for months what even single-cell amoeba beyond Alpha Centaurai had long since realised – that even Andy Cole would make a better full-back than May. By then, of course, it was too late. The damage had been done. On a grisly Ullevi night, David reached his nadir. Blomqvist roasted May to such an extent that watching Reds chanted 'off, off' whenever the ref had words with the hapless creature. When *Red Issue* put together a piece entitled 'Ten Reasons Why United Lost in Europe', the editor had to be physically restrained from typing 'David May' ten times. It wasn't just that May had been atrocious, either, as Ferguson had to take some of the blame for playing him out of position yet again. It was also that his attitude seemed suspect. In this very organ, Rob Shepherd noted darkly that on the plane home, all United players looked deathly, with some appearing to be in shock. Not so David; Shepherd spotted him laughing and joking, seemingly without a care in the world. The fanzine *United We Stand* put this in their next issue and for many May was now *persona non grata.*

We haven't seen much of him since. He had a couple of chances at centre-half and still wasn't much good, heading the ball in all directions but safe ones with his eyes closed like an eight-year-old girl. He did have a good game at Palace and even scored, allowing us to sing 'Ooh-Ay' in earnest at last – for we never criticise him loudly at games, ever-optimistic that he might improve. But that was the night of Cantona's kung fu, when the surreal and bizarre held sway – you could file a decent May display under one of those headings . . .

Of course, we pray the boy comes good, especially with Brucey heading for his bus pass. In the meantime, anyone got a spare centre-back to sell us? Part-exchange?

*(After a winter of press fulmination about Cantona's violence, they were given something properly blood-crazed to get pompous about when England 'fans' did the dirty in springtime Dublin. Remarkably, many of the observations below still seem to apply almost four years later, which in itself appears to prove the following thesis.)*

## When Irish Eyes Aren't Smiling . . .

So yet another England awayday has ended in disgrace. If you were a non-football fan reading the media's coverage, you'd be forgiven for thinking this had come as a bolt from the blue, a virtually isolated reminder of the bad old days when no respectable family would be seen dead near a football stadium. The truth is, of course, that something like this has been on the cards for more than a year; all that was needed was a good opportunity, which the Irish FA helpfully provided by showering Dublin with black-market tickets. That the most visible outburst should occur at an England away game isn't a surprise; the last away game seventeen months ago was studded with violence, so why should it have been any different the other week? The fact is that England's away support has a greater proportion of psycho nutters than any individual club – to such a degree that it can never be assumed the responsible majority will successfully suppress the extremists. An England gathering draws most of the headcases from most of the handiest clubs; moreover, England acts as a particularly strong magnet for those to the right of Newt Gingrich. The result is inevitable – an unusually numerous congregation of unusually right-wing white trash of unusually dominant influence. Given the special political circumstances in Dublin, an absence of rioting would have been miraculous. Only authorities as apparently dim as Ireland's could've been so complacent. (Incidentally, did anyone else find the Irish gusto for slagging all Englanders as 'barbaric animals' rather aggravating? Coming from a nation that has harboured many covert supporters of murderous terrorists for twenty-five years, a touch less self-righteous generalisation would've been in order . . .)

What the media coverage demonstrated beyond all doubt was that those who are paid to be knowledgeable about and to write about footie have no idea what's going on outside their cosy press-box world. Anyone who goes to away games in particular knows that aggro has been steadily creeping back in over the last eighteen months (and has, at last, begun to show up inside the stadia rather than confining itself to town centres or concourses). And whereas once the media would jump on the slightest outbreak and hype it up, they have until recently engaged in a conspiracy of silence over the old voodoo's slight return. Why has recent aggro involving us at Elland Road, Anfield or Maine Road been so remarkably under-reported? Why are the media treating Dublin as the culmination of a very recent, short-term whirlwind that started at Selhurst Park (?!) and went via Ewood and Stamford before the exploding in Eire?

Personally, I suspect that the footie media have become too enthralled to the football establishment and the Brave New World of post-Taylorism. Writers and reporters have hitched themselves onto the family values/all seater/'good news' bandwagon and are happy to treat footie as an extension of Hollywood. They have realised what the new football audience of kids and mums wants to hear – lots of chirpy, happy, exciting stuff about glamour, superstars and pantomime-esque heroes 'n' villains. And thanks to *Fever Pitch* et al., you can be funny too – football is pure light ents, comedy for all, a laugh-a-game presided over by the modern-day Saint 'n' Greavsie, Baddiel and Skinner. Above all, nothing must be written to spoil the image that the media, the FA and club chairmen have struggled to create since the '80s – the world of football is a shiny, happy place for shiny, happy people.

So when incidents occur and trends emerge that threaten to undermine this vision, out come the editorial blue pens. Either that or the footie correspondents try to convince themselves that what they've just witnessed outside a pub, or the Nazi leaflets they've just seen distributed, or the massed 'foul-mouthed' crowd abuse they've just heard, are simply isolated one-offs to be ignored and left unreported. For if they ever attempted to take a wider, long-term view of what's been developing, they'd realise that all is not as rosy as the image-makers' specs make football appear. And that's something they and the authorities don't wish to contemplate or see transmitted to the TV-watching public.

The result of such ostrich-like behaviour is that the truth becomes a casualty – and that important warnings go unheeded. For example, plenty of us have spent the best part of two seasons trying to agitate against the resurgent far-right threat and in particular that focused on the BNP and Combat 18. The national media, however, simply haven't wanted to know, with the honourable exception of Channel 4; now, after Dublin, the tabloids unite to treat Combat 18 as a national menace – but one that has only just emerged. Talk about shutting doors after bolting horses – where were the tabloid Nazi-hunters when they were needed, right at the beginning, to nip the Nazis in the bud? Probably, in the case of *The Sun*, too busy mouth-foaming against immigrants, bastard foreigners and their 'loony left' supporters. *The Sun* directors are clearly either too thick or too cynical to reflect humbly on the irony here: *The Sun* and their ilk now engage in man-hunts to find tabloid-reading neo-Nazi thugs whose political education was largely gleaned from the very papers which now condemn them. Ha bloody ha.

Equally, the media aren't doing any favours for those 'innocent' families who are relatively new to football by applying such a Panglossian tinge to the footie experience. People attracted by the image of clean, family fun who are then traumatised by finding themselves in the midst of seething tribal passions must understandably feel they've been sold a false bill of goods. Any Red could have told a first-timer going into the so-called Family Stand at Selhurst that they were in for a high-decibel introduction to the full range of English obscenities, but they'd have received no such warnings from the football industry and its image-makers. If Dublin and the other smaller-scale incidents have done any good, it is to remind the public that football has not yet been fully surrendered to the thermos-toting families of tennis-club members.

Overall, the media have missed what could be the truly big story – that a backlash is in full swing against the post-Taylor settlement. This movement of opinion is not only against the new antiseptic world of all-seater stadia, family punters and commercialism –

which most true fans remain unenamoured with – but also seeks to revive a *modus operandi* that Heysel, Hillsborough and Taylor were supposed to have buried. There is now, more than ever, talk of old firms reforming or of new ones being established; the word 'kick-off' is increasingly spoken in a context other than a 3 p.m. start; there is renewed interest in the debris of cultural history relating to hooliganism, as evidenced by the success of *Trouble on the Terraces*; and, of course, there is the undeniable re-emergence of the organised, footie-centred far right.

Crucially, there is a sense of continuity too; there are, after all, plenty of individuals (and certain clubs – hello, Leeds) for whom violence never went out of fashion in the first place. If the older hoolie is ready to take up the cudgels once more, there are also younger lads, for whom the '70s and '80s are ancient but glamorous history, who are equally ready to restage the stories of blood-soaked scenes from the terraces their elders have brought them up on. Already those old media faves the firm generals are said to be back in action, organising set-piece rucks for their troops and profiting from the distinct complacency shown by the authorities and the media. It is now over ten years since the real hooligan era fizzled out, which is virtually a generation ago in football terms. The spirit of the times, the *Zeitgeist*, is different from that which held sway in '86–'90, when violence became rather 'uncool'. This is *not* the era of loved-up summers, dropping 'E's, the popped-up Roses, inflatables and the birth of the 'zines. The Roses have become heavy and sinister, crack has replaced 'E' and a Mancunian summer is more likely to be soundtracked by rattling Uzis than by blissed-out lovemaking. Different lads with different values make the running now; the '90s male's lifestyle and mindset, dominated by New Ladism rather than New Man-ism, are far more receptive to the *Pulp Fiction* brutalism that terrace aggro requires. The transformation of the football experience into something akin to a theatre trip may yet be halted in its tracks.

*(Aggro was an old craze coming back in '95; anyone not too busy fighting succumbed to a new, and infinitely more pointless, fad . . .)*

## Coming Soon from the Daily Spurt

FANTASY FOOTBALL LEAGUE FOR SAD BASTARDS
It's the new craze that's swept the nation, kids!

Are you a sad, lonely supporter of a second-rate team with no star players and no chance of beating Man United?

Then Fantasy Football is for you. Retreat into your own make-believe world of fairies, dragons and Man City trophies and create your own little universe where, just for once, you might be on the winning side.

Fantasy Football: the talk of the pubs as fans of inferior teams desperately try to avoid the reality of their utter crapness.

Fantasy Football: brought to you by every bandwaggoning rag in the land – especially popular in Leeds and Moss Side.

FANTASY FOOTBALL – WHERE IT CAN BE 5–1 EVERY DAY!

*(More hype: pleased though the nation was to see United's last-fence failure, May was generally a time for anguished hacks' hand-wringing over the 'outrages' we had witnessed during '94–'95. The author reckoned the following would strike more of a chord with the* Red Issue *public, however . . .)*

## 1994–95: The Season of Shame?

'English Football's Disgrace'; 'Soccer in the Gutter'; 'The Shame of Our National Game'; 'Scandal, Sleaze and Corruption' . . . on and on it goes, the familiar litany of 1995's football headlines. We've had drugs of all kinds, bungs, bribes, kung fu and stamping, deaths in car parks, international hooliganism, sexual shenanigans – in fact, every possible piece of tabloid-fodder imaginable. All commentators and so-called experts have agreed that the combined effect has set back the English game by years. What was once a bright, shiny, happy world of family fun has been transformed into a dark, corrupting throwback to the bad old days of the '70s and '80s. Well, bollocks to all that.

Even though we at United have suffered the consequences of our own moments in the season of shame, I still have to say that most of this 'bad news' has been absolutely wonderful. Far from being a terrible advert for our game, these scandals and affairs have breathed new life into what was becoming the most tediously sterile football league in Europe. Every time a footballer is caught skinning up, sniffing his win bonuses or throwing matches, we get a life-affirming reminder that these footballers are real lads, not role-model automatons. Every outbreak of aggro reminds the world that football still belongs to us, not the new breed of Johnny-Come-Latelys who are seeking to impose their behavioural quirks on the rest of us. And when top footballers are pictured by the 'News of the Screws' marauding about with strippers and baby oil, they should be congratulated for their commitment to the entertainment of the public.

What do the doom merchants want, the screeching moralists who lecture us every time someone misbehaves a bit? They are, of course, all fully hooked up to the family-values, good-clean-fun world of '90s football which is loathed by most of us. They claim that the antiseptic, fair-play, all-above-board philosophy will 'save the game' and build a better future. But just how interesting, exciting and attractive would a Premier League full of Gary Linekers be? A Premier League where every chairman is honest, every fan a non-swearing saint and every inter-club rivalry a friendly one? If football were to be banished solely to the back pages, never to dominate the front with the latest scandal or sensation, it would die. This game isn't just about what happens on the pitch; it's about everything else surrounding it. And most of that 'everything else' tends to be a bit unsavoury, if not downright criminal.

The Devil has all the best tunes, they say: quite right. It's the bad, the gory, the outrageous that is memorable and thrilling. Here's to more of the same next year, doubly enjoyable if it appals the tabloids and the telly. Let's have Liverpool players overdosing on smack, let's have small towns being razed to the ground by Leeds savages, let's have entire clubs being exposed as gambling syndicate covers and let's have some really juicy transsexual/S&M/bestiality sex scandals involving chairmen, managers and players' mistresses. The more people it puts off football, the better: we don't want those sorts in football anyway. Spoil the good name of English football, don't they Des?

*(At United, the scandal and shame continued throughout the close-season too.* The Game *magazine doubtless expected the author to live up to his Fergie-hating tabloid reputation and pen a scathing piece about the Old Trafford summer sales. But as those intelligent enough not to believe what they read in the gutter press would have surmised, treason against our besieged monarch was the last crime he fancied*

*committing, even if Fergie had indeed murdered a couple of footballing princes . . .)*

## 'Now Is the Summer of Our Discontent . . .'

(From *The Game*)

. . . and in parts of Manchester's Red three-quarters, Alex Ferguson is about as popular as Richard the Third himself. Old Trafford's summer sale has given even Allied Carpets a run for their money: in a trice, a quarter of that immortal double-winning side has been vaporised. That would be reason enough for much breastbeating and teeth-gnashing from despondent Reds, especially given that two of the three deportees were at the peak of their career. But add to that the dispiriting, confidence-shattering effect that United's handling of the crisis has had on fans and you have a recipe for revulsion rather than mere regret.

We were not, after all, in the best of summer moods to start with: the loss of the double already had us on a downer. All we wanted was a nice, quiet summer watching the cricketers at the other Old Trafford conquer all, safe in the knowledge that with injuries healed and suspensions served, a full-strength team led by Cole and Cantona would soon be back to wreak vengeance. Instead we've watched open-mouthed as a maelstrom has engulfed us, causing us as much grief as anything that happened during the season itself.

As is sadly habitual these days, United as a club have blundered their way through all this with the lack of aplomb you'd expect from an organisation without any conception of modern public-relations skills. At the height of the fighting, the manager was away on his hols, leaving the chairman to flounder about with his foot in his mouth; then, when Ferguson returned, ostensibly to calm tempers and explain all, he had within seven days managed to drive both Ince and Andrei to spill some devastating beans to the tabloids. In truth, the credibility of the club's public pronouncements had long since been shot to pieces during the initial skirmishes; little wonder, then, that some Reds were now prepared to trust in the players', rather than the club's, version of events. It didn't help the club's image that the chairman should have opined along the way that United fans had no right to sound off about such matters; his proclamation that we were all just customers paying at the gate with no rights to any other consideration did not, to put it mildly, go down well with the 130,000 who pay to be *members* of MUFC and thus expect to be treated as such.

It's now a matter of public record that the transfers of Ince and Andrei – and, allegedly, to a lesser extent, Hughesy – were products of personality clashes between manager and player. Few now pretend to believe that the loss of these players can somehow strengthen United as a footballing outfit; any replacements are by definition almost bound to be inferior substitutes, at least for the time being. Some in Manchester mutter darkly that we'd have done better to lose the manager and keep the players; others talk of Ferguson's Napoleonic Busby complex which has made United a grim autocracy. There are allusions to the King across the water, Bryan Robson, waiting for the call on the other side of the Tees; others talk up the contribution of Brian Kidd, who has now committed himself to United despite the panting courtship from City. United fans have always been split between those who adore Fergie and will follow him to the Thatcheresque abyss ('I want to go on and on and on,' said both Maggie and Alex) and those who've harboured suspicions which are now biliously surfacing.

So, as the song goes, let's look on the bright side, if there is one amidst all this end-of-empire gloom. If Ferguson now has a squad that he is personally at ease with, perhaps United as a team will benefit from the improved atmosphere, from the sense of all being 'Fergie's Boys'. Of course, he has gambled this summer, but then the readiness to take risks has always been an Alex characteristic – and there was no gamble greater and no success bigger than the purchase of Eric Cantona. And whilst it may be true that Fergie's recent record concerning keeping players happy, rotating personnel in team selection and choosing tactics in Europe looks a little ropey, there is one area in which he has been an unqualified success: the breeding of home-grown youth. Talk to Ferguson these days and you'll never be more than a sentence away from a paean of praise for the Fledglings. He has brought these lads on, brought them into the team and now trusts they will help bring home the trophies. It's another gamble, of course: Nicky Butt is not yet a Paul Ince, nor Paul Scholes a Mark Hughes. But as any Red will confirm, there's nothing to match the thrill of watching kids grow into men and from there into stars. If the spirit of Busby and his Babes really is informing everything Ferguson does, it has no less an effect on the fans too; if, come May, the goals of Beckham, Scholes and Butt, defended by the Nevilles, are bringing silverware to Old Trafford, much of this summer's farrago will be forgiven.

*(Blimey, the author was right – although, truth be told, he scarcely believed a word of that conclusion when he wrote it. But then who could have foreseen how extraterrestrially brilliant Eric would be in the spring, or how hilariously feeble Mr Keegan's state of mind would prove to be come the crunch? We were certainly at the end of an era in the summer of '95, and it seemed an apt moment for the author to condense the plot of* United We Stood *into 2,500 words for the benefit of* FourFourTwo *readers wanting a retrospective on the Fergie Years. The author sent Alex a copy of this as a peace offering after their summer misunderstanding; apparently it did the trick. It's one of the author's favourite pieces and it was a complete bugger to get the right construction and the marriage of key managerial developments with relevant matches. Not that anyone cares, of course.)*

## The Gaffer Tapes: 8½ – Starring Alex Ferguson

(From *FourFourTwo*)

As noted film buff and Fergie favourite son Choccy McClair could doubtless remind you, Fellini's *8½* told the dramatically intense and often surreal story of a director's struggle against the odds to complete his life's masterpiece. And happily for this strained allusion, Alex Ferguson's doom-laden Wembley appearance in May marked eight and a half seasons of his own directorial tenure at the Theatre of Dreams, a time stuffed with enough plot twists and climaxes to keep any movie-goer satisfied. Neatly, Alex has ended his eighth full season as he ended his first – in second place behind Kenny Dalglish, natch – but with his star billing so enhanced as to be second only to Sir Matt Busby's. His life's masterpiece may yet be rewarded with a European Cup, but for now let us reflect on how he has become, in Cantona's phrase, the much-worshipped 'head of our family' – the making of Godfather Ferguson, in eight and a half episodes.

### 5.12.87: QPR 0 United 2

For Reds stuffed into the prehistoric away enclosure at Loftus Road, the pre-match talk was not of football but of pub crawls, specifically the spectacular week-long tour of Manchester's niteries by Messrs Whiteside and McGrath. United's greatest drinkers had truly excelled themselves this time, reaching such a state that they were relieved Fergie was keeping track of their progress with an A to Z: 'They were glad at least I knew where they were because they had no idea,' Alex quipped. Neither was fit to play. Despite the Reds' victory, it marked the beginning of the end for the old brigade. Within eighteen months, Strachan, Olsen and Moran had joined Norm 'n' Paul in the exodus from Old Trafford, a quintet which epitomised Big Ron's Cavaliers being replaced by a hard new breed of Fergie Roundheads. The promised Glorious Revolution had finally arrived.

United actually finished the season in second place, setting an Old Trafford record for the fewest defeats in the process, but Fergie had seen enough: 'This set of players had peaked and I knew they would never win the title.' We had all been expecting the purge for some time. When Alex arrived, the contrast with Ron could hardly have been greater. In place of tans, jewellery and wideboy suits came blazers, regulation haircuts and the moral rigour of Scottish Protestantism. The days of the OT Boozers' Social Club were clearly numbered. Of Ron's boys, to whom Atkinson had allegedly got too close, only Robson and the returning prodigal Hughes were to survive the ensuing cull. The howls from the terraces as boyhood heroes were handed tickets to the glue factory were raucous – and enduring, as several of the discarded were saved by other clubs *en route* and revived for years' more service. Strachan, in particular, must have enjoyed his 1992 vengeance. Much later, Fergie would paw the ground sheepishly and concede *sotto voce* that he may have been a bit hasty in one or two cases, especially as the squad soon became so emaciated that you could see all its ribs. Nevertheless, the Godfather had revealed his first traits: a patient fairness in allowing players plenty of time to make their pitch and a chilling ruthlessness in wielding the scythe when his mind was made up, deaf to the screams of horrified observers. Dismantling a runners-up side whilst sitting in football's hottest seat took some *cojones, amigo.*

### 1.1.89: United 3 Liverpool 1

Ah, sweet Scouse-smashing memories. For any '80s-boy Red, this was one of the best. As Fergie began reassembling the United jigsaw, apparently without a nice picture on the lid from which to work, we plunged relegation-wards; hit, too, by a mammoth injury crisis, we faced Liverpool at one of their many peaks live on telly. We prepared for another miserable Bank Holiday but instead witnessed a roasting of the dustbin-dippers that we'd never forget. Special enough in itself, of course, but a historic marker too. For Ferguson had the courage to throw a collection of raw kids into the team and give them free rein – Sharpe, Robins, Martin, Beardsmore and, er, Ralphie Milne. Now there's nothing that excites a true Red more than the sight of a bunch of fresh, thrilling kids in shorts getting hot and sweaty doing their stuff for United, if you see what I mean. The addition of Gill, Graham and Wilson ten days later at QPR completed the full complement of what came to be known as 'Fergie's Fledglings' and together they illuminated an otherwise dank and dreary season. Two of the lads actually scored at Loftus Road, securing a replay on a night that conjured up memories of Docherty's Kids and even Busby's Babes. For the best part of two months, they kept the team afloat; typically, when the big boys returned, they got us knocked out of the cup – with help from Brian Hill – and our season was over. The outstanding image of '88–'89 remained young, gawky Russell Beardsmore slamming the third into the Liverpool goal at the Stretford End. Thanks for the memories, kids.

In the end, only Sharpe and Robins made it into the big time. Injury, bad luck and loss of form accounted for the rest. Looking back objectively, Fergie remarked that they were never quite good enough for a Red future; tellingly, he also noted that they weren't *his* kids but were inherited from Ron, with the exception of Sharpe. However, as we were soon to discover, Fergie had already committed himself to upholding the dearest Red tradition, that of cultivating youth. Long before he took his axe to the old first-teamers, he had already revamped our decrepit scouting system and begun devoting much of his time to the pursuit of young excellence. On New Year's Day '89, he had shown us his intent; as the '90s progressed, he produced the results. Giggs, Scholes, the Nevilles, Nicky Butt, Beckham . . . Fergie's Fledglings Mark Two, as promised.

### 9.12.89: United 1 Palace 2

By now, Fergie had more than three years on the meter, and what had we to show for it? Three months before, City had beaten us by a score I can't quite remember; we were at the start of a four-month run without a home win; we were playing the worst football seen since Sexton; every other Ferguson buy was turning out to be a dud. Incredibly, relegation became a realistic possibility. Back in '74, when The Doc took us down, few clamoured for his dismissal. We could see what he was trying to do long-term, we had faith in his ability to produce eventual success, we could see the finished picture on the jigsaw-box lid. But as United, bereft of the dropped hero Hughes, hoofed up long balls, misplaced passes and got turned over by these nondescript suburbanites, J-Stand had had enough. 'Fergie Out' came the cry; as the banner put it, 'Enough excuses – Ta ra Fergie.' The manager raced home and hid, no longer willing to face the press, the fans, the world. The end was nigh, or so it seemed.

Somehow, the High Noon cup shoot-out with Cloughie was won, ironically aided by a vibrant travelling Red Army, 90% of whom wanted Fergie's testes on a platter; we stumbled and staggered onto a cup run. Still, at Millwall in February, *Red Issue* co-editor Veg 'wanted us to lose, so that we could rid ourselves of Ferguson'; we won – for the first time in the league since November – and the monster lived on. Through sheer grit and determination rather than skill, we made it to the cup final. *Red Issue* sardonically labelled the Wembley event 'Alex Aid: eleven footballers try to keep Fergie out of the dole queue'. For the fans, only a cup win would be enough to warrant Ferguson's continuance in office. The Fledgling Martin duly won it for his boss and, grudgingly, another season's grace was granted. Never has the cliché 'a turning point' been more apt. Behind the scenes, however, the Godfather's one-to-one charisma had already secured his future long before the final. As Jim White, author of *Are You Watching, Liverpool?*, explains, 'When Alex talks to you personally, he makes you feel like you are the most important thing in his world. His sincerity and integrity are overwhelming; he almost always knows how to get through to every variation of personality. He could convince you of anything.' Martin Edwards and Bobby Charlton were under the spell. By guaranteeing Ferguson his future, they gave him his chance to work his man-to-man magic on the players. And within three years the Sorcerer had all the players he wanted, dancing to the direction of his wand. For the fans, this was the sort of egg on our faces that we didn't mind licking off.

**20.10.90: United 0 Arsenal 1**

A twenty-man brawl, if more handbags than fists, was just the sort of top entertainment we all love. The passionate, driven scrapper that is

Alex Ferguson had demanded, 'I insist that my teams have this quality . . . huge, great fighting hearts that just don't want to be beaten.' The foppish, easily dispirited '80s United had gone, replaced by a blazing, hardened beast – and about time too. Later, United would unjustly be labelled a dirty, petulant, over-aggressive side, a product of the manager's lack of discipline, but better that than a collection of gutless, bloodless creeps. Fergie fined a couple of our boys under fierce media pressure but was soon to regret doing so. From now on, discipline was to be internal and private; he was no longer prepared to sacrifice players on the black altar of press opinion. He required absolute loyalty and discretion from his players; it was only right that he should give the same in return. Moreover, collective responsibility was now to be the doctrine: 'I will never betray my staff by marking down individual scapegoats for collective failure.' Like Montgomery and his troops, there was some serious battle-hardened bonding going down here; manager and players tied themselves together around the club standard, yelling, 'Come on then, we'll take you all!' Red fans, genetically programmed to respond to such combative stuff, purred in appreciation.

Where once Fergie had been slated for persevering too long with the hapless and the cretins (*vide* Leighton, Milne, Donaghy), he now began to reap credit for standing by such hesitant debutants as Ince, Pally and Blackmore, who were all beginning to gel with the team. 'I was tuned into the players' psychological breakthroughs . . . because it was similar to my own experience beginning at United,' he remarked. The Fergie learning curve was about to lurch skywards.

**28.11.90: Arsenal 2 United 6**

As Veg says, 'This was the night it all came right, at last.' Arsenal, champions-to-be with only one league defeat, were handed the heaviest drubbing in forty years by a side using wingers, break-neck speed and one-touch pass 'n' move. 'It took him a long time to realise what sort of football we demanded,' remarks Veg, 'but this was no accidental discovery of the true way.' Indeed; by dropping an in-form Webb and rejigging the tactics, Ferguson had gambled astutely. He had found the pattern and the mechanism at last after years of apparently fruitless tinkering; now all he had to do was replace some of the dodgier metalwork to complete his lean, sharp killing machine. With added victories in this League Cup run over champs Liverpool and soon-to-be-champs Leeds, Fergie had at least returned us to where we were at Big Ron's peak: able to beat anyone on our day. Once Giggs, Eric and Andrei had arrived, 'on our day' was to become *every* day. Still, as that year's final demonstrated, and as gratuitously repeated in 1994's counterpart, Big Ron could yet teach Fergie a thing or two about big-match tactics and selection . . .

**20.4.92: United 1 Forest 2**

Or 'Black Monday', as it is sometimes known, when United blew half of their '92 title chance, finishing the job at Upton Park two days later. During the nadir of '89–'90, the team were christened 'Fergie's Fuckwits' by *Red Issue*; now, as we were struck dumb by a series of bizarre selection decisions that ruined our rhythm and style, Fergie himself stood accused of being the 'Fuckwit'. Some, more politely, settled for the appellation 'Tinkerbell', as Hughes and Andrei in particular were left seething on the sidelines at crucial junctures. Thankfully, in our title-winning seasons, this Ferguson disease went into remission somewhat, the bitter lessons of '92 having apparently been learned well. But, like the demented sculptor who doesn't know when to stop chipping away, the old habits resurfaced last season, as Andrei at Goodison, Cole at Anfield and Hughes at Upton Park all discovered. Cue the sound of shattering masonry as the title edifice crumbled . . .

He still suffers the odd tactical stuffing too, whether at the hands of Big Ron or, more emphatically, Johann Cruyff; he continues to have a touching but entirely misplaced faith in players' ability to adapt to different roles, as evidenced by the long-running David May farrago. Then there's the question of his motivational tactics; back in '92, there was much gossip about him overdoing the teacup-chucking and 'Fergie Fury' performances which were said to produce a pressure overload on players. Jim White wonders whether his other psychological tactics and Henry V-style dressing-room speechifying have become too repetitive, hence suffering from the law of diminishing returns. Time will tell; as for the 'Fergie Fury' malarkey, the man himself says he's calmed down now – he only uses the *threat* of the teacups, not the action itself. Royal Doulton are in mourning . . .

**6.12.92: United 2 City 1**

Eric Cantona makes his home debut; his first touch is a brilliant, defence-shattering through ball. Within the month, Eric has inspired five- and four-goal displays against Coventry and Spurs as United's title odds tumble. Ferguson's greatest-ever transfer gamble hits the jackpot, in the face of the Hansen-led Cassandras. The twenty-six-year wait is over; the double follows. Our favourite song for three years now? 'Fergie's Red and White Army'. A rather different tune from 'Fergie Out' . . .

Of course, Cantona was the catalyst, the final piece without which the rest would not have worked quite as beautifully. And yes, there was a large element of luck in our securing his services. Yet, once again, there had to be a man there prepared to take the risk, to go with his purist football instincts, a man willing to take the chance of his empire being contaminated by the seepage from football's most mercurial personality. Signing Eric was what Cantona himself, a French existentialist, might have termed an *acte gratuite* – a self-defining active challenge to the world that expresses your freedom and beliefs. How deserved it is that Ferguson should be the main beneficiary of Cantona's gifts.

There are, however, ten others in a team. Their success demonstrated two further facets of the Godfather's powers. Firstly, (*pace* David May) his transfer-market touch has improved immeasurably. Secondly, his unique, one-to-one managerial style has proved its worth. Few managers risk taking anything other than a uniform, no-favours, collective approach to man-management. Fergie has the confidence in his own managerial ability to buck that trend. 'He'll be sharp and stroppy with Sharpe and Keane, fatherly and solicitous with Giggs and Butt, reverential and indulgent with Eric and so on; he pulls out every stop to motivate each as an individual and in doing that has got the very best out of each,' says Jim White. Success is not universal, of course. Get it wrong with one man and the result can be resentment and estrangement, as has seemingly occurred with Kanchelskis. In general, however, White has no doubts: 'Of all the managers, he is by far the most personally impressive and charismatic, impossible to typecast, impossible to resist.' Alex had found the pattern, found the players and found his managerial method.

### 12.3.94: United 3 Charlton 1

Schmeichel is sent off in a cup tie, a decision almost incontestably correct. In now archetypal Fergie-team style, United blaze back to win with passion anyway, but Fergie emerges to slag the referee. The media piranhas dive in for a feeding frenzy – yet another hothead Fergie outburst, to go with his 'Jimmy Hill's a prat', 'Galatasaray should be closed down' and 'Teams leave Anfield choking back the vomit'. If you need any more reasons as to why we now love the man, look no further. He thinks, talks and reacts like one of us, like a true Red. No room for objectivity, for mature consideration or for being a good loser – he shoots from the hip, defends the indefensible and takes defeat as badly as McEnroe. Yes! This is exactly what we want from a United manager. We expect the impossible from our leader, in many ways. We want a Busbyesque father figure to respect, a street-fighting hardcase to empathise with and a football-loving connoisseur to tantalise all our senses. Ferguson, somehow, does the lot. Again, he is unusual amongst managers in that he makes almost no effort to cosy up to the press corps or, indeed, the world at large. Amidst the vulturish hacks, he is the soul of discretion, offering favours to few. All he cares about is United's staff and players; the rest of the world's existence is merely to be tolerated.

As we spent most of '94–'95 behind the battlements, dominated by the siege mentality, what a man to have to hold us together as we huddled for comfort around the Red flag. Naturally, the siege might not have been so harsh had Ferguson's attitude not alienated so many outsiders in past years, but we don't mind. We like it in here, repelling barbarians outside Old Trafford's walls. No one likes us and we really don't care; we've got Alex and Eric – what more could we desire?

**16.3.94: United 5 Wednesday 0**

Eight episodes done: this is the half. To be precise, the first half against the Owls, when United scored four and threatened ten. Everything Ferguson has worked for was on display, whether in the commitment, the one-touch movements, the outrageous charges forward or the superb goals. 1994–95 might have witnessed the return of some unpleasant side-effects of Fergie's rule, from the tinkering and tactical botches to the transfer errors, but we'll all be turning up once more in '95–'96 in the hope of being privileged enough to see more football like this: Ferguson-style.

If Ferguson is the Godfather, then Matt Busby was God himself. The late founder of the modern dynasty will never be replaced as the ultimate supremo. Alex, however, at least sits at his right hand.

Recently he has talked of retirement, handing over the family to Brian Kidd or Bryan Robson, but whatever they achieve they will be hard-pressed to match the cinematically dramatic story of the Ferguson Years. There still remains the quest for the European Cup, which would be a fitting conclusion for the man an unusually eloquent David Meek described thus: 'He has the best qualities of all his predecessors: the decency and application of O'Farrell, the scholarliness of Sexton, the fun and humour of Docherty and the awareness and approachability of Atkinson.' With a European Cup on the sideboard, an added reference to the best of Busby would be warranted too. For the modern Fergie's Red and White Army, it would be the least he'd deserve.

# 1995–96

*(Biblical students will recall that Lucifer was once an angel sitting at God's side before he got relegated to the Nationwide League [Hell Division]. Eric had travelled the other way: vilified by the world as Satan's spawn, the ultimate Red-mist Devil, in January '95, Old Trafford's faithful worshippers had since canonised and then, finally, deified him. As the '95–'96 season kicked off – without Eric –* FourFourTwo *asked the author to attempt an explanation.)*

## King Chronicles: Deifying a Devil

(From *FourFourTwo*)

For Man United fans, the close-season took off where the campaign proper had ended – applying thumping one-twos to the solar plexus. Hard on the heels of the double defeat came the knock-down sell-offs: the Guv'nor and the Ledge exited stage-left from the pantheon of heroes. But then there are heroes and there are heroes, differing degrees of divinity on a Hinduesque basis. For however shattering these two losses were, at least *Dieu* remained. As one hardcore Red put it, 'I'm angry about Ince; I'm sad about Hughes. But if they let Eric go, I'd be lookin' at a double manslaughter charge.' Messrs Ferguson and Edwards, I think he was only half-joking.

Since the Selhurst Park débâcle, Eric has often been referred to as a 'cult hero', which gives the misleading impression that Cantona-worship is an obsession for a minority. If you've attended any United match this season, however, you'll have learned the truth. At the risk of *FourFourTwo* ending up on bonfires in the Philippines and Deep South, Eric is currently more frenziedly adored in the Red three-quarters of Manchester than Jesus, Take That and Ryan Giggs combined. This is no cult – it's mass devotion that drenches thousands in the juices of love.

The media have a propensity to calculate anything Red-centred in terms of merchandise and money, so let us measure it thus. Tour the barrows of the Old Trafford market-place and you will currently find twenty-three varieties of Cantona T-shirt. The *Eric the King* video is the best-selling player vid ever. There are more club shirts with 'Cantona', 'Dieu' or, er, 'Le God' stamped on the back than all the rest of the team combined. His autobiography took up residency in the top-ten lists and even sold well when it was only available on French-language import. The indie record label Exotica released the song 'Eric the King' as a low-key single and were astonished to see it shoot into the indie top ten *en route* to becoming the best-selling indie footie record ever; a Cantona album is due in October. If you're soulless enough to see these things in purely bottom-line terms, the man's pre-eminence is fiscally unchallenged.

For the lads on what were once the terraces, the devotion is more simply expressed – in song. During his long, painful absence when the consequences of his kung fu conspired to cost us our double, did we hold it against him or allow him to slip from our thoughts? Of course not; with perhaps typical Mancunian perversity, our sessions of vocal hosannas doubled and trebled in frequency and intensity. Not a match was allowed to pass without our reminding both Eric and the world of our chosen religion; the 'Cantona Medley' became the mainstay of the K-Stand songbook. At the last count, there were eight fully fledged Cantona songs, all of which you are likely to hear sung in any particular game. And whilst it may be true that the high priest of Ericism, Peter Boyle, originates most of them, they are taken up by thousands within moments. How gratifying, then, that in the face of media criticism of our 'shameless' behaviour, Eric should have cited our efforts to support him as a prime reason for re-signing. To Rob Shepherd, Patrick Barclay et al. it may seem an 'obscene obsession', but as any Red of the political kind would argue, the ends are deemed to justify the means. Eric will be back with a vengeance and that is all that matters.

If, as Basil Fawlty said to Sybil, your specialised subject is the bleedin' obvious, you might explain this Gallophiliac frenzy with a simple reference to his footballing ability: he is the best player at the club, ergo he is the most adored. That, however, would be as howlingly simplistic as crediting the Beatles phenomenon to their unusual chorus chord-shifts. Nor is it enough merely to add that his pivotal role in ending our twenty-six-year title-free starvation was enough to elevate him to the heavens, important an aspect though that is. It may be true that for Red intellectuals, the star-quality baggage that comes with Cantona – the philosophy, the painting, the style – adds hugely to his appeal, making him truly admirable in a way that your average, monosyllabic, *Loaded*-reading, provincial trundler can never be, however good a player. But for Reds, particularly of my post-'60s generation, there is something more elemental to it than all that.

Firstly, those of us who were too young for 1968 and the Holy Trinity of Best, Law and Charlton have something to cherish that inhabits the same plane as those '60s legends, something about which we can rhapsodise to our kids, an era to mythologise for evermore. At last we have been there in person to witness a team that could give the '60s side a match – and, in doing the double and retaining the title, a team that in some ways has outstripped its illustrious forebears. Cantona was the jewel of that team, a veritable Koh-i-noor and the catalyst of the success; moreover, at last we have our own contemporary hero fit to be mentioned in the same breath as Best and co. However much we loved Robson, Hughes, Whiteside and Hill, none ever quite reached that pinnacle. But Eric, surely, has done so.

Secondly, Eric has become more than mere flesh, even more than a holy talisman. He has, especially since Selhurst Park, become the personification of United. It isn't just that our own siege mentality has produced an empathy with his own personal beleaguerment; it's because in Eric we see a distillation of everything that we like to think we are. We see style as important as function; we exalt the individual over the collective; we rejoice in the very qualities the English are supposed to disdain – glamour, sexiness, arrogance and hot-tempered exhibitionism. Not for us the moralising, humble and dogged Protestant work ethic of the rest. We always reckoned United were not quite of this world; now, Eric and ourselves are United as spiritual Continentals stuck in a downbeat English league. *Vive la différence* – and *vive l'entente cordiale*!

*(LMTB and season-ticket holders were, as ever, delighted to receive a letter from Ken Merrett at the start of '95–'96, a masterpiece of patronising aggravation – but was the following a more truthful first draft?)*

## 'Dear Member . . .'

There seems to be some confusion as to what is, and is not, acceptable behaviour at Old Trafford. To clarify the position, we set out below our policy.

- Standing for anything other than a goal is NOT ACCEPTABLE

- Singing any song apart from those officially sanctioned by Keith Fane or Ken Merrett is NOT ACCEPTABLE

- Wearing offensive T-shirts, i.e. anything not purchased from the Megastore, is NOT ACCEPTABLE

- Being, or behaving like, the bloody working class is NOT ACCEPTABLE

The majority of United supporters are people who want to enjoy their visit to Old Trafford in a sterile, church-like atmosphere and do not wish to be disturbed by you proletarian bastards in the cheap seats. We, as a club, wish to encourage that feeling.

There have been suggestions made that we are opposed to singing or other forms of vocal support. NOTHING COULD BE FURTHER FROM THE TRUTH. We recognise the value of positive support; the players need it and we welcome it. However, chants of 'We hate Leeds' (or anyone else for that matter) are not helpful to our players and let us all down. Only the manager is allowed to say 'I hate Leeds', 'I wish they'd get bloody relegated', 'You sheep-shagging scum', etc. Do as we say and not as we do.

Towards the end of last season, we received a letter from the Association of Football Families. One paragraph (published below) speaks eloquently of the type of supporter who is an embarrassment to this club and a disease which, if not removed, will fester and drive good, decent people away from the clubs and the sport they love.

> Although we at the Association were pleased with the results of the recent Premier League survey, we are anxious lest it deters clubs from addressing this major problem. There is a minority of 'supporters' who don't know how to behave at the modern football ground. They sing throughout the game at the tops of their voices in horrid working-class accents and sometimes use words like 'sh*t' and 'cr*p'. Some have traces of alcohol on their breath, which suggests to us that they have been in a public house that morning rather than in church. Some, instead of wearing the nice club shirts, have T-shirts on that poke cruel fun at our friends from Maine Road and Anfield. We have even experienced these individuals laughing at us because we are carrying twelve club-shop bags or because we sing along to the official club record. When our members change seats, they still

find people like this all around them wherever they go. Sometimes you wonder if these hooligans are in the majority.

This letter is written in a spirit of conciliation and goodwill, even though it might appear we're declaring war on you vermin. We take no pleasure in expelling people from our stadium; however, if we must, we will, and we'll be keeping all your season-ticket money. Decent, well-behaved supporters are entitled to nothing less. The rest of you are entitled to nothing.

Yours in sport,
K.R. Meritless.

*(The one moment of light humour during the summer was the revelation that United had received what is now termed a 'cod-fax' concerning Andrei's transfer. A 'representative of the player' assured United that it came from the Donetsk vice-president and that it contained a waiver of the £1.1 million cut which Donetsk could have claimed from the deal. A week later, a fax arrived from the president saying, 'Where's my fuckin' money, comrade?' Red faces all round and a three-week tug of war with Goodison that threatened to produce the football court case of the year ensued. Now we already knew that those in power at United are often not that bright or worldly-wise, but this gullible acceptance of the year's fishiest fax was very heartening. We wondered if we could con United into believing some of the following faxes if we sent them in?)*

## Fishy Faxes

*FAO: MUFC Medical Staff*
*From: Dr Batson D. Seeling*
I write as Mr Brian McClair's personal physician. I have just examined him and am informing you that he's a bit poorly. In fact, he has both arsey cancer and viral knobbytitis and may not live much longer. I haven't told him yet as I don't want to depress him. I strongly suggest that to avoid contamination of other players you do not let him into Old Trafford ever again and, in view of his limited shelf life, you should consider selling him immediately. Try Bolton Wanderers – they won't have any players left by November and will be so desperate that they'd even buy Brian.

*FAO: Chief Executive, MUFC*
*From: De Zoete Welder Merchant Bank, Head Office*

We act for our clients, the True Red Consortium consisting of *Red Issue* and IMUSA, who wish to buy out your shareholding in MUFC and thus take control of the board. We assume, judging from the level of salary and dividends you have paid to yourself, that you are as keen as ever to maximise the financial yield from your position at MUFC. We therefore offer £50 million for your holding, which is way above the market rate. As blue chip merchant bankers, we can assure you that we have determined that our clients do indeed have such assets and will guarantee they're good for it. Michael Knighton is NOT involved. All we suggest is that we conduct the transaction on your favourite Paul Ince Payment Pattern, i.e. you hand over the share deeds now and we'll settle up with you in two years' time, honest.

*FAO Ken Meritless, Secretary*
*From: World Council of Methodists*
We have been watching your splendid career as a part-time lay preacher in our Manchester chapels and feel it is time to offer you the position of Moderator Supreme over all our world churches. You will then be at liberty to inspire hundreds of thousands all over the world with your cries of 'Sit down and shut up', 'We don't want your sort in here' and your classic 'We all love Leeds'. We must insist, however, that to give this post your full attention you must resign from your MUFC post and announce that you will never darken Old Trafford's doors again. Yours in sport . . .

*(Somehow one doubts either of the Kens is ever going to figure in anyone's list of favourite United people. Pat Crerand, however . . .)*

## Redheads: Paddy Crerand

(From original *Despatches* book)

If you ask Pete Boyle why he's currently writing as many songs about Pat Crerand as about King Eric, Pete simply replies, 'Respect is due – by public demand.' Apparently, so many Reds asked the Boyle to immortalise Crerand in song that he felt duty-bound to do so. In a recent fanzine poll, Paddy was voted Red of the Year; in Gothenberg, he was virtually mobbed by well-wishers on the Allevyn and had to duck out down backstreets. At a club where every individual has at least some critics, no one I know has ever heard a word said against him. Although he'd probably slap me for being sacrilegious in saying so, he has moved into the Premiership of the Respected to take his place alongside Sir Matt and Eric.

How has this happened? After all, he hasn't played for a quarter-century, his main public visibility these days being via radio commentary; many of his fans are too young to have ever seen him play. The country is full of ex-United pundits – and it's not as though he was our greatest-ever player either, his name being absent from the Holy Trinity litany of Best, Law and Charlton.

Ah, but therein lies the rub, already exposed. To describe his current standing as that of just another media pundit is laughably inadequate, as we shall see. First, let us remember where he's coming from. The *cognoscenti* of Red history and those who were actually there during that decade will tell you that Crerand was the key to the success of that great side – and, in some ways, the embodiment of its special qualities. It is a happy coincidence, given the way his personal life developed, that as a professional he was so reminiscent of Busby the player. The two of them epitomised that classic model of football history – the cultured, civilised Scottish half-back who thrived on skill and intelligence rather than mere pace and force. Never physically quick, a supposed fault that cost him his place under O'Farrell, his speed was all in the mind and the touch. For vision, instinct, courage and pure craft, there was no one better. Decades before we were enthralled by Eric's ability to see and execute the ball that all others were blind to, Paddy was knocking them off every few minutes. But then genius was in ample supply at Old Trafford then; only at mid-'60s United could such powers be taken for granted. The roll call of the Holy Trinity should, to be accurate, have been expanded to a quartet; some will tell you that although United could still function when one of the golden trio was absent, the loss of Crerand was always to be keenly felt.

He took a few weeks to settle at United, but once his man-of-the-match performance in the 1963 cup final was under his belt, he transformed United into title challengers and winners. Fittingly, given his latter-day support of Eric, his impact and his role were Cantonesque – by becoming the brain of the team, in Bestie's phrase, he acted as the alchemic catalyst that turned Old Trafford gold. He too displayed the fight and temper of a man who won't accept injustice, perhaps a product of a superior morality that places a man's own moral code above those imposed by lesser mortals – like refs and administrators in general. Whatever, that battling, brave commitment was precisely what we all want from our midfield generals. It was Crerand who, in the devastated aftermath of European semi-final defeat in '66, rose from the dressing-room bench to promise Matt that we would win the '67 title and then the European Cup; he did as much as anyone to ensure he kept his promise to his 'adopted father'.

His relationship with Busby was always a key element in Crerand's life. Matt, drawn to streetwise, larger-than-life characters, would have liked him anyway; add to that the Crerand integrity, honesty and decency which Busby always looked for in himself and others and it comes as no surprise that the Crerands were always favourite guests at Matt's modest Chorlton residence. Moreover, they had both been forged by similar life experiences: neither born with silver spoon in mouth, both proud upholders of a Scottish/Irish Catholic ancestry, both fierce individualists who nevertheless overcame the collective Anglo and Protestant bigotry ranged against them. When Crerand explains his relative lack of Scottish caps in terms of the bias against Celtic/United Catholics, it is not an excuse but the plain truth. And when you hear the Dunphy story about Paddy throwing a pint in the face of a reserve who was singing 'The Sash', you understand that his sentiments run deep. He doesn't just passively belong to a tradition – he actively defends it. So it is with Paddy and United: if you're not prepared to man the barricades at moments of strife, then you've become part of the problem. Crerand never looked for trouble – life was always for enjoying to the full – but when the calls came, he took up the trident. Benfica in '68, The Doc in court, the Red-hating media in '95: they've all felt Paddy's prongs.

It's a tantalising historical 'what-if?' that Crerand was considered by Busby as his successor in 1969 before McGuinness got the job; Paddy was playing too well to be moved upstairs in those pre-player/manager days. Throughout that often torturous decade, Paddy was one of the few to emerge with clean hands from the behind-the-scenes skulduggery. Typically, he behaved with Busbyesque impeccability. As usual, his judgements were spot-on: Wilf got the job too soon and under the wrong conditions; O'Farrell simply wasn't the right man for the post in the first place. Both managers dropped Paddy but, unlike other ageing heroes, he wasn't motivated by this to become a back-stabber – neither ex-manager will finger Paddy as a malcontent. The Doc, notoriously, engineered Paddy out through a series of unsubtle slights and snubs; he paid for it later, firstly when Paddy alerted Matt to the Brown situation, later when he responded to Willie Morgan's libel-action call to arms. It was a rare direct intervention in United politics but, in retrospect, one that was wholly justified. Taking up a managerial role at Northampton, Crerand was his usual no-nonsense self; facing a board he believed had reneged on previous assurances, he simply cleared his desk and walked out. If they'd assumed he was the archetypal duck 'n' dive, give-and-take merchant, they were hugely mistaken.

Throughout the '80s, Paddy did most of the usual ex-player stuff: he ran a pub in Alty, got involved in a travel firm with Big Norm, did a spot of hospitality at OT and so on. But, fundamentally, he remained a fan, going to as many games as possible and taking advantage of radio-commentary offers to combine work with pleasure. So he'd joined the punditocracy – hardly remarkable. Yet as the years have gone on, he has increasingly stood out from that over-populated and generally mediocre class. Passionate, opinionated, utterly biased, highly observant and unafraid to offend with the truth, he was every Red's choice of ideal match companion. As time went on, other would-be standard-bearers for the legacy of United have fallen by the wayside: Law on mundane autopilot for ITV, Bobby lost to the clutches of the board, Best staggering about over bottles and birds in between rank videos. Paddy's the last authentic voice from another era.

However, it's what he says and what he stands for that matters. As his voice became more widely sought-after by the media and the football world, what makes him special became clearer. Because he talks to us, the fans – and, more importantly, listens – he is in tune with the spirit of United like few others. Because he is genuine, open and democratic in the broadest sense of the word, we seek him out, and because of his reputation as player and man, the club has no option but to defer to him too. He is able to straddle the worlds of 'official' and 'unofficial' United – thus remaining both hugely well informed and highly influential – in a way that no one else can. Even when supposedly constrained by the self-censorship of 'official' United, for example in his *Man U Mag* column, he says what no one else would dare say with complete forthrightness. He's probably not cynically sly enough to realise and exploit the fact that he can do this because his status makes him virtually untouchable; he just does what comes naturally – that is, talking honestly and without guile or fear.

So we have learned to appreciate that in United's internal debates, he is the only man of stature who will willingly put our case and do so because he knows the issues and will make his own mind up. But when it's United against the world, he alone can speak for all of us, club and fans. The Cantona Affair saw Paddy at his best, stepping into the breach when no one else could or would dare. That awful night, as our coaches crawled away from the scene, Paddy took up our standard on radio and put all the pro-Eric arguments that later became our common currency. For twenty-four hours he stood virtually alone, reviled by the rest of Britain for his defence of our God, as he appeared wherever he could to stuff some common sense down the throats of the lynch mob. He stood fast on that beach-head, clutching the Red Flag, deflecting the flak until the rest of us could catch him up and support him; for that and his continued campaign on behalf of Eric alone, he would deserve all our thanks.

Many of the traditions and qualities that United had under Busby have long gone. The old brotherly club is now an inhuman plc behemoth, the ground a sanitised plastic family playground, the newer fans often a strange breed, uneducated in the ways of the Reds. Links to the soul of the club, that of the departed Sir Matt, should be cherished wherever they are found. A friend of mine who's been lucky enough to get to know Paddy well thinks his strength and popularity derive from a simple quality: 'He lives life on the Busby principle. They share so many characteristics and beliefs that the respect Paddy is held in is no surprise at all.' When we sing 'United, we love you', I often wonder what we mean by 'United'. The fans? Too many are entirely unlovable. The ground? Give me the 1976 version any day. The players? Heroes today, villains tomorrow. The club? Edwards, Merrett and co. – are you joking? No, I think 'United' is a spiritual concept, not a physical one. It means something about the way you behave, the way you play, the way you think, the way you support. That spirit, occasionally, is visible in certain individuals. Matt was one such being – and Paddy Crerand is another.

*(Even in a season as apparently triumphant as 1995–96, there are always moments when doubts surface about the manager's judgement – in Fergie's case, it's usually a query about tactics or selection. So lest you think we've been a tad hagiographic towards the gaffer . . .)*

## Daily Spurt Video Offer

FERGIE'S TACTICAL MASTERCLASS – PART TWO

In Part One of this series (available on MUFC Video for £18.99 with free Ryan Giggs tampon remover), we saw our manager expound the virtues of five-in-midfield, as seen at Upton Park, and five-in-defence, as witnessed at Villa Park. We also learned how, when things don't go right, NEVER blame the system you picked but say that the players were shit instead.

Today, Alex unveils some new formations that might see action this year.

*The 'One-Nine-One'*

'As youse all know, I am very concerned about "swamping", especially away from home. I don't like risking our midfield getting overrun and it seems from what happened at West Ham that five-in-the-middle just isna enough. So when we're up for a battle this year, I'm going for nine in midfield to be sure, in three rows of three and all holding hands so we keep our shape. Whoever's up front must also be prepared to chase back. Stevie Bruce will stay in defence, as I'm convinced his timing, speed and touch are as good as when he was twenty-five, just like I'm convinced that David May is a model of versatility.

'Youse will notice that a 1–9–1 means we won't actually have a permanent goalkeeper, but as I said to Peter Schmeichel at the Nou Camp, sometimes youse have got to sacrifice yourself for the team. So we'll play fly goalie, with Choccy McClair running back from his lone up-front role to cover. His work rate's amazing, he covers every blade of grass, etc. etc. . . .'

*The 'Five-One-Four'*

'This might be the one we'll be going for in home games. My excellent new five-at-the-back which we practised so successfully in the Midlands will feature David May at sweeper, proving how versatile he is – and you need someone totally reliable and nerveless back there.

'Nicky Butt, as I've said before, will be the best midfielder in the galaxy by Christmas. I have no doubt that he will rise to the challenge of being our only midfield player in this formation and will enjoy showing how right I was to sell Paul Ince, who only ever *seemed* to be our sole midfield star.'

*'The Whirl'*

'This isn't quite the same as that thing the Brazilians and Dutch did in the '70s but it'll be just as exciting. When the kids are having no joy, we can abandon 4–4–2 and switch to this, which basically involves playing the natural game the kids learned at school.

Therefore all eleven will rush madly around in a whirling pack, chasing the ball, refusing to pass it and dribbling as far as they can go before falling over and grazing their knees. It will mystify the opposition and I'd like to stress that this is *not* the same system we used in the late '80s.'

*The 'V' Formation*

'We'll be using this against Everton and Inter Milan. Basically, May will be the pivot at the back with the two legs of the "V" stretching out to Giggsy and Lee on the wings. The message will be clear: a big V-sign fuck off to those bastards Ince and the Russian from the whole team, including those who went to Incey's farewell party, you'll notice. It'll leave the space in the middle to draw them in, then Roy and the boys will close in and kick the shit out of them. Not that I'm at all paranoid or defensive about the summer sales, of course . . .'

Look out for part three in the series, entitled 'Fergie's European Tactical Triumphs', which will be broadcast in its entirety during the four-minute slot after *Channel 4 News.*

*(But if slagging Fergie is a rarity, popping at Edwards remains, quite rightly, the monthly staple of every United writer . . . By the way, extremely young readers should know that* Raise the Roof *kicked prime-time ass long before Mr Tarrant started asking his now infamous question.)*

*It's Saturday night on Granada!*
*It's time to stop shouting 'woof woof' and 'slag' at* Blind Date*!*
*Because it's time now for:*

## Raise the Roof with Bob Harness!

BOB: 'And tonight's star prize is a villa in Majorca, worth an astonishing £300,000!

'Well, Martin, a part-time businessman from Wilmslow, you're through to the final round and you've chosen the category of Man United administration. That's a very specialised subject; I hope you know your stuff!'

MARTIN: 'I've got an O-Level in Economics, actually.'

BOB: 'Well, you just need to answer four questions correctly in sixty seconds to win the villa, so let's Raise the Roof!

'What happens to the rest of the money owed to United from the Paul Ince deal when Inter sell him?'

MARTIN: 'Erm, ah, pass to the next one please, Bob.'

BOB: 'How come Liverpool are getting £25 million for a five-year kit deal when United signed away eleven-year rights for £11 million?'

MARTIN: 'Umm, tough one – help me, Robin . . .'

BOB: 'No conferring, Mr Launders. Now, Martin, next question: is it a wise use of fans' money for United to commission an opinion poll, which must cost at least £80,000, to find out how many Reds are in Britain?'

MARTIN: 'Er, I'll have to think . . .'

BOB: 'When are United going to put everyone out of their misery and tell us if and when Kiddo is going to be the next manager?'

MARTIN: 'Umm, can I have a "P" please, Bob?'

BOB: 'Bad luck, Martin, it's tough under the spotlight, isn't it? Good job you're not the man in charge of United, though, isn't it?! Never mind, you go home with our best wishes and, of course, Bob's Bungalow. And, after all, you've already got a luxury Majorcan villa, haven't you, you snidey bleeder?'

MARTIN: 'I'll have an "E" please, Bob . . .'

– ANOTHER SHITE ITV PRODUCTION –

*(Clearly the Devil was making work for idle hands, but, come October, at last the wait was over . . .)*

### King Chronicles: Red October

1 October 1995, to be precise: two suspensions, a court sentence, a media lynching and one rather alarming Parisian walkabout later,

the King returned to his supplicant minions. It seems hardly coincidental that the duration of his sojourn was approximately that of a pregnancy. No birth has been so anxiously, so frenziedly, awaited; 34,000 expectant parents looked on, hoping he'd emerge from the womb-like Old Trafford tunnel as beautiful as they'd dreamed he'd be. And, like every parent who prays the kid'll be all right, all limbs and senses in perfect order, our exhilaration at witnessing the rebirth, the second coming, was surely tempered by similar worries. Would his touch be as good, his vision unimpaired, his genius undimmed? The pompous media-crats decreed that Cantona 'owed' us, that he had a debt to repay to the faithful – thank you then, Eric, for taking only sixty-seven seconds to dispel our every concern.

That Eric's own particular contributions – making the opener and scoring the match-saver – were ridiculously, cinematically dramatic shouldn't have surprised and astonished us as much as it did. It was, after all, quintessential Cantona. To reword Sherlock Holmes: with Eric, you must remove everything that is predictable or normal – whatever is left, however incredible or seemingly impossible, is what Eric will do.

The rest of the day's carnival was, in contrast to Cantona's effervescent quantum physics, Newtonianly predictable: the tricolour-drenched crowd was good, though never '70s-great; the media multiple-orgasmed themselves dry; Pete Boyle got extra-strengthedly pissed; Lee Sharpe was fucking hopeless. All played their supporting roles tight to the scripted word, leaving Eric to ad-lib and free-form at will. Liverpool, too, played their usual part of recent times, outclassing and outpassing us for sixty minutes, superior in almost every key position but Eric's. If you could detach yourself sufficiently from the emotional maelstrom that Eric's return engendered, you'd have written off United for the season on this performance, our first match of '95–'96 against a truly good side. But who could detach oneself from the cosmically magnetic Cantona Force? However much Liverpool exposed our loss of Ince, Hughes and Andrei, the moribund state of Bruce, our overdose of youthful callowness and our lack of tactical and teamplay cohesion, as long as Eric remains, so does the dream – the dream that he can lead those around him to maturity and dominance.

To be realistic, we all know we can count on nothing. The mercurial magic that makes him so brilliant also makes him unchainable. By the time you read this, he may already have left. He may go next summer, winter or spring; he may die happy here at the age of 120, having devoted his life to us. Who knows? But remember Eric's existentialism: he, surely, would tell us to forget the past – it cannot control us – and to dismiss notions of destiny or eternal commitment. All that matters is here and now, how we define ourselves every day through our present actions. When a loved family member almost dies, you appreciate and enjoy his or her presence so much more intensely afterwards – you've come face to face with what you could have lost. However long Eric stays at our side, live each day as if it could be the last: to the max. Whether this is his swan song, his Indian summer or just the start of the brightest supernova of his career, envelop yourself in it. Go to every Eric game, sing every song, join every hosanna – because we'll never see his like again.

*(Nevertheless, terrace disgust at the increasing corporate trough-feeding continued unabated, fuelled further as IMUSA's propaganda department and* Red Issue *cynics hit home . . .)*

## It Could Be You! (not)

There were delighted faces all around the boardroom after the latest Profits Lottery came up trumps for the local Cheshire Fat Cats Syndicate. 'We've hit the £20 million jackpot!' beamed one ex-butcher. The winners, who picked their lucky numbers by using the numbers of their off-shore deposit accounts, benefited from it being a 'roll-over' year: 'The pot just got bigger, what with players being sold, ticket prices soaring and no trophy-winning bonuses,' explained the syndicate's resident preacher and spiritual guide. Now the only problem they have is how best to screw the fans (*surely 'spend the booty'? – Ed.*).

'Obviously, we've got to clear this with all the players in our syndicate first,' said the leader, 'but cos me and my best mates paid for most of the tiny original stake back in the beginning, it's really only up to us actually.' Their plans for the millions are said to involve the following:

- Supporting mistresses and second families: £3m
- Paying for David Weak puff-pieces: 8.35p
- Extensions to Balearic villas (*put in accounts as new training facilities*): £2.5m

- Bribes to keep certain personnel from going to MCFC and Derby: £3m
- Continued instalment pay-offs to Ukrainian mafia: £5m
- Treble inflation-rate pay increases all round: £2m
- Building new MegaExecDoubleBarmaidBlowjob restaurant (*top ten shareholders only*) which provides free prawn cocktail and double share option per diner: £1.5m
- Petty cash balance forward (*spending money*): the rest

Asked whether they'd continue to play the Lottery despite their win, one syndicate member replied, 'Of course. It's great fun, especially when you're guaranteed a jackpot every year . . .'

*(As IMUSA fought the good fight throughout the autumn and winter, they increasingly found their most annoying and wormlike adversaries to be not the plc but the* Manchester Evening News *and some of its personnel in particular, which prompted this closer examination.)*

## Redheads: David Meek

(From the original *Despatches* book)

At the end of the '94–'95 season, David Meek retired as the United correspondent for the *Manchester Evening News*, a post he'd held since the Munich Disaster. Supposedly the doyen of the Old Trafford press pack, his final days were fêted with awards, tributes and commemorations as he prepared to spend the rest of his days freelancing, a deal to columnise for the *Evening News* safely tucked in the wallet. But should United fans continue to regard him as the great omniscient oracle of OT, still the journalist to rely upon, to respect?

Talk to any members of the United-watching press pack about David Meek and, for once, you'll get a uniformity of opinion: 'nice bloke', 'decent fella', 'salt of the earth' and other such blandishments trip easily off the admittedly sometimes forked silver tongues. It's what they don't say that's interesting: never do you hear 'top-flight writer', 'tremendous story-breaker' or 'fearless crusader' – in short, none of the epithets that hard-bitten hacks normally dream of earning. Curious, that.

But no more curious than the *News* reporter's job is to begin with, perhaps. Meek, as holder of the position throughout these decades of media explosion, has shaped this role to such a degree of concrete irrevocability that Stuart Mathieson and his successors would struggle to deviate from the appointed path, should they ever wish to do so. It's hard to exaggerate the centrality of the Meek Model in the lives of locally based Reds. Not only are the match reports in the *News* and *Pink* read by the majority of Manc Reds, the midweek news items are the primary sources of information for all, be they fans or other media. Then there's the radio and TV appearances, supplemented by whatever syndicated or commissioned articles can be rustled up in other papers and magazines, that allow for further comment, 'insight' and guidance, all gratefully hoovered up by news-hungry fans. Add to that the unquantifiable tips and spin-doctoring that may be given to other less privileged hacks behind the scenes – and the fact that MUFC is the most secretive club in Britain – and you can appreciate that the position of the *News* correspondent allows the incumbent enormous influence over the way United's affairs are perceived by the outside world. True, the phenomenal growth of tabloid interest in MUFC over recent years has meant that what were once local-only stories now appear on national back pages too; consequently, several national journalists are beginning to catch up with the *News* in terms of influence and access. Nevertheless, the *News* man remains *primus inter pares*, wielding an almost automatic credibility that the nationals have yet to earn.

Meek, however, always had one disadvantage compared with the tabloid guys. He was, essentially, on his own, solely responsible for the United coverage in the *News* and thus the individual answerable to both the club and the readers for his coverage. The tabloids have at least two United specialists each, normally a Mr Nasty squatting in London, ever ready with an invented shock-horror story, balanced by a Mr Nice up in Manchester, always prepared to give the club the benefit of the doubt and happiest when running 'good news' pieces. That's a grossly simplistic synopsis of what are actually very Byzantine and unfathomable cross-relationships, but the results are effective enough. Tabloid stories hostile to United that enrage the club can be blamed on London; the Manchester correspondents can then maintain their friendly links with favourite United sources by saying 'It wasn't me, guv'.

The *News* man has no such luxury. Cross the club in print and the consequences, in terms of the reporter being able to get his job done easily, can be awkward. Cross the readers, however, and what is the penalty? Say he runs a piece backing hikes in ticket prices, defending the board and attacking complaining fans. Some fans will be angry; one or two might even get past the 'Postbag' guards and have a letter printed. So what? Where else is the Mancunian reader going to go for his United latest when the *News* has a monopoly? If the reporter is of the old-school type who never talks to or quotes local fans anyhow, he has even less to worry about: in the pecking order of groups not to be offended, the fans come a long way behind the manager, the board and the players.

You can see where this is going now, can't you? Many years ago – twenty-three, to be precise – there was a defining moment in the coverage of United by the *News*. David Meek is now perceived to have run a very brave piece defending Frank O'Farrell during the last days of his benighted regime in which he argued that everyone, including those within the club who were unhappy with Frank, should give the man more time rather than agitate for his dismissal. Meek pointed out that the McGuinness situation had been handled cack-handedly and that lessons should be learned; now was the time to issue a statement of support for Frank and accept that the club as a whole was responsible for the current demise, not just O'Farrell.

The perception of bravery stems from the fact that, as many in Manchester's better-informed circles knew before the article appeared, the board had already decided to sack O'Farrell two days previously. It looked as though Meek, who presumably also knew this, disapproved and had gone as far as he could in public to make his disgust plain. Certainly that was the club's view: the board immediately informed Meek he was banned from the team coach and some difficult weeks followed for the hapless reporter. Hapless? Well, it turned out that he'd had no idea that the decision to sack O'Farrell had already been made. Quite accidentally, through not being well informed, he'd made himself look much more courageous than he'd surely ever intended; from a cock-up emerged a crusader.

Addicts of hypotheticals might like to conjecture as to how Meek might have behaved had he known O'Farrell was already dead in the water; more cynical students of his later career might contend that a 'So long, Failure Frank – and thanks for Martin Buchan' would've been a more likely headline, if Meek's volte-face over Paul Ince last summer is the yardstick. (Remember how one week he was lauding Ince for having topped the year's ratings chart and talking of his glittering future as next captain? Within the month, Ince was the bossy, too-big-for-his-boots liability, as Meek implicitly backed

Fergie's view that Ince had only played 'four good games' that season. As Meek always boasts of his 'behind-the-scenes' knowledge, how come he didn't see fit to tell us about Ince's alleged failings long before his departure?) To be fair, the 1972 Meek Model seems to have been a patently courageous and independent-minded version. He wasn't cowed and refused to hide himself away, being justly rewarded by certain players and officials who continued to brief him quite openly. Eventually, relations warmed up once more, and if Meek wasn't literally back on board the coach, he was at least back within the family fold as a prodigal son of sorts.

And therein lies the rub. The episode was a watershed but it could've been a moment of much different consequence. Brian Redhead, then editor of the *News*, was outraged at the way the club treated Meek and offered to 'go to war' with United over this and the larger issues it raised. Meek was grateful but declined the bellicose option, preferring to work it out on his own. I spoke to Redhead about a year before his death and managed to raise the subject. He ruminated on the episode and, although he had nothing but praise for Meek's bearing throughout this little cold war, wondered whether it might have been better after all to slug it out with United. I suggested that such a fight might have altered the way United–*News* relations were conducted forever – instead of the cosy alliance there seems to be between the two bodies, we might instead have benefited from a much healthier scenario of mutual scepticism and mistrust. Redhead didn't demur. Instead of reporters gratefully accepting the stories United choose to feed them, they would be forced to dig and forage and thereby give us stories of substance rather than bland PR-sheen news releases. Similarly, the club would have to account for its deeds – or misdeeds – to properly inquisitive and impartial reporters rather than luxuriate in the contented knowledge that the last paper who'd ever give them a hard time is the *News*.

Sadly, the aftermath of 1972 panned out very differently. Lessons appear to have been learned all round but not, I would contend, to the educational benefit of United fan readers. Think back over all the traumatic episodes at Old Trafford since then: three managerial sackings, of course, but also the myriad scandals and outrages that included boardroom battles, personal tabloid disgraces, controversial sales and purchases, rip-offs, libels, court cases, violence, exploitation, profiteering and so on. It's a cliché that life at Old Trafford resembles a soap opera, but truly we host more drama and suspense than *Brookie* and *Corrie* combined. But can you recall any of these crises or debates featuring a campaigning *Evening News* at the forefront? How many serious stories that might embarrass MUFC have been broken by the *News*? How many articles can you recall that have backed a fans' movement against the board, the management or a particularly unpopular player? Look through Crick and Smith's *Betrayal of a Legend* and remind yourself of some of the activities engaged in by United's leaders – how many of those were even noticed, let alone criticised, by the *News*? Judged on such a survey, who could blame any onlooker for thinking that the *News* – and, as their central player, David Meek – have been so reluctant to tackle the thornier issues that they appear to be nothing more than eunuchs at the Old Trafford harem? And who can blame Reds for holding their noses and turning to the tabloids et al. for their United fix because they can't trust the *News* to give them the full picture? What happened to the old maxim 'all the news that's fit to print' – when did the suffix 'as long as it doesn't annoy the Kens/Fergie/Edwards' get appended?

If you don't like to dwell on ancient history, let us stick to those events of the recent past for which you'd have expected our local paper and our local man to make the running. The outrage in Istanbul? Well done for top coverage to (*ugh*) David Mellor and the fanzines. Commercialisation and social engineering at Old Trafford? Channel 4, *Newsnight* and the football magazines. Pursuing explanations for last summer's sales? *The Star* and *The Mirror*. Reporting the important progress of IMUSA? Well, every medium except the *News*. The *Evening News* calls itself 'a friend dropping in'; MUFC plc must think it's the best friend they've ever had.

As the man at the helm, David Meek is the one who must answer for such a selection of material. He cannot plead ignorance of his readers' concerns, concerns which stretch to rather more than merely news of who is injured, who's in the team and what the manager thought of the latest performance. He has read the fanzines from almost the beginning; indeed, it was his pompous condemnation of *Red Issue* that gave them their biggest sales surge ever. He does, therefore, know that his readers are interested in the greater, 'political' aspects of MUFC – he has simply chosen not to reflect that in his journalism. Having laid down this gold standard, he has set a course from which his successor has not yet shown any signs of daring to deviate. Such is the legacy of twenty-three years' reporting of the old-school style, the school that Meek's admirers claim he personifies *in excelsis*. Personally, I think it's one of the few traditions around Old Trafford that I'd like to see the back of, but without a fundamental re-examination of their journalistic rigour at the *News*, I suspect we're stuck with Meekism for some time to come.

Meek himself remains as much on the scene as ever. Indeed, his weekly *News* column gives him even more opportunity for opinionated grand-standing than ever, although it is noticeable that denizens of the new post-Hornby football press such as *Goal* and *FourFourTwo* have not been rushing excitedly to him for copy. Freelancing is a tough world for old-school warriors, and in the new fan-friendly media environment, being perceived to be an Establishment crony can't help.

Meek's treatment of the Independent Man United Supporters Association this year serves as a good case study to illustrate the thesis behind this piece. Before the argy-bargy over the summer sales rumbled onto the back pages, Meek had already made a couple of telling stumbles resulting partly from his continued reluctance to maintain the sort of meaningful dialogue with fans' bodies that national journalists tend to daily. On the Monday before Eric Cantona re-signed for United, Meek told his readers to expect the worst: he confidently predicted God would be pledging to Milan on the next 'Black Friday'. Unfortunately for Meek's credibility, the more informed fans already knew through our own sources that Eric would, in fact, be staying. The truth was a phone call away for the *News* but it was 10p they'd never bring themselves to spend. That same month, Meek penned a centre-page tribute to Martin Edwards in the *Pink*, glorying in the new 'Gold Trafford' and telling fans it was time to pay homage to our leader, whose fine stewardship had proved all the doubters wrong. The timing was hilarious – days before, IMUSA had been formed precisely because dissatisfaction with MUFC had reached such an uncontainable peak, with the broken promises on ticket prices and the new ban on standing the proverbial final straws. Meek appeared to be blissfully unaware of both the fans' mood and the sheer bad timing of his piece; never has a serious article produced such mirth.

Once IMUSA was under way, Meek went in with the boot on four separate occasions, each time blundering to such an extent that he'd have been better off getting the boot itself to write the piece. That Meek was hardly hosting a ticker-tape welcome for IMUSA was no surprise. (Fans threatening to think and act for themselves, disturbing the cosy circle of boardroom, dressing-room and press box, promising to cut out media middle-men by using their own sources to get info to members? No thanks, lads.) That IMUSA was misrepresented quite appallingly on each occasion was almost to be expected, given that he never bothered to interview any members first. That he should twice cause me in particular to consult libel lawyers in London was a bonus; in both instances, I was informed I could sue but graciously settled for reply articles and letters in the *News* and for the satisfaction of hearing that the editor had had to send out letters of apology to complaining readers.

So pardon me for not kneeling at the altar of Saint David as the rest of the football writers' world has done, but give me Steve Curry or Jim White any day. If you are one of the many who were never that keen on Meek to begin with, don't waste time criticising him for the trivial annoyances, the innumerable times he's repeated a bum steer from United and predicted the wrong team line-up, or the fantastically bizarre player ratings that always seemed to give the ref and McClair twice their worth. What really matters is that he could have done so much for us, the readers, the long-suffering and often ally-less United hardcore. But when it mattered, when we needed support for our overwhelming sentiment against a particular decision or development, when we were desperate for the unvarnished inside story, David Meek wasn't truly there for us. He now tells us, to paraphrase a recent column, that he is free to say the unsayable, to lay into issues that the club themselves cannot touch. It makes him sound like Oddjob to the club's Goldfinger – 'We abhor violence against our foes, Mr Bond, but our friend Mr Meek is less fastidious . . .' Isn't he also now free to do the same for us, the increasingly dispossessed traditional support, those who want the truth, however hurtful, rather than club PR-speak? Will he now do so, or are the habits of a lifetime too hard to break? Sadly, I suspect that last question was purely rhetorical.

*(Apology to non-Mancs: if you don't live in Manchester, most of the references below will go straight over your head . . .)*

## Daily Spurt: The David Piss-Weak Column

When you've been a United expert for eighty-five years like I have – although those pot-heads at IMUSA wouldn't agree, would they? Woolly-headed students! – you get to know a few things. Like when The Doc succeeded Dave Sexton (or was it Wilf? Or the other way round? Check that before printing, sub-editor), there was an awkward moment when they caught me in mid-lick, so to speak. It's a difficult job, extracting your tongue from one managerial rectum before placing it up another, and when Martin 'Gold Trafford' walked in, it was an embarrassing moment, to be sure! Even more than the time I got banned from the team coach. Did you readers know about that? (*They fuckin' should do, you mention it every week – Ed.*) Not too long ago – was it 1990? 1985? (*1972, actually – Ed.*) – I wrote a damning, hardline, brave piece about Frank O'Ferrett, headlined 'Oh, go on, please give him another week'. And they kicked me off the team coach! That shows what a tough nut I can be – although those heroin-injecting sociology teachers at IMUSA would probably disagree!

Of course, I had to give Louis a blow-job every morning for the next five years to make it up, but it was a matter of principle, y'see? And that's what those Colombian drug-mafia sexual deviants at IMUSA don't understand. There's a principle involved: you must support the manager and everything he says or does without question all the time. Even if you're a supposedly independent journalist. Even if the manager were to shag everything that moves, or take ten-figure bungs, or even pick Brian McClair in the starting line-up. And when those child-abusing mass murderers at IMUSA said in the papers that 'The fans deserve to know the truth', we all know what they meant – they were really saying 'Kill Ferguson and his family and ritually burn his testicles in Albert Square'.

Well, I've been behind the scenes, and at the risk of being thrown off the team coach again – did I mention that story? – I'll say this. Fergie is my man for life and I won't have any truck with disloyalty. Unless the chairman ever removes him, of course, in which case I'll have a 'Fergie was toss' piece ready by nine the next morning.

In my view – and I've been behind the scenes, so I know – Tommy Docherty was the best manager ever in the history of the world. He was always a straight-talker, y'see, unlike that Dave Sexton who was manager before Sir Matt. Dave had a problem with the press; he never talked about his players in public, so it made all our jobs impossible – we actually had to work to get the stories! Imagine that! The Doc and Fergie were great for us; they just tell us what to write and we print it. Anyway, I'm a firm believer in straight-talking, just like The Doc did about Eric Cantona. And I like to think I follow the Doc method. Look at Paul Ince: when he topped the '94–'95 player ratings, I wrote a no-nonsense piece saying that he was the brilliant guv'nor, best in the club, the obvious next captain. But when he left for Italy, I listened carefully to all the arguments, especially those voiced in Glaswegian accents; I'd been behind the scenes and in my view Ince was a traitorous shit who'd played like a fart all season and we'd never miss him. Straight-talking, y'see? Perhaps those dangerous terrorists at IMUSA – did you know that five of their committee are grandchildren of Hitler? – should take a leaf out of my book here. But they'd probably smoke it, wouldn't they?!

In my view – and I don't think I'll get thrown off the coach for saying so this time – Mr Gold Trafford deserves a bit of hero worship from the ungrateful fans. Did you see those fantastic profit figures? Now how was that achieved, if not by the financial brilliance of the board? To listen to those drug-addled hideous monsters from Venus who lead IMUSA – you don't think they're actually human, do you? – you'd think the fans had contributed to those profits somehow. In my day, there was none of this 'consulting the fans' business. You paid your two-and-six, waved your rattle and if a club official deigned to boot you in the bollocks on his way past, you felt privileged he'd noticed you. These so-called United supporters who think going to every game entitles them to something should think on.

*(Meanwhile, the last 'season of shame' seemed to be extending itself well into '95–'96 as grainy video images of Liverpudlian goalies crowded* The Sun*'s front page.)*

## ***Daily Spurt Undercover Report Exposes More Sleaze***

'YES, I TOOK BRIBES' – RALPHIE MILNE

Following the shocking allegations involving Bruce Grobbelaar, United star of the '80s Ralphie Milne has stepped forward bravely to admit his own dreadful sins.

B*LL*CKS

Speaking from a makeshift shelter in a wood outside Bristol, the former Red winger owned up to the lot. 'They used to call me the new George Best,' remembers Ralph, 'and United had their eye on me from the minute I broke into the team at Ashton Gate. Alex used to tell me not to play too outstandingly well in case someone else spotted me before he'd tied up the deal.'

BOOZE

Milne got his dream move, but he'd scarcely had time to warm his boots when sinister forces took hold of his life.

'I fell in with a bad crowd at Old Trafford,' moaned Milne, 'who spent all their time taking me round the drinking clubs of Manchester and putting all their beers on my tab. I was too young to resist and before I knew it I owed local gangster bar-owners thousands.'

WIGGY

Milne was at his most vulnerable when he was approached by a shady local character, 'a small-time businessman with an amazing Shredded Wheat wig,' recalls Ralph. 'He promised he'd pay off my debts if I played crap for the Reds. I was on a sliding scale, with money being paid on the basis of which Old Trafford stand my crosses landed in.'

Ralph became less than popular with the OT crowds, who never realised that a devastatingly brilliant footballer lay just below the surface. Ironically, the businessman never paid up and Ralphie was forced to flee the city. 'He phoned me one night and told me he wasn't going to pay. Apparently all his cash was tied up in instalment payments for something he'd bought in Wolverhampton in 1979 – so I was finished.'

CHOCCY

Milne's remarkable story has prompted others to come forward; Paddy Roche, Tommy Jackson and Tom Connell have all announced that they too were potential superstars ruined by temptation. No current stars have yet been implicated, although leading figures in the butcher's trade speak darkly of enormous pie-related debts.

## Daily Spurt Legal News

Following the tempestuous Botham–Imran libel trial, another ball-tampering case has come to light which needed the attentions of Sue, Grabbit and Runne.

A United player has been accused of messing up matchballs to an unacceptable degree by an anonymous colleague with a French accent who acted after receiving 46,000 complaints.

'The culprit has been squashing the ball by treading clumsily all over it, by falling arse-first on top of it and most frequently by slamming it against advertising hoardings, seats in the stand and passing airliners,' said the prosecution barrister.

The accused defended himself, saying it hadn't been deliberate and that such ball-tampering had been 'part and parcel of the game' for years, especially with expensive bought-in United strikers.

The trial judge Justice Ferguson found the defendant guilty and sentenced him to a summer of humiliating transfer speculation. Mr Cole is twenty-four.

*(The late and unlamented* Goal *magazine liked to think it was the authentic voice of the terrace but it was* FourFourTwo *who first took an in-depth look at the independent supporters movement; the author looked at IMUSA's groundbreaking contribution, described by one* Guardian *journalist as 'a model of modern activism' . . .)*

## IMUSA – Here to Stay

(From *FourFourTwo*)

Given Man United's recent on- and off-field success, the emergence of a critical IMUSA may seem odd, even churlishly ungrateful. Indeed, there are Reds of a Stalinist hue who will not countenance a word said against any aspect of MUFC plc – but then, how often that kind turns out to be the comfortably-off, priority season-ticket holder. For the ordinary lads and lasses, bound together by tradition and mutual angst in their Stretford/Scoreboard End strongholds and away ground enclosures, treated as so much turnstile fodder down the years, there was nothing odd about the emergence of IMUSA; indeed, the only surprise for them was that the inevitable had taken so long to occur.

United did once have an independent fans' body of sorts but the club hierarchy subsumed and emasculated it, ousting the leader in a grubby *putsch.* Since then, whilst the club has transformed itself from an underachieving family concern into a Mammon-friendly corporate behemoth, concerned fans have been forced to watch play from the sidelines. Impotent and unrepresented, they often feel that they are the victims of certain toxic side-effects produced by the impressive fission that generates the plc powerhouse.

The acutely simple *raison d'être* of IMUSA has always been to give back to the fans a unified voice. Not that IMUSA ever pretends to speak for all United fans, as their club-crony critics claim. Whilst no one is excluded from membership, the short-hand 'true hardcore Reds' bespeaks their target membership: those fans who, despite United's success, remain deeply worried about the direction of the club and share a sense that they are being marginalised, ignored, priced out and downgraded. And though many do indeed come from a stereotypical 'traditional supporter' background – young, working-class, vocal males – they have been joined by people from every possible demographic segment, including those normally typecast as being in thrall to the Brave New World of post-Taylor modernisation.

IMUSA formed last March after the United–Arsenal match, a 3–0 victory marred by an atmosphere-shattering tannoy announcement that bellowed 'Sit down or get out' at the jubilant goal-celebrants in the East Stand. The issue of how fans should behave at Old Trafford is but one of a whole raft on IMUSA agenda, many of which will be familiar to any disgruntled fans at 'modernised' clubs: exorbitant ticket-price rises, the abuses of away-match allocations, the enforced club monopoly on European travel and the apparent dominance of business considerations over football's, all of which can be said to stem from the complete lack of proper fan–board consultation. But the controversy that raged over the club's announcement that anyone standing up during play – even in traditional behind-goal areas – could be ejected and banned for life serves as a microcosmic paradigm of the way MUFC and IMUSA interact. A policy introduced without warning or consultation on the strength of a handful of individual complaints produced outrage amongst the vast majority at the two ends. Traditional methods of remonstration were used as a first step – a stand-up protest, a leaflet-drop, a public meeting – but the opposition remained within the family. When the club refused to back down, IMUSA regretfully took the final modern resort of going public; as the leaders are all experienced media operators, they knew how to use both local and national press and radio to further their agenda. After a brief campaign, the club relented; but, most importantly, IMUSA followed up with some aftermath reconciliation by submitting detailed proposals on how to avoid problems with fans' behaviour at Old Trafford and by offering their full support in order to achieve the club's and fans' common goal of satisfying customer demands.

Certainly, IMUSA's work with the media has produced very visible results: high name recognition, good agenda exposure, an IMUSA quote being a *sine qua non* of any serious United story. But modernity is the key to everything with IMUSA, which is ironic, given that they stand for many traditional values. They employ techniques such as computerising, Internetting, opinion-polling methodology, running a media-monitoring and supplying unit and so on; but they have also eschewed old-hat oppositionism. By using the language of their quarry – the board and plc shareholders – in their arguments and documents, they seek to demonstrate that they are not the 'enemy within' but a potentially invaluable conduit to improve producer–consumer relations. Their current glossy proposal brochure, ready for the November AGM, would not look out of place in any corporate HQ. As even quondam arch-critic David Meek concedes, 'They're a smart and articulate lot.' Whatever anger and resentment Reds have felt in the past, business is business and IMUSA knows that co-operative solutions are all that a plc wants to hear. That's what they offer – for now, at least. Because as chairman Chris Robinson, not a man known to make idle promises, states clearly, 'We're not going away. This is no short-term pressure group.'

*(Three years' development later, IMUSA had fully matured just in time to take on the battle they were perhaps always destined to fight. One wonders who else would have had the strength and skill to lead Reds against Sky if they'd fallen by the wayside. Thankfully Robinson had been right: IMUSA were here to stay.)*

## *Daily Spurt News*

UNITED IN 'NO DISASTERS' SHOCK HORROR
NORMAL WEEK OUTRAGES FOOTBALL

Manchester United rocked the football world to its foundations this week by failing to make any cock-ups, insult its fans, sell any star players or stage an on-pitch fight. Gutted hacks cried into their expense-account whiskies as ashen-faced United officials admitted, 'It's true – all we've done this week is a spot of training and played a couple of matches.'

SHOCK

Fans were in shock as they turned to the back pages and found other clubs in the headlines.

'What is going on at our club?' asked one fan outside the

Megastore. 'I didn't send back my season ticket for this. I demand the board gets back to its job of screwing up United now!'

Blame was being squarely laid at the door of manager Alex Ferguson, who is alleged to have told United staff, 'Can we please stop fucking about and start being a football club again?'

LAUNDRETTE

Journalists were stunned when they even failed to get either Mr Edwards or Mr Launders to say something stupidly insulting to the fans. 'I can't believe it,' wailed *The Spurt*'s Lunchtime O'Booze. 'Usually you only have to put a mike in front of either of them to get their feet in their mouths. They're simply not doing their job.'

COCK UP

Harassed United officials promised they'd do their best to get the club back on course. 'I'm sure this competence is only temporary. Give us a week to get back in touch with Inter Milan about Eric and to bring David May back into the team and normal cock-up service will be resumed,' said a spokesman.

NEW MAY CONTRACT DETAILS REVEALED

In the wake of Eric Cantona's mould-breaking 'pay-as-you-play' contract deal, United have taken the opportunity to apply the same principles to other players, starting off with David May.

'We've made Davey's a little different from Eric's,' announced finance chief Robbin' Launderer. 'Basically, he'll start each week on £5,000. If we're forced to play him, for example when every other defender in the club has a broken leg, then he goes down to £4,000. Every shit header then costs him £500, every bottled or botched tackle £250, and every goal he's to blame for a grand. I suppose it's not so much 'pay-as-you-play' but 'fork-out-as-you-fuck-up'.'

May's agent, B. Magoo, was reported to be less than happy with the deal: 'David will be fucking bankrupt by Christmas.' The club have denied that Lee Sharpe and Brian McClair are to be offered similar terms.

*(Based on the secure assumption that the Blues would succeed in making it 'twenty-two years and won fuck all at OT' in the '95–'96 FA Cup tie, we helpfully compiled all the excuses they'd want to use in the weeks afterwards. These excuses could be used time and time again. For the*

*rest of the month, it was open season on the Blue muppets. Like it ever stops . . .)*

## Cut Out 'n' Keep Blue Excuses

1) You cheating Rags make your pitch too small so we can't play properly and, er, being a big club, we get the biggest pitch and yours is titchy cos, er, you don't come from Manchester . . .

2) It was the floodlights: yours are crap, we couldn't see the ball properly, we're a massive club with the biggest and best floodlights ever of all time and yours are rubbish cos, er, you bought them outside Manchester, where you don't live, blah blah . . .

3) You bastards never give us enough tickets, how can we win with no support, you give all yours to Cockney twats, well, yeah, we got 8,000 this time, but that's shite, we're such a giant club with a travelling army of 25,000 true Mancs, burble burble . . .

4) We don't care about poxy cups, it's the league that matters for big clubs, yeah, now we can really concentrate on, er, finishing higher than Bolton, who wants to go to Wembley anyway, it's a shithole, we're saving our money for the Intertoto, we'd have pissed on you at Maine Road, the draw was a fix, wibble wibble . . .

5) We wanted to lose actually, yeah, now you'll fuck up the league 'cos of fixture pile-ups, yeah right, we don't need trophies to prove we're the biggest, at least we come from Manchester, and Newcastle will piss on you now, Toon Army, let's all buy black-and-white scarves and be really funny, Turkish Delight anyone? babble babble . . .

6) . . . er, um, – we never do well in the cup when there's an 'a' in the month?
(*Now there's the truth . . .*)

## Daily Spurt News: Crimewatch Update

There was little surprise when it was revealed that Ballbarings-busting futures dealer Nick Leedson is a Man City fan. At the moment Leedson is, like many City fans, in the nick – is that why

City can't even draw 20,000 to important cup ties? – but his colleagues in Singapore have revealed the cause of his downfall.

'Sadly, Nick got heavily into the City futures market. We warned him that he was letting his heart rule his head but he wouldn't listen,' said an insider.

Leedson is alleged to have invested over £1 billion on a stock exchange sporting index – he was the only trader in the Eastern hemisphere who took up an option that City would finish the season in the top six. There are even worse losses to come that the new owners of Ballbarings must handle, said our source. 'Nick even stuck several hundred million on City winning a trophy before the decade is out. The local traders don't know much about football but even they knew that this was a sure-fire loser. They couldn't get in on it fast enough. Ballbarings will be paying out on this forever.'

Manchester City have hotly denied that Leedson had anything to do with the Steve Daley deal or the employment of Malcolm Allison. Meanwhile, Leedson refuses to concede he might have made a mistake on the City trophy futures deal. 'We're a big club,' he burbled from his Frankfurt cell, 'and will win several trophies in the next few years, mark my words.' Lawyers handling Leedson's case are considering an insanity plea as the best defence.

### *Daily Spurt News: Manchester Health News Update*

The news in a recent survey that Manchester is the fourth most depressed place on earth has come as a surprise to most of its inhabitants, particularly Reds who've had the time of their lives for the past couple of years.

The *Daily Spurt* can explain the findings for proud Mancunians, however. The percentage of Mancs who are depressed or who have mental disorders is 24.8%. We suggest that figure is probably the exact percentage of Mancs who are Bluenoses. As any City fan after the 8–0 double and cup knockout must be virtually suicidal, and given that most Blues are clearly mentally defective, we think the mystery of miserable Manchester is solved.

### *Daily Spurt News: Today in History*

With Uwe Rosler and those 'hilarious' German bomber T-shirts in mind, we look back to a *Daily Spurt* edition from World War Two.

The *Daily Spurt*, 12 March 1941

FIFTH COLUMNISTS SUSPECTED AFTER RAID ON OLD TRAFFORD

Air-raid wardens at the scene of the football stadium's devastation suspected local traitors were responsible for guiding Hitler's death bombers to target Old Trafford.

'Local residents report shifty-looking, possibly drugged characters hanging about just before the raiders arrived. They were carrying torches which we think were to illuminate the target zone,' said an ARP sergeant.

'They wore strange insignia, presumably the symbols of some sick sect – shirts with "6–1, 1926" on the front in blue letters.'

Officials are puzzled as to the location of this group, although sightings have been reported in some south Manchester ghettos. They refused to confirm or deny local reports that the collaborators were heard shouting 'Bomb the Rags! Bomb the Rags!' during the raid; police wouldn't elaborate on the possible meaning of leaflets they left behind headed, 'Who's got the biggest pitch now, then?'

*(If we can just butt into this micro-edition of the* Spurt *to point out that the following might well be the* Red Issue *ideal in a nutshell: Blue-baiting, dashes of 'Carry On' and sly digs at Fartin' Martin [remember Debbie Miller?] . . .)*

## Daily Spurt Exclusive

DEBBIE'S A PREMIER STRIKER – 'I SCORED EVERY TIME!'

Forget the 'News of the Screws' and Martin Edwards; we've found a girl who's played on every pitch going! Buxom blonde bombshell DEBBIE MULLER's been on intimate terms with all the Premier Big Boys and she's confessed all to the *Daily Spurt*. She's no stranger to Manchester, either: Debbie is a well-known 38/24/36 figure in Moss Side, as pouting Deb explains.

'Yes, I met Alan Ballsup at a top hotel in the city (Vera's B&B in Ardwick) and it was lust at first sight. We toasted each other with tumblers of bitter and fell onto the bed. He was such a gentle, considerate lover, although he had a bit of trouble finding the centre of my goalmouth, if you know what I mean! He said it was a common problem where he worked, so I guided him in myself.'

GOING DOWN

But it all ended in tears and confusion for Debbie.

'One night I plucked up the courage and asked him if he would "go down" on me but he just went wild. He shouted that he was not going down under any circumstances. His voice was screeching like a stuck pig's and I was really scared. I tried to make him feel better and said it was OK, I had every confidence in his abilities, but he just burst into tears and wailed, "Franny never tells me owt like that!" Well, I assumed he meant he had another woman, so I had to give him the boot. He just laughed strangely and said I wouldn't be the first to do that to him. It was all very bizarre.'

BLOW MY WHISTLE

Things began to look up for luscious Debs when Francis LeeOnePen took her under his wing, plying her with wine, exotic holidays and naughty awaydays in his Roller. Their sex life was perfect and her loving pudding-head satisfied all her oral needs – but she began to have her doubts when things took a slightly perverted tone. 'He just loved diving down on me but it was getting a bit out of hand – he was down there all the time. I got a bit worried when he asked me to blow a whistle every time he went down on me and shout "Penalty!". It seemed to turn him on all right but I thought it was a bit odd, to say the least. Then one day he asked me if I'd like to meet his horses and I knew it was time to get out.'

IN THE BOX

It wasn't long before Debbie was introduced to the boys in the dressing-room and started administering post-match relief.

'Terry Pheelup – what a wild boy he was! Loved his S&M, especially when I put him in a dog collar and dragged him around the bedroom on a lead. I had to call him Rover and I let him sniff my bum. I had to dump him after he bit a huge chunk out of my arse. But he was a real animal in bed.'

Which was more than could be said for the other City boys.

'Some of the lads who played up front were useless, though – didn't have a clue where to go or what to put it in. They'd stick it frantically wherever they could – anywhere but the target! I complained about being left frustrated and unsatisfied but I think they'd been told that before.'

RED HOT PUS

Deb's a regular on the Kippax now and says she feels at home with the other City girls: 'We all have similar standards.' She's only strayed once, when she was taken to a Scouse reunion and fixed up with a young Liverpudlian called Robbie. 'It was a nightmare. They asked me to do a favour for a physically disadvantaged lad but nothing could have prepared me for what lurched through the bedroom door. I ran off screaming – it put me off sex for at least a week. The smell of pus was overwhelming.'

Debbie's now embarking on a career as an actress. 'I've got a part with a film company called Electric Blues; I think it's something to do with City with that name.' Well, there are a lot of knobs in it, whatever.

*(That's enough Bitter-baiting: given their circs these days, it's like invading Grenada. From the ridiculous to the sublime – what is it about Scottish managerial success in England such as Fergie's? How come Tartan bosses are so good? That was the question a* Total Football *special asked; here's the answer the author supplied as regards our own top Jock.)*

## The Gaffer Tapes: Great Scot

(From *Total Football*)

I asked an Anglo-bigot acquaintance of mine to characterise his stereotypical Scot; 'Drunken, sentimental dosser with a cultural cringe,' was his succinct reply. (Doubtless there'll be a 15 June Wembley police cell with his name on it.) Not an analysis that would be much use in explaining the uniquely Scottish dimension in the success of Alex Ferguson. For if he does indeed fit a Tartan archetype, it's the complete opposite: this is a man bred on the spirit of tough, confident, hard-working Protestant austerity. Throw in the elements of left-leaning, working-class vanguardism he gleaned from his shop-steward days and the physical strength needed to safeguard one's passage down the meaner Clydeside streets and you have a man who's not to be messed with. Give him a mission – in his case, to break first a Glasgow duopoly and then a Merseyside monopoly – and you've got a twentieth-century William Wallace on your hands. Football is littered with broken-spirited former adversaries who've learned this the hard way.

A contemporary once described a fearsome sixteenth-century clan leader thus: 'The loyalest man who ever lived, yet he'd slice your head off without trace of tears.' Fergie runs his own Red clan in precisely the same way. If you're a 'Fergie boy', he'll protect you, cherish you, persevere with you however bad the going. McClair, Cole and Cantona are all, in different contexts, just the latest examples. But come the crunch, for the good of the whole, you can be executed without a sliver of sentiment. Robson, Hughes and Bruce have all felt the ruthless axe-blade when softer managers would have relented. That peculiarly Scottish mix of Protestantism and socialism can produce a man who simultaneously understands and maximises individual potential yet never loses sight of the power of the collective. No other manager dares to treat players on such a personally tailored *ad hoc* basis, yet none can assemble such a concretely cemented team unit. Some trick – some manager.

As for the never-say-die spirit that inspired both Robert the Bruce and countless historical rebellions, Fergie is clearly subsumed in it. Endless batterings throughout the dark years of '86–'90 seemed only to fortify him; repeated European humiliations in recent years have merely made him even more determined to sign up at OT once again and launch new Continental invasions. That curious lack of sentimentality helps; he's often said that for him the moment of victory is only fleetingly delirious. He has no time for nostalgic reflection, only the drive to strive ever onwards.

'Scottish cultural cringe'? Mention that to him and you risk receiving the infamous 'Hairdryer' verbal assault. This is a man who only half-jokingly talks of the 'Scottish master race', who is confident of his own status amongst its elect and who knows that he's worth the 700K a year Martin Edwards must now shell out to keep him. He would never so boast, but he's taken his place alongside Shanks and Matt to form a glorious triumvirate which proves that although England has the players, it takes a Scottish iron rod to turn them into teams.

You can't talk about Ferguson without mentioning the infamous Tartan temper. Compare him to that quintessential Englishman Dave Sexton, who managed United from '77 to '81, a nice, mild-mannered chap who couldn't bear scenes and even found it hard to stand up and give a team-talk. No such hang-ups for this dominant Scot, whose skill with the flying teacups and, er, underpants is legendary. Once described when angry as 'the most terrifying sight since Joe Jordan's roar', he can be as gloriously emotionally expressive as any hot-blooded Scottish legend. Cross him and you'll be lucky if you're forgiven any time before the sun explodes. You don't have to be an Anglo-bigot to observe that Scotland loves its grievances, positively revelling in historical angst; Fergie may not stomp about muttering 'Culloden' but there are plenty of pros and journos about whose life insurance lapses if they tread within a mile of Old Trafford. Nothing keeps a United star playing to the rules Fergie has set down like the knowledge that transgression brings forth the Eternal Wrath of Govan.

But it is, ironically, where Fergie cannot tread that his Scottish-sourced influence is felt most keenly at United. The pure passing game was invented north of the border; the giants of the Scottish game have passed the creed like a cult down the generations, producing the twin apexes of the pre-war national team and the late '60s Celtic supremos. The football produced by the Scots Shanks, Busby, Stein and Ferguson has been the best of the last thirty years because it has conformed to their country's core credo. Fergie's a true believer in this Scottish religion; at United, amidst Sir Matt's children, he's found fellow worshippers.

*(Mind you, having said all that, Alex still attracts more controversy than all those illustrious forebears put together, '95–'96 being no exception . . .)*

### *Daily Spurt Exclusive: FA Probe 'Filthy Perv' Poaching*

The FA have started an inquiry after complaints from southern football clubs that their youngsters are being preyed upon by a sinister Scottish poacher. Arsenal claim that they've already lost a young boy called Matthew Wicks who disappeared up north; other clubs report sightings around their training grounds of a 'red-faced middle-aged geezer' who crept around 'muttering in a strange dialect, chewing furiously'.

Friends of Matthew spoke of the moment the frightening man approached. 'He suddenly announced, "I've come to get my hands on your Wicks," and we feared the worst,' said one boy. 'Then he started fishing about inside his long Umbro coat and I thought he was going to get his thing out but luckily it was just a contract. We never saw Matty again. We think he was paid to go with him to his Stretford boys' harem.'

A lad at Oldham, where the prowler has also struck, remembers his cunning technique only too well. 'He'd come up and show us his glamour pictures – boys our age dressed up in red nylon looking flushed and happy. Then he'd ask if we wanted to come and play with his boys, Nicky, Gary and Paul. He said he'd make it worth our while and that we'd really excite the punters. It was so blatant – I'm surprised he didn't want it there and then and offer us puppies and sweets in his car while he was at it.'

Sources in the game have long suspected that any boys who fall for the Scot's promises run the worst possible risks. 'Some seem to do OK, but a few years ago a whole load of boys – Russell, Tony, Deniol – simply disappeared completely. We think a bit of digging up the garden may soon be in order.'

*(The football business boom hit stratospheric heights during the season and shot off into outer space after the Euro Championships, but the author thought he'd spotted the seeds of destruction. It'd be another couple of seasons before the national media began to see the same signs. Intriguingly, a spy in Umbro HQ doing work experience reported to us that this* FourFourTwo *article had been clipped and placed in the in-tray of a leading Umbro exec marked 'We should keep an eye on this'. Judging by the latest sales figures in the sector, it seems they must have taken their eye off the ball . . .)*

## 'Turn to the Left, Turn to the Right . . .'

When United thrashed Chelsea on a wet Wembley Saturday in '94, all things Red (and black, yellow and green) were bathed in the glow of total fashionability: the best players, the best style, the best lookers . . . and a million trend-hoppers jumped on board. But the *Zeitgeist* is a tough tiger to ride, and despite – or perhaps because of – the best efforts of the Man United merchandisers, some now wonder whether United have become left behind as the club of choice for the nation's nerds and misfits. Walking through an anonymous dreary outpost recently (oh, all right, Wrexham), I watched a damp, grey-shirted United kid being teased in the street by a collection of smart-threaded pre-teens; 'Man U Mongo!' was their repeatedly yelled catchphrase. The lads were an assortment of Liverpool, Wrexham and – tellingly – Newcastle fans dressed in best Blur-wear and it has to be said that the wretched Red looked quite a state in his badly designed Megastore garments. Talking to the mini-Toon, he confessed that he used to like Man U 'until all the saddos got into them too'. Now, young United fans being despised in the provinces because the locals are jealous is one thing, but when they're merely being laughed at for their naffness, it won't be long before such sentiment is reflected at the MUFC cash tills.

Actually, the signs are already there. Leaks from inside the club warn that the merchandising boom has already peaked. The newly opened Megastore may have been a success but the general demand hasn't been quite as overwhelming as expected – the pre-existing Superstore has been virtually empty even on matchdays and is tipped for a New Year early bath of the permanent kind. Remaindered T-shirts and books litter the retail emporiums – it seems there is a limit to the amount of tack that even the most devoted can devour. The latest blue-and-white 'misprinted deckchair' and the all-grey 'John Major' kits, whose designers have been dubbed 'Dumb and Dumber', have apparently not excited retailers as much as the classic red; a Stretford kit specialist described their performance in his shop as 'Crap and Crapper'.

The more acutely perceptive of United's hardcore, who wear that 'Sharp' logo on their chest the least but deserve that adjective the most, were making the connections here a long time back. The élite of the barrow-boy fashion gurus supply chic shirts to the clued-up, using quality material featuring bang-up-to-date designs which United's T-shirts can't match, as well as creating faithful replicas of old '50s and '60s classics. As one of this fraternity told Jim White at the height of the merchandising boom, 'The naffness and god-awful tackiness of the club's operation will be their undoing. If we're not careful, even City's boys are going to look cooler than our lads, and in the long run, bad taste doesn't pay.'

Indeed. The glut-the-market, stick-Giggsy-on-everything tactics have long offended the more aesthetically aware observers but it was always assumed that no one goes broke underestimating Joe Public's fashion sense. However, now that United have become a byword for provincial naff, that assumption looks less assured. The 12–26 age group is where the merchandise-money really pours in from but that demographic category also happens to be the most susceptible to the vagaries of street-cred trends. As a teen mag recently noted, there is currently no greater schoolyard fashion *faux pas* than being seen in a United away kit; others have even suggested that the entire footie-related accessory industry is about to be the victim of a fashion-police bust. Dressing like a footie player is on the way out; paragliding, mountaineering and snowboarding togs are coming in. Ryan Giggs salopettes wouldn't have quite the cachet of his branded footie boots, would they? And even amongst those sticking with football, it is Newcastle who are flavour of the season – Man United are no longer the only stylish team with a gorgeous Frenchman and a dark, moody young winger. Whither lies United's future if tomorrow's hardcore have already been alienated by their apparent crassness, over-exploitation and downright lack of cool?

Interestingly, there are signs that United themselves have sensed the change and are refocusing attention on match-going punters rather than non-attending out-of-towners. The club have divested themselves of their shares in 'Fred the Red' and their market-leading magazine is said to be in for the same treatment, hived off fully to the Zone media group. It's perhaps only symbolic but it speaks of a distancing of the club from its commercial off-shoots to concentrate on football fundamentals. As for the hardcore fans, this apparent drop in popularity is often to be welcomed. The lessening in ticket demand has meant that some home and away tickets have been on general open sale for the first time in years, which suggests that the club will also have to freeze prices if they hope to fill a 55,000 capacity. And for the most fashion-conscious Reds who take their lead from the fanzines' Lauren-worshipping 'House of Style' and 'Cultcha Vultcha' columns, any diminution in the number of style-free geeks following the Reds is good news. Feel the quality, not the width . . .

*(United then went and bollocksed this theory up for the time being by extravagantly claiming a double double, thus attracting yet another horde of glory-hunters over the summer. Every pot of silver has a cloudy lining. Still, what a glorious day that was . . .)*

## King Chronicles: The Cantona Double

(From *Cantona*)

Wembley Coach Park, about 5.30 p.m. Dozens of Reds down for the 1996 cup final on the infamous Burnage Boy Bus are reeling around the departing charabancs in frenzied celebration, both dazed and delirious. Twenty-four hours of intense substance abuse had played its part, of course – but the mainlining effect of Cantona's eighty-fifth-minute winner topped anything they could snort or drink. 'The Curryman' approaches me, his dancing eyes testament to a night of John Belushi/Led Zeppelin behavioural impressions. Five seconds of lucidity intervenes: 'The only way it'll ever get any better than this,' he declares with a slur, 'is if Eric scores the winner in the European Cup final.' *In vino veritas*, indeed: yes, it was that good.

Eric said precisely the same thing as 'The Curryman' the next day.

It had been a week of personal epiphany for Cantona already – Footballer of the Year one day, the news that he would become a father again the next. (Some suggested that Eric should have shoved that award straight back up the orifice through which so many of the prize-givers talk, but he contented himself with some entertaining toilet metaphors.) That he should display such technique, control and timing in scoring the goal that brought us the double double was, as he wryly remarked, ridiculously and cinematically glorious. Yet already he was looking to the future; just as Ferguson admits the moment of victory's delirium is fleeting, Eric had already focused on the greater challenge ahead. Because at Wembley, he and United had come full circle.

Just in terms of the '95–'96 season, there is a pleasant circuity in Eric beginning and ending with personal triumphs against Liverpool. Back in October '95, Cantona was stepping into the unknown, a good ninety minutes that day no guarantor of future success and certainly no impediment to those on his back still betting on disaster and looking for the negative. By May, the transformation was complete, thanks to a self-imposed ban on tackling, decency from fellow pros and an instinctive self-preservation. Now the Cantona bandwagon groans under the weight of all who've clambered aboard to seek the reflected glory of Eric's successes and illuminate the positive. Eric says nothing, his actions on the pitch obviating any need to crow or gloat.

That Eric should score the double double winner, then lift the cup itself, may well have been the fairy-tale that the cliché-mongers cite but it was also entirely logical and correct. Since he personally seized the initiative in late-winter, driven by all of the soul's demands which we have discussed all season, he has in turn driven the team and club forward to a triumph that few dared predict. The famous series of one-goal winners was in itself enough to grant him the title of Champion of Champions; add into the equation all that he created and the leadership he gave as a captain-elect and there can be no surprise at the overwhelming volume of votes he has received in every United player-of-the-year poll. The quality of some of his interventions has been astonishing, given the context. His devastating blows against Spurs, Arsenal, Newcastle and Liverpool must surely be included in any summary of greatest Cantona strikes. Martin Edwards, ever the accountant, has remarked a touch prosaically on the twenty-one points Eric's goals directly won. But genius is unquantifiable. You can only make an approximate measure in terms of your feelings and emotional responses. They already called Eric *Dieu* long before this season's final assault. Where are we going to find the words to express what he means to Reds now?

So, full circle – Wembley '94 to Wembley '96. Now, as then, Eric's goals win the double on the day, just reward for a season's dominance which has already been recognised by a Player of the Year trophy. Europe, and greater glories, await on the horizon. Last time around, a UEFA suspension, Romario 'n' Stoichkov and a combination of thug, authority and media conspired to drive the Cantona mission off the rails; now we're back on the grid again, in pole position. If Eric can continue to fly at his current elevated plateau for another season, then 'The Curryman' and co. should book their liver transplants for May . . .

*(I know, I know – so painful to remember that eager hope when you know what would actually happen in May '97 . . .)*

# 1996–97

*(The author now began to write pre-season preview pieces for the football glossies, mainly because he knew flippancy wound up other fans, even those who read the quite groovy* Total Football *. . .)*

## Mystic Red '96

(From *Total Football*)

Blinded by the gleam of the European Cup, we might give some dark horse a shot at our title; expect a few nation-pleasing silly United defeats on Saturdays before Euro ties, but watch our challengers' arses collapse around Easter as usual. Poborsky, whom we trust will cut his hair seeing as his first name's already girly enough, will either be a one-chip wonder or the new Kanchelskis. This means he'll either a) score a dozen improbably outrageous goals and be a K-Stand hero or b) stomp back off to his Budvar-brewing hometown in a stew of temper and homesickness, claiming Fergie tried to murder him. If Shearer has signed and avoided the Old Trafford Strikers' Curse, United might just astonish our fans and disgust Britain by doing well in Europe, with a brave semi defeat the minimum expected. Peter 'Streaker' Boyle will have a top-ten hit with 'Knobs out for the Lads' but, as United's unpopularity reaches virulent heights, Ned Kelly's team Security boys will have to consider Uzi purchases. We will treat the Cola Cup with complete disdain, possibly fielding teenagers in slippers. This will allow Liverpool the chance of one trophy this season and thus prevent the Monopolies Commission from banning us from domestic tourneys.

*(With the mass influx of foreigners into OT that summer, we'd gone from barely being able to pick eleven decent players to having a humungous Euro-style squad. This meant lots of players were going to have to take their turn 'rotating' and spending time twiddling their thumbs; fortunately, with Diana dropping a hundred charities in July, there would be plenty of opportunity for the lads to get a bit of part-time*

*charity patron work under their belts. We had some suggestions of posts that Reds could fill.)*

## *Man U Moonlighting*

**Ryan Giggs**: Patron, Friends of Strippers and Drunk-Drivers Association. Can entail 'hands-on' counselling, horizontal trauma therapy and liaison with the police. Ryan is now available after resigning from his Talentless TV Starlets support group.

**Andy Cole**: Joining the Victims of the Giggs Friendship Curse (founder members Lee Sharpe and Paul Ince), having also discovered that anyone who buddies up with Ryan mysteriously becomes *persona non grata* or simply *footballa tres mierda* at Old Trafford within two years.

**Nicky Butt**: Fund-raising celebrity for the Minor Head Injuries Appeal (Chinese Restaurant Branch), though his mate will do the actual work . . .

**Roy Keane**: Taking over at the helm of The Robson Memorial Trust, which specialises in training and advising young players how to handle the twin demands of drinking and playing like a demon. Already holds the coveted Robson Award for running the cup final then out-drinking all-comers for eighteen hours without collapsing once.

**David Beckham**: Gorgeous Becks has graciously agreed to run a free totty-testing service for fellow professionals – if Dave likes the taste of 'em, they'll be good enough for Ryan and co. when he's done.

**Lee Sharpe**: Cannot understand why the boys at Lifeline keep phoning up with job offers.

**Terry Cooke**: Terry has angrily refused invitations from Kanchelskis to form a wingers' 'Fucked-about-by-Fergie' society.

**Brian McClair**: Chair of the DIY Victims' Support Group; involves therapy sessions to discuss the sexual perversions of pinewood-fondling, spontaneous ejaculation on sight of B&Q or Texas signs and the strange effect plane-sanding has on nasal emissions.

**David May:** Sole member of Redhead-Bluenose Schizophrenia Trust for United-paid City-supporting players who turn into completely different creatures when moved ten yards across the backline.

*(Nostalgia trips became all the rage as we disaffected oldies felt increasingly marginalised, so we'll slip in this detour to Tripoli, Libya, 1989, a piece that won the author a little writing prize in* FourFourTwo. *All right, hardly the Booker, but then there's not much on offer in the category 'facetious, biased football scribbling', is there?)*

## Feeney, Gaddafi and Me

Now that we're top dogs, we spend a lot of time slagging off the anyone-but-United brigades. When we cock up, they have a party; we sneer that they're sad, small-time bastards who hate us more than they love their own team. And that's probably true of many of them. But don't you remember, when we were shit and Liverpool were kings, the sheer joy of seeing them derailed? It didn't mean we didn't love United enough, but sometimes, at the end of a season when we'd done fuck all, the only climax available concerned Liverpool. And if you can't have a shag – United winning a cup – then a good wank's the next best thing – Liverpool falling at the last. As every lad knows, some very special wanks can even be better than a third-rate shag. Is it disgraceful to confess that I once got more ejaculatory pleasure from Liverpool losing a title than I did from United winning the League Cup a few years later?

Tripoli, Libya, 1989 – and I'm in the middle of three years as a part-timer because I'm working abroad as a teacher. The job's four weeks on and one off, so I still get a few games in per season, but basically I'm at the mercy of the BBC World Service and three-day-old copies of *The Sun*, from which the censors cut out every pair of tits. (That's pictures of breasts, not mentions of Mickey Phelan or Ralph Milne.) Paddy Feeney is God to every footie-loving ex-pat, the voice of the Saturday afternoon sports show which gives you thirty-five minutes of second-half commentary, score flashes and the full-time scores. From these scant sources, you've got to build your own mental picture of what's going on at the club. However confused you regulars were by the bizarre goings-on between '87 and '90, it was nothing compared to my mental state. Imagine hearing that infamous 5–1 scoreline on a crackly old radio in the midst of an Egyptian desert, as I did. You saw it with your own eyes, but for hours I believed I'd been the victim of an aural mirage.

Virtually all the foreigners in Tripoli live on a giant compound eight miles outside the city centre. This was to prevent the local girls from being distracted by the blond, blue-eyed hunks inside the compound and getting sucked into decadent Western ways. Actually, the motley crew of balding, beer-bellied oil workers who constituted the majority of the encampment were no match for the dark Arab Lotharios outside, but we were happy to be isolated. At least we could home-brew to our hearts' content, be rampantly unfaithful to our spouses with the imported nurses and generally misbehave – all of which would have got us arrested and imprisoned outside the walls.

As the sun plunged into the Med this particular night, there was a buzz around the site. Tonight was a special event – the World Service was breaking decades of tradition to broadcast live football from England *midweek*: the Championship decider between Liverpool and Arsenal. The Muslim call to prayer from the muezzins echoed eerily across to us from the city but the only holy voice we were awaiting was Paddy Feeney's. For a week, the entire foreigners' corps had done nothing but home-brew. Huge industrial vats of the stuff were being lugged from house to house by figures scuttling through the darkness in preparation. Libya was on a war footing – virtually a monthly event back then – and heavily armed troops were at every crossroads, ready for an American invasion. But for virtually half of the Brits on campus – the United regiment – there was something to be feared more than stray Yankee friendly fire: a Liverpool title and another double. And they were odds-on favourites.

That second half lasted an eternity. Listening to football on radio is famously far more stressful than watching it on TV or live. Worse, we had the short-wave flutter to contend with, as waves of distortion would seem to take you from Arsenal attack to desperate defence within a second. Outside, the Libyans – who, uniquely, have no interest in English football – were completely mystified. They couldn't understand why virtually every house was tuned to the same radio station, producing a crescendo of commentators' voices rolling out to the sea. Later, one told me they thought we were listening to war-readiness propaganda from the Americans. At eighty-nine minutes, they must have shat themselves as a deafening roar went up around the site: Thomas had scored. Seconds later the campus roads were full of mad Brits running about like dervishes: for a few moments, Salford and Tripoli were as one. In the middle of a sweltering Arabian night, on a coast bristling with ready deadly weaponry, United boys were having the party of the year. I was puking for two days afterwards, of course, but I'll never forget the sight of an Aberdeen Red oilman, dressed only in filthy underkeks and carrying the biggest barrel of home-brew he could lift, legging down the road and jumping into a machine-gun post to shout 'give us a kiss' at the startled soldiers. Sad, part-time fun at its best; sometimes there's nowt wrong with it.

## Daily Spurt Local News Round-Up

OFF THE RAILS

Liverpool City leaders, who last week announced plans on *Look North* to build a new low-cost tram system, have been explaining how they can manage to construct an entire network for 30% of the price of Manchester's Metrolink.

'We intend to use the best of Liverpool's local skills and ingenuity to achieve these superb savings,' explained Councillor Bazza Sinbad. 'We're going over to Manchester to fuckin' nick theirs.'

KRAPSHOT KRAUT

Following the shocking assault-rifle attack on President Clinton's White House, the FBI have arrived in Moss Side to hunt suspects. 'We think we could be dealing with a psychotically deranged Bluenose here,' said agent Jed McBurger. 'The assailant took over twenty shots from close range but missed with every one.'

CAUTIOUS CAUCUSES

Security forces in Vladikavkaz have been puzzled by the media fuss made over their supply of thousands of troops for the visit of Liverpool FC to the war-zone. 'What did you expect?' asked Boris Marshallov. 'We have learned that when Scousers are around, it's best to have as many police on duty as possible.'

*(As we edit this collection, the battle for the 2006 World Cup is back in the headlines again, ages after we were supposed to have lost out to the Germans. An apt time to restate the following, then . . .)*

## Deutschland Über Alles

The recent revelations that our German cousins have got their towels on the World Cup sunbeds first have delighted everyone. After all, there's nothing the Brit tabloids and their xenophobic readership like better than bashing the Huns, donning the old tin hats and pretending it's 1940 all over again. Personally, I take my hat *off* to the Krauts. And I wish them all the best in their bid. *München 2006 Jawohl!*

I hasten to add that I don't like Germans or Germany, however racist that sounds. I do know that it's both pathetic and deeply suspicious to have had so much pleasure over the years from supporting *any* team in a match against them – the orgasmic 1982 World Cup final springs happily to mind. But if there's one sight guaranteed to aggravate me even more than a squadron of arrogant Krauts jackbooting around a beach, it's the chauvinistic temper tantrums of the Little Englander. To see the cretinous trio of Major, Blair and Kelly wrapping themselves up together in St George's flag to wave their puny fists at the Krauts was vomitory enough; the way the media expected us subjects to 'go over the top' and bash the Hun as if by instinct said a lot about our national inferiority complex. That so many tabloid readers sent in their worthless hyperbolic opinions was sad, but predictable. We're a nation of noisy but neutered bulldogs, unable to accept that the Doberman next door is our superior. Because the truth about the 2006 World Cup is this: Germany deserve it cos they're better than us at virtually everything.

Look what happened the other week, classic Kraut cunning totally outsmarting bumbling Brits. They'd been planning this secretly for years and had laid down all their battle plans. Our only 'weapon' was having Bert Millichip in as a UEFA adviser. 1914 and 1939 all over again or what? Like going in against machine guns and Panzers with rifles and horses. Germans plan everything a decade ahead; Brits improvise on the spot. *Of course* Herr Sauerkraut got their UEFA alliances sorted – just as in 1938, when they snapped up the Soviets into a pact after we'd spent years spurning a desperate Stalin. There's no point bleating about surprise blitzkrieg attacks: if Bert and co. had been awake, they'd have seen it coming. In 1914, Britain was shocked by the headlong tumble into war in a matter of days. Yet some observers had predicted the precise date a year before, knowing that as soon as the Krauts finished the critical Kiel Canal for their Navy, they'd be up for the scrap. So Mr Kelly shouldn't be surprised that the Germans are already booted up and in the trenches; this is how they establish superiority early on.

Facts: the Germans work harder than us (check their productivity figures); they're the best organisers in the world; and they'll happily submit to rigorous structure and discipline for years on end. (The less-welcome by-product of these characteristics is that they'll sprout dictatorships and SS-fodder the minute the West's back is turned, of course.) But for FIFA, they'll guarantee the most militarily efficient World Cup of all time. How soon the Little Englanders forget the true farce that was Euro '96. Ignore the hype: that tournament was an embarrassment. A complete breakdown of security and segregation; vastly overpriced tickets; general commercial exploitation; a complete lack of customer care and liaison; and a calculated conspiracy to hide from the public the fact that there were virtually no sell-outs and that cheap seats could've been had by all. We've all spent years slagging the *Dad's Army* incompetents at Lancy Gate – now we suddenly argue that the world and FIFA should put their fate in the FA's liver-spotted and shaky hands? We just can't be trusted to get it right. The Germans will match seats, prices and people with flawless precision, beat the shit out of nasty southern English hooligans and imprison any locals who try to take advantage of their honoured guests. You know what they're like about hospitality; it's a chance to earn post-war brownie points, so the place will be full of Enfield-clones apologising for the Blitz and offering half-price beers.

Like I said, the Krauts are superior. We only ever beat them with other people's help, e.g. US GIs or Russian linesmen. They're taller, healthier, richer, better at footie, better in bed and better beer-brewers. So let them shoulder the 2006 burden whilst we have the piss-up at their expense. Tourneys at home aren't really fun anyway – it's like holidaying in Cleethorpes instead of Ibiza. Besides, you want to misbehave in someone else's house, not your own. So, suggested war plan? '*Achtung*, Fritz: we surrender.'

*('Free as a Bird' Beatlemania swamped Britain for a week or so during '96–'97, as the* Spurt *was quick to note . . .)*

## Daily Spurt Showbiz News

YEAH! YEAH! YEAH! (HIC) –
THE FAB THREE ARE BACK!

Fans all over the world were delighted to hear that the original Fab Three from the '60s were getting back together – despite the brain death of one of the members.

Mega-bucks offers from several sad satellite and video companies cashing in on the nostalgia boom will be bringing back the trio for endless reunion shows to wank over old footage and pretend they never hated each other.

Bobby Maccacharlton, who found further fame and fortune after the split by joining top-earning group 'The Bastards on the Board', will link up with old colleagues 'Ringo' Law, the big-nosed fans' favourite, and the mercurial genius George Ono-it's-Best; the fact that the latter has been semi-comatose since an unfortunate incident with three crates of vodka in 1980 has not deterred the group.

'Technological advances have allowed us to clean up Georgie's contribution and make him sound as good as he did in 1970,' beamed a Rotten Apple Corps executive.

The reunion will feature an exclusive performance of an old George routine found by a former Miss World in a drinks cabinet; it's called 'Pissed as a Newt'.

## *The Dark Side of the Moon: The Man U Experience*

*(An occasional series in which* Red Issue *operatives go behind the OT scenes)*

. . . and apparently, this 'Experience' takes place inside Bowlers nightclub, not Old Trafford, or at least it did on 3 April. Over a thousand 'lucky contestants' who won teen-mag and radio competitions nationwide are assembling in temporary stands around the dance floor, ready to enjoy 'one of the most exciting football events of the year'. Someone tells me over 250,000 entrants wanted to be here – and nobody's paid a penny to get in, either. (Me and my mate from the Dog haven't either – press pass freebies ahoy.) Already I'm panicking: what's United's angle here? Surely they can't be doing this out of the goodness of their black hearts – hiring Europe's biggest club and promising that everyone will get to meet every first-team player? Perhaps they're going to bus everyone over to the Megastore for compulsory shopping afterwards.

First we have to endure an hour of inane build-up from Zoë Ball and Vince Miller, half an hour of big-screen video highlights and a bizarre twenty-minute performance by the world keepy-uppy champion, with audience participation. (I'm not making this up. It's like something extra-tacky out of *The Simpsons*; my mate thinks Truckosaurus or the Box-Kite Parade will be next on the floor.)

Meanwhile, Zoë Ball's libido is swamping the arena. Bearing in mind half the crowd are under eleven, her slobbering over every mention of Becks, Keano or Giggs seems a tad inappropriate. As she,

Vince and several video cameras roam around the stands, plucking out unfortunate victims for the 'what's yer name/have you come far?' routine, she addresses virtually every dad as 'hello, sexy', 'ooh, you're good-looking' and so forth, setting every mother's molars grinding. A six-year-old behind me asks her dad 'What's sexy mean?' and the poor sod of a father squirms throughout a completely inadequate five-minute explanation. It was the only entertaining question-and-answer exchange of the day.

Vince prowls across the floor looking for photogenic interviewees and announces, 'I'm looking for a young girl.' ('Aren't we all?' remarks my companion.) Finding an eight-year-old cutie, Vince and three camera crews surround her. Unpleasant allusions spring to mind as she's bathed in TV lighting and breathed all over by Vince. At the end of a banal chat, Vince asks if he can have a kiss. The little girl says no. At last: we have discovered someone in the arena with taste. Zoë has a go at keepy-uppy and tries a couple of headers. Bet she's used to juggling balls near her mouth, boom boom.

Finally, after two hours of excruciating sub-Butlin's 'entertainment', the players arrive – impressively, the entire squad and management less the on-duty Keano and Pob. Each enters the arena after a personal build-up from Zoë and Vince. When Ms Ball reads from her cue-card that next up is 'the popular left-back who scored the cup winner in 1990', we wonder how ex-Red Lee Martin has got roped into this. Out trots Denis Irwin, looking faintly embarrassed. *The Zoë Ball Big Book of United History* would surely be a most entertaining read; earlier she kicked off proceedings by announcing that United were founded in 1892 and later blithely proclaims that she couldn't name the 1968 European team even if her life depended on it.

Eric seems bemused by the tackiness of his surroundings; Jordi looks bored already and on stage adopts a sitting position that my girl describes as 'homosexual'; and Ryan, announced with a hormone-exciting fanfare, hares across the dance floor in two seconds flat, leading a disappointed Vince Miller to note that he was too quick for the cameras. Suddenly, I think I've discovered the angle: the entire afternoon is being videotaped, with copies surely to be offered later to all the audience at a tenner a pop. Ryan's refusal to mug for the lens has probably just knocked a quid off the video's worth. Ah, but how would United get everyone's addresses? By making everyone fill in a name-and-address card if they want to be sent a card with all the players' autographs on it. Doubtless accompanied by a video offer, merchandise catalogue and exclusive 'MU Experience' £20 T-shirt offer.

The much-vaunted question-and-answer session is wonderfully banal: 'When's Ryan getting married?', 'What time does Phil Neville go to bed?' and 'How does Peter feel when the ball goes in the net?'. The tabloid hacks, who have long since realised everyone is on dullard autopilot, have even left the bar by now and headed back to their lairs. Eric drops the one morsel of slight interest – that despite his disbelief in God and superstition, the upturned collar was initially a spur-of-the-moment thing but soon became a 'good luck' charm because United never seemed to lose when he had it up. (True – only one defeat in his first thirty games.) A girl standing next to the *Evening News* hackette remarks that she never knew McClair was Scottish. Another tells the crowd that her family left their London home at four in the morning to be here, although she's never been to a game. A grown-up in front of us tells his son that United won the European Cup in 1975. I realise that Zoë Ball is indeed the perfect compere for this crowd after all.

Orgasmic peak is reached – it's time to meet the players, who are now looking distinctly glazed-over and, in one or two cases, near death. The crowd, in single file, pass down the players' line to claim their allowance: one handshake and strictly no photos or small talk. My mate ignores this and starts asking the players if they've got any Dortmund spares, and is rewarded with an arrest attempt by Ned's boys. (Meanwhile, Jordi's handshake is even limper than his performances. I am seriously worried about the guy.) Eric recognises me, winks, and I am pathetically chuffed to bits. And, looking around at the sea of beaming young faces, my cynicism melts. These kids will never forget the day they met every one of their heroes. They didn't have to pay a penny for the opportunity and they'll end up with written proof of their good fortune to wave in the disbelieving faces of schoolmates. The afternoon was tacky, cringe-inducing and symbolic of much of what is wrong with United – but at the centre of it was a bit of the magic that only Red shirts can weave. In a way, it was just like a matchday: a kernel of beauty on the pitch surrounded by tat, commercialism and theme-park crap. It was, indeed, the Manchester United Experience. Pity long-serving season-ticket holders don't get the same sort of privilege every year or so.

The best was yet to come, however. My guest, who'd had quite enough of Zoë Ball's bimboesque performance and always votes for her as the *Red Issue* 'Celebrity C**t of the Month', went over to her to let rip. 'Why don't you stop embarrassing us in public all the time?' he roared politely. 'What were you doing in a bloody Liverpool shirt and why do you keep exposing yourself as a cock-hungry glory-hunter?' (Or words to that effect.) Hilariously, Ms Ball was mortified. 'I only wore that shirt cos it was a kids' charity event,' she wailed, only making matters worse. 'I don't go to the players begging for tickets or anything,' she pleaded, before confessing that the guys at ITV Sport often sorted her out. 'I got such a lot of stick in Porto, but is there anything wrong with me starting supporting United so late?' The Withington Red sneered, thrust a copy of the *Cantona* book into her hand and dealt his parting shot: 'Read in there about what real fans get up to – maybe you'll learn something and stop humiliating yourself.'

As we retreated to the bar for some £1 vodka-beers, we heard Zoë get onto the mike, address the throng and tell how she'd just been accosted by some 'real fans'. (Shit, real fans in the arena – surely an alarm should've gone off?) Incredibly, she then apologised to everyone for wearing that Liverpool shirt and promised to behave herself in future when talking about United on telly. And this was in front of the entire squad, too. Remarkable.

But, but . . . two days later, Zoë appeared on *Live and Kicking* wearing a competition prize: Alan Shearer's England shirt. Sigh. My mate has now declared his intention of becoming Zoë Ball's stalker. What with her main target Dave Beckham being revealed to have rather Spicy tastes, it looks like this is not Zoë's lucky month. But don't despair, Zoë. At least the *Red Issue* 'Celebrity C**t of the Year' award is surely yours?

*(Postscript: The kids never got their autographs. After eighteen months of parental complaints about the delay, the club sheepishly wrote to them admitting that it would no longer be possible for the signatures to be sent. One suspects the players were too busy buying Ferraris. Within the letter came an invitation to visit Old Trafford for a training session, when they'd also have an opportunity to visit the Megastore. Arf!! As for the following, written soon after the event, we didn't have anyone in mind at all, oh no . . .)*

## Daily Spurt Interview: Red Celeb Bimbo

So, tell us about your first visit to the Theatre of Dreams.

– Eh, what's that?

Old Trafford.

– Oh, yeah! Well, I remember it so vividly, as though it were yesterday.

Is that because it *was* yesterday?

– Yes, it was actually! And what a thrill! I'd been waiting so long, dreaming about the day I'd finally get here – ever since my agent phoned last week and said, 'Oi, you'd better get yerself a soccer team, every celeb needs one these days.'

I see. And what made you choose United?

– All my babe friends follow United: Zoë, Ulrika, Victoria. We're just one big crazy gang, y'know! We're mad, we're bonkers, we are! Always trying to outdo each other with our wacky stunts!

Like what?

– Well, Zoë's boyf supports United, so Vicky got herself a United *player* for her boyf, then Ulrika got a Red Devil tattoo on her botty, so guess what – I got my clit pierced with a lickle metal Devil! Wicked or what! We're 'avin' a larff, aren't we?! And you'll be able to see it in next month's *FHM* 'Cheap Sluts Get Their Waps Out' photo special. Tasteful piccies, mind you: no animals or poo.

And how are the United crowd taking to you?

– It's so sweet, they love me here, always laughing and joking with me, showing that funny sense of humour they have up here. Like when I did that prize draw on the pitch with that hunky Keith Fane and they were all booing and pretending to hate me – what a larf! I could tell they loved me really, y'see, cos they were chucking coins towards me in appreciation, and one sweetie even threw his full bottle of beer at me to drink, bless him. Bad aim, though – almost hit me head!

Do you get annoyed at being stereotyped as a girlie who knows nothing about football?

– Yeah, it's really hurtful, innit? Just cos I don't know the names of the United team that won the World Cup in 1969, some people get the hump. But I know loads about this club: I can tell you Ryan's cock size, where to go to pull the fledglings and how to force the dressing-room door so I can be ready in the bath when the team comes in.

Any plans to get more involved in the game now you're a true Red?

– Ooh yeah, loads: got a video out soon, a book (which one of those nice boys at Zone is writing for me), a radio series and a TV special.

And we'll be seeing you at Old Trafford again for a United match soon?

– God, no, it's far too cold up in that stand for me in my *faux*-leather mini and boob tube. But you can be sure I'll be watching the boys on telly like a real fan. We're the ones in Red, right?

Thanks for taking the time to talk to us, the *Man U Mag*, every lad-rag, tabloid, tacky telly show, etc etc . . .

## *Daily Spurt News*

END OF AN ERA: SADNESS OF FERGIE DIVORCE

The nation was united in sorrow as Fergie's divorce was announced, ending a spectacular and often controversial marriage. The days when we all swooned at their whirlwind romance in the '80s are long gone – now the couple spend barely any time together, their last liaison lasting barely forty-five minutes. Fergie, who's been linked with many dashing young men over the last few months, has finally decided to choose freedom and confirmed the divorce to excited pressmen last night.

'Yes, I can't deny it – we are no longer in love. I have finally realised that what everyone else has been saying for years about my man is true. Brian McClair is a hopeless performer and no longer turns me on.'

Fergie will be keeping custody of his brood of eighteen-year-old kids whilst Brian retires permanently to his rest home at Gigg Lane.

## *Sour Puffs*

(From *The Box*)

Football is the new rock 'n' roll, as every publisher, editor and TV producer has long since recognised. You know the familiar litany:

Italia '90, *Fever Pitch*, Sky Sports money, Premiership hype, blah blah blah – and, at last, the advertising industry has caught up and started *Zeitgeist*-surfing with a vengeance. Try watching Sky or ITV for an hour without catching sight of some wooden footballer trying to flog you something; it can't be done. For the star players, the attraction is obvious and comes bundled in thousands. But for the denizens of Adland, the appeal is scientifically specific, as rising star GGT account director Mike Falconer explains.

'We were, as ever, a touch late on the scene because we reflect rather than pre-empt societal trends; Euro '96 broke down the final barriers. But football adverts offer a unique demographic combination in the '90s: a universal referential touchstone, yet also an arrow straight into the prime targets of ABC1s and 18- to 34-year-old males. It's an irresistible hat-trick.'

Car manufacturers, cereal makers, sweetie sellers and the rest of the Chamber of Commerce have duly waded in, snapping up every star and wannabe to front their product pitches. (When your local non-leaguer's ugly left-back crops up on your cinema screen to remind you to buy some popcorn in the foyer, you'll know saturation point has been reached.) But do the Soho trend-hoppers actually know what they're doing with football?

Recent ad-howler examples abound. Particularly sad is David Platt's minty effort, primarily because its 'star' is a) no oil painting, b) an Arse-trundler and c) nearing the nadir of an extended decline. Surely not even Highbury zealots were tempted into the sweetie shop by this? (Also, I remember Tictacs as being devices to mask ciggie smoke from parents. As Plattie *is* your dad, he'd be lecturing you on tar content, not handing out the mints.)

Even the goal-hanging Honey Monster gets it wrong in his 'hilarious' duet with Kevin Keegan. Newcastle scoring a winner at Wembley? Not unless this is 1955, pal. Moreover, the admen hadn't realised that the self-aggrandising Toons are actually not as nationally loved as Mr Monster; slumping Sugar Puffs sales in Middlesbrough, Sunderland and Salford testified to a case of one set of admen falling for the hype of another.

Worst of all – and I say this with the heavy heart of a Red – is the Karel Poborsky ad for Strike cereal. Scarcely was the ink dry on the new arrival's contract when the tonsorially challenged Czech appeared on our screens telling us he'd come here 'to win things'. Like Pontin's Reserve League medals, I suppose. It will serve as a classic caveat to all advertisers dabbling in football: it can be as dangerous to be premature as it is to be unfashionably late.

As Falconer remarks, 'It's a minefield; there's a lot of shit out there. Football looks a safe bet when you enter the arena but to escape with your credibility intact is actually very tricky. That 18–34 core audience are canny, cynical and critical; you patronise them at your peril and certainly don't risk going into battle uninformed.'

Indeed. The best ads have been those that clearly know their subject and stars, then have the humour to exploit every foible. Cantona's Eurostar ads and Lineker's crisp promotions are nicely judged and made with creatives' love – Walkers are rumoured to have increased their market by 30% on the back of Gary's winsome hamming. Falconer also highlights campaigns such as Reebok, Coke and Nike, which tap into football's universality, as being well regarded within the pony-tailed industry, though these require big, multinational-style budgets and large-canvas creative vision. So the cheapo one-gag insularity of the Pizza Hut penalty commercial would hardly do for Adidas.

At the end of the day, Brian, the mass-market ad's golden rules should be obvious. Only use players whose personalities have transcended their narrow club appeal (so Roy Keane and Julian Dicks might be problematic); remember that true Brits prefer humour to pretension every time; and make sure you market-research genuine fans before you make that client presentation. They might just save you from proposing Tony Adams as the frontman for a new hatchback ad . . .

## Redheads: Ryan Giggs

Back in the autumn, the United star against Juventus – in the second half at least – was Ryan Giggs, whose sinewy runs caused chaos and drew two markers onto him. He took the plaudits the next day, but there was a tinge of relief amidst the congratulations, almost as though fans had just regained their hope for the future of the former wunderkind. The older he gets, the more enigmatic he has become – and the more uncertain the relationship between him and the Old Trafford faithful.

Loftus Road, 1994–95: a cat-suited Dani Behr is tottering back to the Tube after watching current inamorato Ryan Giggs play. 'Oi, blondie,' yells a Mancunian voice from the darkness, 'stop shagging Giggsy cos it's shagging up his game.' Once again Reds were concerned that 'delicate' Ryan's fragile equilibrium was being disturbed by carnal intrusions. And Giggsy's career at United has been a curious combination: outrageously ultra-confident peaks separated by lows of beetle-browed self-doubt. Blaming the birds for the latter is a bit tough on both shagger and shagged – it's far more likely that it's been a function of the neurosis which weekly being dubbed a genius since the age of thirteen has produced. But it's symbolic of the odd relationship between the still overwhelmingly male Red home-and-awayers and this most precocious of players.

Gruff old baldies sometimes mutter that Ryan is a 'girlie's footballer'; not only is he most popular with the female teenies who've made him a *Smash Hits* superstar, but also on the pitch he can be as maddening as any temptress. Spectacularly orgasmic purple patches, such as that sexiest of spells during the last title run-in, are too often followed by grouchy pre-menstrual slumps such as that which he suffered after United's first title.

As Giggs is the twenty-seventh young flyer to be dubbed 'the new George Best' – and the first to half-deserve it – it is wryly amusing to see him building a reputation for scrapes and alleged totty-based naughtiness, whether it be messing with strippers, drunken models or footie groupies. But George always delivered on matchday; he was mercurial yet still reliable. The fascinating aspect of the unpredictable Giggs is wondering not only what on earth he might do next with those extraordinarily long, curling feet but also, pre-kick-off, whether he's going to be a participant or a spectator. He can play an absolute howler on a Saturday, then on Wednesday dazzle and become the toast of Europe. Kids today, hey? Kissing their gran one minute, sellotaping bangers to her cat the next.

Except that Giggs is no longer such a young lad; to the new Fergie Fledglings, he's an older-brother figure and a player beginning to assume team-dominance responsibilities. Some at United think this will be the making of him, that after years of talk, yet unrealised, that he will become a European superstar, this season could finally see the fulfilment. It seems ridiculous, given his achievements, that he has a way to go yet before United's lads put him on the highest Eric-level pedestal, but such are the man's natural blessings that only a consistent Cantonesque brilliance will suffice. United fans have always seen him as special; there is an unmistakable protectiveness towards him from the stands which assures any clogger who tries to crop him years of unrelenting abuse. But pure idolatry still yearns to be unleashed. And there are many who won't wait much longer.

*(Followers of British politics couldn't have failed to notice how much Tony Blair had been cosying up to Alex Ferguson during '96–'97. Apparently, Blair was much taken with Fergie's management techniques and was given to quoting examples of what Fergie had said and done at United as a lesson to Labour's leaders. After New Labour's election victory in May,* Red Issue *sketched out a plausible scenario for the Fergie-influenced future of Tony Blair's Britain.)*

## New Labour United: First Term

December 1997: European Union Summit. Britain fails to qualify for the last-eight stage of the EMU. Fumes Tony, 'We are choking back the vomit. We would easily have gone through with our strongest team but they invoked the devolved three-foreigner rule, forcing our Scottish stars Robin and Gordon to stay at home.'

July 1998: Top midfield general Cabinet star Robin Cook is shockingly transferred to the new Scottish Parliament; some say he went willingly, enthralled by the prospect of becoming Scottish President and earning big bucks, whilst others claim that he was pushed out by Tony, who could no longer stand Cook calling himself 'The Boss Haggis'.

May 1999: Despite the loss of Cook, Tony calls and wins a snap election, having also replaced Prescott, Cunningham and Brown with members of his hand-picked 'Young New Labour' faction. David Dimbleby is forced to apologise for claiming Tony would 'never win an election with kids'.

August 1999: Tony denies being obsessed with becoming the European President and neglecting domestic affairs despite stuffing his Cabinet with foreigners who have more experience in dealing with the sneaky Krauts and Eyeties. The secondment of Czech Václav Havel to the Treasury on the strength of his performances in the 1989 European Post-Commie Liberation Championships does not go well, especially as he refuses to have his unfashionably hairy moustache trimmed.

September 1999: Bad inflation (6.3%) and unemployment (up 5%) figures follow within seven days of each other. 'It's just a blip,' says Tony. 'The fact that the inflation score was so high doesn't reflect how well we played on prices. It was just one of those days.'

April 2000: Chancellor Kohl pips Tony in the election for Reichführer of the European Union. Tony promises he'll go one better next year, that his team of advisors is better than Kohl's, and that the Germans cheated by appealing for penalties against Britain under the Maastricht convergence criteria. Eric Cantona is later sacked as Minister of Cultural Affairs.

May 2001: Tony finally wins the European job after Kohl's stomach explosion forces his retirement; Tony is then appointed Director of the Labour Party, allowing his deputy to become British Prime Minister. Though our pundits do concede this might be wishful thinking . . .

*(A week after the election and the day after Eric lifted the title trophy against West Ham, the author wrote this in anticlimactic mood for the* Sunday Tribune. *We didn't yet know what a busy week it was going to be . . .)*

## 'Sit Down for the Champions . . .'

(From the *Sunday Tribune*)

Back in August, we were asked by a football magazine for our predictions as to how Manchester United would fare this season. 'A brave semi-final defeat in Europe, and just enough domestic complacency to give our rivals at least a chance of sniffing the title,' was our verdict. We hadn't counted on Newcastle and Liverpool producing quite such passion-free witlessness, thus making our amble to a third title in four years even easier than usual, but undoubtedly an air of inevitability has hung over 1996–97. Whatever the hype-*meisters* of Sky and the PL spin, we know that this is a poor league; such is the United squad's skill and experience that it was always going to take much more than Anfield's male-model preening to dislodge us from the summit. Keegan's self-combustion demobbed the Toon Army early; Wenger's Arsenal had their ridiculous pretensions exposed by us one thrilling February night. United were a team in transition, with a captain on autopilot and all eyes on Europe – yet we still won with a week to spare. It is said United fans are too arrogant, but, given what's happened, how could you expect us to be humble?

You could draw parallels between our attitudes and those of the Conservatives before their humiliation last week. So accustomed are we to domestic dominance that we allow ourselves to become almost entirely entranced by the European Question – for single currency, read Champions' Cup. The anyone-but-United brigade will be praying a similar Toryish fate befalls us. But here's the truth: we *are* utterly obsessed with the Holy Grail of emulating the heroes of 1968. The emotional highs and lows of the league campaign – hammering the Scousers and Tykes, being savaged in Tyneside – were effortlessly outstripped by the Continental counterparts, thrashing Portugal's champions and getting stuffed by Turkey's. Before Christmas, when the team appeared to be playing from memory to artless and sometimes point-less effect, few fans got too worked up about it; winning in Vienna and saving up for Oporto were our twin obsessions. Fergie was lambasted in the press for dismissing the league as 'a competition in which we can make up ground later', but he was right, wasn't he? If, as one critic contended, the European Cup is 'an albatross around Fergie's neck', then he has 55,000 Reds willing to share the burden. Your correspondent promised the Lord that he would forgo conjugal relations for a year if He allowed us to get to Munich's final. (The bargain was presumably rejected as being an abuse of prayer.) He'd only have offered a month's abstinence for the Premiership . . .

Strangely, the true domestic drama has happened away from the self-styled Theatre of Dreams. The greatest results and the most memorable supporting have occurred at places like Elland Road, Ewood Park, Anfield and Highbury rather than at Old Trafford. Indeed, there are plenty of time-served lads in Stretford who'll argue this has been the most boring OT league season in years and that the drug of adrenaline on which supporters depend has only been available on awaydays. It isn't merely that the current team is not yet as viscerally exciting as 1994's – nor, indeed, as those of 1985 and 1976 – but that the new 55,000 super-stadium has not delivered what we want. 'We' means the hardcore fans, of course; the plc board has garnered precisely what it desired by the million. Naturally, fans appreciate the income to buy the superstars we demand, but they crave blood-boiling atmosphere even more. Going to football, as opposed to being an armchair supporter, is about a sense of event, of occasion: it's vibrant, live theatre as opposed to second-hand, filtered cinematics. At times this season, the atmosphere and support at Old Trafford have veered dangerously close to the disgraceful, prompting supporters' groups, certain players and even the management to protest that 'something must be done'.

Old Trafford's officials aren't listening, however, as they're ensconced inside a metaphorical bank vault, counting the proceeds made from the Faustian bargain with The '90s Football Experience. The deal? Fill the ground with day-trippers, families and the wealthy; price out the traditional fan; enforce a code of audience behaviour akin to that of an opera house; compensate with big bonuses and dividends all round. One day, one of the self-proclaimed geniuses who take the gullible media's plaudits for building the modern United will see the correlation between United's lacklustre home form and the absence of atmosphere. They might even grasp the dreadful long-term significance of denying young Mancunians a place at Old Trafford. And if, God forbid, United have a few bad seasons, they will certainly come to learn the folly of placing the New Breed's interests above those of the home-and-away hardcore, when empty seats will testify to the fickleness of the '90s football 'consumer'.

So don't be surprised, or find it churlish, that we select two non-football moments as our domestic OT highlights of '96–'97. Firstly, the night during the Arsenal match when a tannoy announcer bellowed at us to 'sit down or be ejected'; the entire ground rose defiantly to its feet to sing 'Stand Up for the Champions' and start a campaign that will never end until it is satisfied. And secondly, last Thursday night. With the title safely won, United's East Stand lads were at liberty to subject their mortal enemy Alan Shearer to ninety minutes of the most sustained, vicious and yet hilarious abuse heard at our ground this season. A new chant was devised every two minutes, joined full-throatedly by the 8,000 hardcore behind the goal; the New Breed and United's officials may have tut-tutted and muttered something about bad sportsmanship, but we loved every minute. So at least twice this domestic season, we felt we were at one with our fearsome forebears from the '60s, '70s and '80s – united by United. We may not love the club as embodied by its bean-counters and executives; we may not love every player in a Red shirt; we may even not love every Johnny-Come-Lately who tries to define himself as a United fan. But we love without limit the proud rebel heart that is the *spirit* of United – and that's worth more than any single silver trophy. Though a European Cup in 1998 wouldn't do it any harm . . .

*(Hang on, we can't go a whole season without a final pop at Leeds and their bestial kind . . .)*

## Are You a Sheep-Shagging Yonner?

Help yourself get diagnosed and cured if you suspect you've got village idiot/country bumpkin tendencies with our quick-test questions; it's never too late to get yourself sorted and become a sophisticated metropolitan lad. You might need treatment if:

- You have ever used lard in bed
- Your lifetime goal is an inside toilet
- You get a free calendar every year featuring farm appliances in provocative poses
- Someone asks to see your ID and you show them a newspaper photofit
- Your condom supply isn't kept in the bedroom but the barnyard
- Your tractor has curtains before your house does
- Your mother has lost her teeth opening ale bottles
- The stash under your bed consists of a box of Kleenex and a pile of *Livestock Monthly* back copies
- You can't understand why the black guy in the *Pulp Fiction* back-room scene is so cross with the sheriff and shopkeeper
- You've ever caught your sister smothering your ram's knob with mint sauce
- You have to sign your Leeds (or Bolton, or Blackburn) membership cards with an 'X'
- Your idea of a quality night in is a six-pack, a can of cockroach spray and videos of Munich crash footage

So, if you've answered 'yes' to more than half, see your nearest Mancunian for treatment advice – or 'do a McAllister' and get out of sheep country . . .

*(Can't put it off any longer. 'What profit a man that he may win a trophy but lose a king?' as Will never said. What a roller-coaster week that was . . .)*

## King Chronicles: 'Adieu'

(From *Man Utd: Tribute to a King* and the *Daily Express*)

*The afternoon that he retired, I personally found some sort of release in writing about Eric. Because I am his most recent biographer, I found myself swamped with media enquiries; I did some telly and radio the next day, although I knew I couldn't blurt out any of the darker stories I'd heard. If Eric wanted such things to emerge from the shadows, he'd have to do it himself. Like other Reds called upon to comment that day, I just wanted to express our admiration for him – and to ensure that we fans would not be portrayed like suicidal Geordies were the day they sold Cole. I chose to write the two small farewells below, the first in the Daily Express, because that's Fergie's paper, and the other in the Man Utd Mag because, sadly, it's the publication that reaches the most Reds. I'd like to think that this is how most Reds I know felt about his departure.*

The legions of Man United haters who will this morning be taunting Cantona fans about their hero's departure should really save their breath. For Reds have always known this day would come, such is the nature of the man and his existentialist world-view – and they've always been mentally prepared for it. We won't be crying in the streets like a bunch of girly Geordies but instead will display stoic forbearance. Back in 1995, when not a week went by without a 'Cantona to Quit' headline, we used to say that if he went, we would simply respond with, 'So long and thanks for all the fish.' (We loved his sardine analogies so much, we put them on a million T-shirts.) Like any passionate love affair, the Red–Eric relationship could always have ended at any moment. Even so, today certainly feels like the end of a monarchy, the abdication of a king. Sorry to offend royalist readers, but many Reds will miss Cantona more than any Windsor.

Even at Old Trafford, you only get players who make such an emotional impact once a generation. Duncan Edwards and George Best were such players, embodying everything that was immortal about their respective classic teams. Eric Cantona has been that player for my generation. I honestly doubt we'll see his like again. He is inextricably intertwined with the magical experience of May 1993, when United ended their twenty-six-year quest for the league title after Eric added that last special ingredient. Only a successor winning the European Cup virtually single-handedly could hope to compete with the impact Eric made. And the greatest football any Red under thirty has seen is that which he inspired during the 1993–94 double season, nine months of brilliance which, despite being so recent, are now acquiring almost mythic and mystical status. Long before he became our captain, he was *notre Dieu.*

To understand his iconic status fully, you must see Mancunian youths strutting around with figurative collars up, oozing the kind of self-confidence and *savoir-faire* in which Eric specialises. Few footballers have been so loved for who they are as much as for what they do. And honesty always mattered to him, so he's done as he promised, going out at the top. We are spared the sight of a hero cascading down the other side of the hill. There may be recriminations to come. But today, surely, is for thanksgiving.

* * *

All of you reading this are Reds; most of you are, like me, too young to have seen George Best or Duncan Edwards. So when we're asking ourselves what Eric Cantona meant to us, we can skip the formalities and take it as read – Eric was simply the best we've ever seen. More than that; without his inspirational, catalysing presence in the team over the past four and a half years, much of our success would have been not just unobtainable but inconceivable. Don't bother trying to argue the toss; this is fact, not opinion. When supporters' spokesman Andy Walsh led the Red public's appreciation on 18 May, he was right to divide the credit for our '90s dominance equally between the management duo and Eric Cantona. For, after all, it is *players* who win matches – and no Red won as many matches for us as the King.

There is nothing new to say about his skill, flair and achievement on the pitch. We've all exhausted our vocabularies over these years trying to encapsulate what it was like actually to witness his moments of outrageous divinity. His presence in the team made going to United a compulsion, not a choice – you could not risk missing what he might do. Perhaps we should add, however, that recently he has given us leadership too, leaving a legacy of a champion team at its highest European rating for nearly thirty years, a team increasingly manned by 'kids', who became footballing men under his tutelage. Who amongst his detractors from the early years would have thought it possible that he could have become such a paternal figure, offering guidance and inspiration rather than uncontrollable temperament? Even we fully paid-up *Cantonistas* hadn't reckoned on that.

But personally, I'm going to remember him as much for the man he was as the player he became. When you're a kid, anyone in a Red shirt is automatically a hero to be worshipped unconditionally. Then you grow up, get wiser, then more cynical; pretty soon, players are often there to be admired on the pitch but ignored off it, the modern footballer often being a byword for naff cluelessness. The cultured Cantona, of course, was the rule-proving exception – an iconic hero for all ages, even for the critical, knowing, cool lads in the Ralph Lauren gear. He always was both a player and a man for all seasons.

# 1997–98

## Mystic Red '97

(From *Total Football*)

Writing in mid-June as I am, I have no idea what our team is going to look like come 10 August. Indeed, I'm not sure that I'm particularly arsed either, for that afternoon will mark our Premiership debut at Spurs, a prospect that only induces world-weary *ennui.* We have been the best team in England for six straight seasons and our easy supremacy begins to jade. Too much of our domestic programme feels like drudgery, filling in the weekends between those special Wednesday nights. For what I really care about is how our team will look in September, when it's time for the 10,000 travelling Red Army to pack their bags, fortify their livers and head for the Continent's fleshpots. Naturally, I'll still enjoy our needle matches against the likes of the whining Scousers, the crying Geordies and the knuckle-dragging Tykes, but our true peers surely reside abroad. The Championship has become merely a passport that must be renewed annually by finishing in the top two; it's now a means to an end, rather than an end in itself. When you've grown accustomed to Nou Camp, Communale and Westphalion, Oakwell, The Dell and Selhurst Park pall a tad in comparison.

There is an air of uncertainty around Old Trafford this summer. It's a reflection of the larger picture, beamed to us on digital satellite but still dark and fuzzy at the moment. Out there ahead of us is pay-per-view TV, a possible European Superleague, the increasing dominance of player- and sponsor-power and the intervention of capitalism's big beasts. It is not too fanciful to envisage a near-future scenario which posits United under new ownership, franchised across the world, playing its first team in Europe and its reserves in a domestic feeder league, beamed to 20 million armchair fans whilst 55,000 actual match-goers spend the entire weekend at the Old Trafford Leisure Park and Hotel complex. The Premiership thinks of itself as the bright, shiny future, but for the big two or three it might just be a stepping stone to a vastly bigger stage.

In such a context, this is a make-or-break season, whereby our footballing and financial performances will largely dictate how the next decade looks. Is the plc able to make the sort of commitments in terms of transfer fees and wages to compete at an exalted European level? Is our team, the core of which would be expected to see us through the next seven or eight years, going to be good enough or did we flatter to deceive last season, possibly as a prelude to being 'found out' in this year's expanded, harder-to-win European Cup? And whilst such crunch issues are being settled, the club have to handle two rods they made for their own back: battling predators in the City who'll seek to take advantage of our plc status and buy themselves a cash-cow; and fighting their own increasingly discontented and mistreated hardcore fans. Amidst such existential crises, forgive me for not being agog at the poxy Premiership's destination.

*(During the season's opening month, Wimbledon, a club notorious for its lack of fans, proposed to move to Dublin where there's a surplus of easily pleased long-ball fanatics. Other clubs, we suggested, might also be planning American-style location changes to acquire what they can't get at home.)*

## Movin' On Up?

**Manchester City** will be moving to Jersey in order to find backers to save them from bankruptcy. They reckon that pleading to minted businessmen to 'save your only local club' might work with the doddering yokels down there – it certainly hasn't worked with smart Mancunians, has it? Also, there's room there for even bigger pitches and there's no chance of being completely outclassed by local rivals, the Red Lion Regulars. (*Latest score: Red Lion 2 City 0 – Lee missed pen*)

**Liverpool** have been fretting that the Kop is nowhere near what it was and that the lack of atmosphere is affecting the team. Therefore, in an effort to reunite all those Koppite regulars of the '70s and '80s, all future home games will be played by rota at HMPs Walton, Haverigg and Wymott, where most Liverpudlians over twenty-one now live full-time.

**Blackburn Rovers**, in a pathetic attempt to win back King Kenny and prevent ultimate relegation, will relocate to Formby Golf Course next door to Kenny's house; hopefully this means the grumpy tw*t will manage to fit in some work whilst he's enjoying stroke-play with Hansen.

**Newcastle** will be staying put but will be moving from the Premiership into the St James' Park League, where they will play against their Reserves, Juniors and the rest for the Lord John Hall Cup. This ensures they will finally win a Championship trophy and keep those overwrought girly Geordies from committing mass tearful suicide. (*Latest score: Reserves 3 Newcastle 1 – Shearer penalty*)

**Leeds United** will relocate to New Zealand for obvious fan-pleasing reasons and also hope that, if they're quiet enough, Howard Wilkinson won't be able to find them again. The club will, however, remain twinned with NSDAP Nuremberg (*est. 1933*).

**Bolton**, however, are refusing to move. Apparently, living in a decaying armpit amidst racist Neanderthals suits their traditions down to the ground.

And finally, **Manchester Council** will rebuild the heart of Manchester around Old Trafford because they're sick to death of their 'representatives' at Maine Road embarrassing the fuck out of our city by being so shit-awful.

*(Every early-season tipster had one cert: Roy Keane was going to be the nation's dominant player now that Eric had left.* Total Football *commissioned the following cover story on the same basis. Three weeks later came Elland Road. If it does indeed turn out that he'll never hit his 1997 peaks again, this might serve as a snapshot of him at the summit . . .)*

## Redheads: Roy Keane

(From *Total Football*)

Here's a glib wannabe-paradox for you: Roy Keane plays for a club called United, in a role that requires him to hold the team together, yet the mention of his name divides opinion wherever you go. At Old Trafford, he can't escape the ancestral lineage. He's already the latest in the Robson-Whiteside-Hughes tradition of granite-hewn leaders, players around whom team-mates can rally, men upon whom managers can rely. Brilliant he clearly is; even the most twisted and bitter Manc-hating Scouser will concede that. But it has become a media cliché that you can't talk about Keane without immediately raising the question of his temperament. As with the leader he's replaced, Eric Cantona, the demons he supposedly breeds within apparently make him as much Anti-Hero as God. It was once said of Cantona that 'he left a trail of sulphur behind him'; with Roy, it's the tang of cordite as he roars from one battle to another, all guns a-blazing. Typical consequences: a stupid red card at United for punching a Middlesbrough opponent leads to several complaining letters to the fanzines and papers; a summer dust-up with Eire sees him booed whilst playing for his country against Iceland. To those who believe in the Charlton/Lineker philosophy of gentlemanly football, players such as Keane are always going to be anathema. Sadly, such prudes are grossly over-represented in the media, whose denizens circle Keane vulturishly, waiting for the next explosion.

Fortunately, the vast majority of those who pay his wages would prefer to concur with Eamon Dunphy's view of Keane's, erm, 'over-committed moments': 'All it shows is how much he cares for the shirt and for the cause.' Which is, of course, precisely the reason why hardcore fans of every club love their hard men – they play with the passion of a fan, rather than the clinical detachment of the careful pro. But it probably shows something else too: that this is a man who had to battle his way up the ladder. As a young lad back in Cork, Roy was small for his age – it's the one facet everyone remembers from his youth. At, say, fourteen, he had the skill and vision of an eighteen-year-old but the physique of a kid. Week after week, he'd have to take on the bigger, harder lads, all of whom would be seeking to put this flash prospect in his place, viz. on his arse. Rockmount AFC, who moulded Roy for eight years before he ever went near Cobh Ramblers, were breeding him tough, plonking him into the middle of the park as playmaker and expecting him to handle the close physical attention *mano a mano*. Consequently, long before Cobh and semi-pro status, he had a reputation as a lad who'd take on all-comers; he'd never give the ball away and he'd never back off from a challenge. Although a summer job lugging beer kegs and crates in Blackpool helped develop the odd muscle or two, it wasn't until he began full-time training at an FAI course in Dublin that he really began the transformation into the physiological marvel that he is today. As with Robson before him, the terrier needed beefing up before he became a beast big enough for the First Division jungle.

Roy has benefited from the genetic inheritance of a warrior clan too. The name 'Keane' divides opinion in Cork as well as over here; talk to some locals or Irish journalists and they'll tell you hair-raising stories about his tribe, using adjectives of which the only printable one is 'fiery'. If you want to go looking for it, there are some patches of bad blood about their region of Cork. But the majority always remained fiercely proud of him, doubly so when it became clear that Roy would not be deserting his roots. He goes back home as often as he can and brings Cork back to Old Trafford if he can't; many a legendary tale is told around Manchester about the exploits of The Cork Boys whom Roy would bring over *en masse* for weekends of *craic*-ery. It is undoubtedly a mutual admiration society: as Roy told RTE's Dave Hannighan, 'I'm proud of where I come from – in fact, I count myself as a Cork man first, and an Irishman second.' To Alex Ferguson, always a devotee of roots, family and loyalty, this mentality is music to the ears. As everyone around Old Trafford knows, Roy is certainly a Fergie Favourite, an adopted son in the McClair/Cantona tradition. And when you're protected by Fergiepower, the odd carp from the critics can safely be ignored.

Nottingham Forest's scout Noel McCabe knew he'd seen something special in this lad – something even rarer than Roy's unusual mania for training, during which he'd drive himself to the limit, turning what everyone now calls his 'engine' into a V12-plus. That in itself spoke of his dedication and ambition, as well as meaning that he left his contemporaries flailing behind him in any kind of physical contest. 'We just couldn't keep up,' remarked one. 'Roy was always three laps ahead – in every sense of the phrase.' To possess a portfolio of all-round skills as well seemed gratuitously prodigious: Forest whipped out fifteen grand pronto, doubtless marvelling at the rare failure of Man United's multi-tentacled Irish scouting network to spot him first.

At the City Ground, it would be the other, under-reported side of Keane's temperament which would impress – his total unflappability and cool footballing vision. With only ten minutes of reserve football under his belt, Cloughie tossed him into a first-team debut (at Anfield, of all places) with about fifty minutes' notice. A Forest coach remembers that Roy's face blanched for five seconds when Clough told him; the momentary shock subsumed, Keane then went out and produced one of the best debut performances he'd ever seen. The fans and local press, who'd been told Keane was 'one for the future', were now told he'd get a brief run in the team before a long rest. But Roy never did relinquish the shirt. By the end of 1992 he'd appeared in two Wembley cup finals, been named Forest's player of the season and was on every decent manager's Ten Most Wanted list – including Alex Ferguson's.

Fergie had noticed Keane back in 1991, being jolted out of his seat when this brash lad dared up-end Bryan Robson in front of the Stretford End; by 1992, he was offering Forest the man now more famed as Shelley Webb's husband in part-ex. It would take a record fee, and some unpleasantness with Blackburn, before he finally made Keane his in 1993. Fergie had no doubts about Keane's ability; his only question, which he posed to Jack Charlton, was would this shy Cork boy be big enough a man to take on United? 'Buy him, now – you'll never regret it,' declared Jack, who's always had a way with an adman's tag-line. Sure enough, and – unlike so many other Forest/ United transfers – Fergie's never had to look for a money-back guarantee in the small print.

A few minor bedding-in problems before Christmas '93 were easily resolved. Firstly, Roy bought a house after six months of microwave-fuelled rootlessness; secondly, as Roy told RTE, 'Bryan Robson taught me how to become a box-to-box all-rounder instead of continuing the more limited role I'd been used to at Forest.' By the end of 1994–95, Ferguson now remarks, 'I thought Roy was beginning to outshine Paul Ince; we felt Roy was maturing into the biggest future influence at the club.' Exit one Guv'nor, amidst much weeping and wailing – but Keane would repay the faith loaded upon him by his boss. You don't hear calls for the return of the prodigal Ince so often these days, for United have a new midfield governor. The difference between the two maestri, which we all suspect Fergie invests with great significance, is that Roy would never call himself 'The Guv'nor', however much he might deserve the title. That's not the style of a shy, unassuming Cork lad.

Those who don't know Keane off-field – and who, like mouthy Alan Green, label him 'a lout' – would be surprised at his off-duty demeanour. Unlike some United players we could mention, he loathes drawing attention to himself and prefers to stick to a close circle of mates and family he can trust; you're not going to see him in the tabloids schmoozing with rock stars and two-bit actresses. Sure, he admits he 'had one or two scrapes when I was living in Nottingham', and he still likes a pint or two, but the media have been slow to catch up with the reality of the 1997 incarnation of Roy Keane – he's settled down with his wife and kids and is rapidly becoming an Old Trafford elder statesman. His eyes are no longer on the next all-night bender but on the long-term future as the team's leader. As an occasional drinking partner remarked when I put the question of Keane's reputation to him, 'He behaves just like an ordinary twenty-five-year-old bloke – no better, no worse. The fact is that he's amusing, generous and modest, happier out of the limelight than being the centre of social attention.' Indeed, his local barman back in Cork suggests that one reason for some of the dust-ups he's had around town over the years is that punters mistake his shyness for aloofness; others decide that his on-pitch character must make him fair game for bawdy baiting. Not that he complains: he's always known the price of fame.

The 'problem' of his on-pitch temper remains. A grinning Fergie told RTE, 'He reminds me of Robbo, the way he gets involved. But Robbo always knew when to stop – the moment before the ref starts fishing in his pocket. Roy just keeps on going, doesn't he?' Fergie won't criticise players publicly but you can assume this is a subject often discussed behind the dressing-room door; indeed, the fact that Roy was only sent off once – and quite unjustly too – during 1996–97 suggests progress is being made. But the Cantona comparisons are apt, whereby Eric would proclaim that he needed the 'inner fire' to make him the player he was. Keane might try to mitigate his volatile temperament but the fundamentals won't change. With Cantonesque defiance, he declares, 'I'll never change. If I did, I'd be half the player I am now. It's part of what makes me. If it means I'm going to get the odd sending-off in the future, I'll have to deal with it.' Typically forthright – just because he's modest ('I've been lucky to be in a good team and to have had opportunities come along at the right moment'), it doesn't mean he is unsure of himself or his opinions. Indeed, one difference between him and Cantona is that Eric always gave the impression of a man still looking to discover things about himself. Remarkably for a twenty-five-year-old, Roy Keane seems to know exactly who he is and what he believes. And one such belief, tailor-made to please his manager, is the work ethic. As he told RTE, if you put in the effort and application, 'you can then deserve the rewards that come to you'. One '60s United veteran recently described Keane as the best player to wear the Red shirt for a quarter of a century. That will be the first of many accolades to reward the boy from Cork over the next decade. The vacant throne at Old Trafford awaits.

*(The funniest spectator blood-sport of the month was undoubtedly watching the Maine Road circus trying to appoint a new ring-leader, as potential candidates headed for the hills and incumbents resigned every full moon. We did our bit by advertising the post for them . . .)*

## Daily Spurt Classified Ads

MANCHESTER CITY'S MANAGER'S POST

The directors of MCFC, the only very big club in Manchester itself, wish to appoint a new manager; previous experience in any division preferred, though we'll consider any ex-pro Blue with time on his hands.

Our top-line executive package befitting our status as the club with the biggest pitch includes the following:

1) A salary of no less than £183 per week will be paid, financed from the running profits of our new SuperFrannyBurger catering division. Pay your own national insurance; income tax is up to you to sort out (if you want to pay it, that is . . .).

2) Bonuses will accrue every time you mention the following phrases at press conferences: 'The chairman has been tremendous', 'Our fans are the best in Britain', 'There's money for players if I want it' and any phrase including the words 'big club'.

3) A transfer kitty of £26.50 will be made instantly available, to be topped up by whatever the chairman wins on his accumulator that day at Ladbrokes. The kitty will be augmented if the top-secret 'Kinky Fund' becomes available.

4) An attractive benefits package will be provided, consisting of:

- Unlimited free toilet paper (sponsor: 'Wipe Yer Fanny With Franny's')
- 20p off every pint of Greenalls you can drink (Monday nights only)
- Money-off vouchers to be spent in our Oasis Restaurant-and-Spud-U-Lick
- Free choice from a range of Brother knitting machines (slightly spoiled seconds)
- Free parking in any Moss Side car park (note: leaving your car not recommended)

5) The full range of our ex-pros' talents will be yours to choose from, as will top-notch advice from Tony Book, Asa Hartford and Mike Summerbee, whose efforts over the last few years have helped produce such remarkable results.

6) The period of this contract will run for exactly eight months – the longest we've ever committed to a new manager – or until we are taken over by one of the consortiums who are scaring the shit out of us, i.e. next week, possibly.

7) All we ask in return is the details of any offshore bung account you might possess. Can you lend us a few quid out of it? It's to pay the manager . . . oh, go on, I'll sort you out next week . . . honest, there's a £10 postal order due from sales of the City Mag . . .

*(Meanwhile, the battle for the soul of our stadium continued as the club wrestled with the East Lower rebels. An astonishing night's atmosphere against Juve led to the issue topping* Channel 4 News *and the club changed tack by the week as they attempted to keep us in line. Cue more delightful correspondence from the blazers? . . .)*

## 'Dear Member . . .'

ENJOYING OLD TRAFFORD – WITH YOUR HOST, KEN RAMSDEN

Hello boys and girls. I know we all enjoyed the Juventus match and we at Old Trafford want to assure you that we are not opposed to customers trying to improve the atmosphere. But we mustn't have any more of that naughty standing up, must we? Anyway, Mr Ferguson has insisted we try and help you, so these are some of the exciting ideas we have suggested for the Themepark of Dreams™.

- Special Premiership Flag Day. Recreate that Juventus atmosphere! Just the same plan, except that we don't want any flags bigger than two foot square. And no poles, please. Flag edges must be rounded and smoothed – we don't want any bruising, do we? – and come with a Fire Safety Certificate. Amusing slogans are permitted but must have approval from Taste Stewards, who will be on duty. You will be allowed to wave your flags for three seconds every five minutes. Specially created flags featuring Fred the Red and the caption 'Sit Down for the Champions' will be on sale for £7.99 (25p discount to members with ten vouchers).

- Stadium Singalongs. Our wonderful DJ, Mr Keith Fane, has formatted a pre-match programme of your favourites, picked for crowd participation with sensitive care. So sing yourself hoarse with Oasis, 'You'll Never Walk Alone', 'Football's Coming Home' and 'The Sash My Father Wore', a selection Keith is sure will get a loud reaction! As a special treat, we'll be playing a recording we made against Juventus of 'Stand Up for the Champions'. (Anyone standing up during this will be ejected and arrested.)

- Public Address Cheerleading. In future, there will be no need for hooligans in the East Lower to stand up and start songs; we will be starting them for you via our state-of-the-art tannoy system through which trained announcers will prompt you into a relay of favourites. (There will be a strict rota of 'Red and White Army', 'United' and the occasional 'Champions'. No others will be permitted.) To aid your enjoyment and safety, we will be more pro-active in our crowd communication, allowing us to broadcast pre-recorded common announcements at the touch of a button. (Such as 'Sit down or be ejected', 'East Lower Block 3, you're all under arrest' and 'Mr Boyle, put your trousers back on *now*'.)

- Improved half-time entertainment. We know you get very excited at seeing Red celebrities, so instead of the cash-dash draw, we'll be inviting all the celebrities attending a match onto the pitch, passing round the microphone and thrilling to their stories about watching United on TV at the Groucho Club and all the great moments they've experienced being Reds since 1994.

- Finally, for your family peace of mind, we have seized upon the findings of the recent Premiership Fans' Survey to which over fifty of you replied and banned all forms of swearing. You will be allowed one 'damn' and one 'blast' per game but all other four- and five-letter words will result in immediate season-ticket confiscation. (We have, however, decided not to act upon the survey's other findings concerning excessive ticket prices, lack of atmosphere and overpaid directors.)

Here's to a great new future together!

Yours in sport,
Ken Ramsden

## ***The Dark Side of the Moon: Fergiepower vs. the Press***

There's obviously been some terrible mistake but MUFC and VCI have allowed a *Red Issue* contributor to come along to the manager's new video launch to do an interview for *Total Football* magazine. Excellent: a chance to slip behind enemy lines and see the Fergie–press relationship at close quarters, not to mention having a tête-à-tête with the great man himself. I'd made a mental list of things best not to mention – Paul Ince, Sunderland away, Barcelona, *Manchester Evening News* phone polls – but after a bit of pre-lunch champagne swiped from the Premier Lounge on the way in I've already forgotten it and am beginning to feel both bolshy and light-headed. I'm afraid I'm not much of a 'professional'.

The sight of the circus inside the Players' Lounge where Fergie is to conduct the launch doesn't help. The assembled reptiles of the media are helping themselves to bundles of free videos and canapés whilst barking self-importantly into mobiles. Mutual cock-sucking is the name of the game: 'Ooh, great piece on Asprilla yesterday, John,' 'Hey, loved that interview on Sky, Paul' and so on. A couple of them are moaning about all the (free) Premiership games they have to attend and how the facilities at such and such a ground are shit – 'Yeah, I had to go half an hour after the game without a beer,' remarks one, and my heart somehow fails to bleed for him. More than ever, I think how good it would be if all press boxes were closed down, forcing the fuckers to buy their tickets and rough it with the rest of us – then maybe their reports wouldn't so obviously be the products of heads-up-arses.

Then, as the main attraction slips through the door, I get a flash of Fergiepower, the metaphysical force that is going to sober me up completely in about twenty minutes' time. Some men have a presence that dominates a room, no matter what the egos of those within. Having seen a few stars up close in my life, I'd only really seen it emanate this strongly from Eric Cantona and Morrissey; Fergie's equals theirs. Hacks who were taking the piss out of him moments before cower into silence, some visibly shrinking from his aura. As a Red, I love it, seeing the reptiles fawning; as a prospective interviewer, I begin to worry.

The ridiculous state of modern football now dictates that most access to stars comes via events like these. Some kind of merchandise is being promoted; the star is here to talk about that and nothing more. Whoever the sponsor or manufacturer is dominates proceedings and determines who gets what goodies. No one from the club is here to keep order – this is a VCI affair, the video manufacturer's rep the final arbiter granting you three minutes here or a quick photo there. And you all have to stick to the charade, of course: try and talk generally about football and you're out. So the hacks spend twenty minutes padding soft and tedious questions over to Alex about his 'Dream Team' video: 'Was it hard to pick eleven, sir?', 'Do you wish you could've led this team out at Wembley?', 'Was Bryan Robson a good leader?' and so on. Alex does his best and sounds fairly interested but the overwhelming impression is that this, for him, is a time-wasting chore. I'm praying for someone to ask 'So no Ralphie Milne, then?' but the pack are under his spell. The guys at the front are kneeling at Fergie's desk, figuratively as close to giving him a blow job as you can get. When a hack's mobile goes off, the poor sap looks so mortified that, if you'd offered him a sword, he'd surely have fallen willingly upon it.

It occurs to me too that all these guys will file glowing reports about the video, whether they've seen it or not, knowing that the beady hawk eyes at VCI will be tracking every follow-up. Slag the video and there'll be no invite to the next VCI product launch, perhaps? And if you're not invited, you've no chance of a one-to-one with the stars. Admittedly, with Fergie there are other avenues. But some players these days are almost solely accessible through product launches: offer the kit sponsor a three-page photo shoot and you might just get five minutes with the player. Maybe this seems right to some modernist types, but what happened to speaking to one's fans via the media just for the public-service value? In the week following the launch, I notice a certain *Manchester Evening News* correspondent manages to get three separate plugs for the 'Dream Team' video into his reports for the paper, two of which are wholly gratuitous. The guy may not actually be on percentage points from sales but his brownie-point total with VCI and the club can only have increased . . .

The bird representing VCI who's in charge of the whole proceedings pulls me aside at the start: 'Don't be boasting to any of the other journalists that you've got a one-to-one with Fergie – it'll cause me problems and make them jealous.' It turns out only two of us are to have private audiences where we'll actually be allowed to talk about something other than VCI products. She reminds me every few minutes how lucky I am, and how I should hang back at the end for my 'special treatment'. Jesus, I'm beginning to think she wants her pussy licking out in gratitude or something. Not that I would normally object, but she looks like Graeme Hogg in glasses. Needless to say, being very immature for my age, I seek out the rep of my least favourite tabloid and na-na-na in his face about my impending interview. The spineless twat soaks up my abuse without a murmur. (The editor of his paper was once actually nicknamed 'The Human Sponge' by a former editor for his legendary ability to take any amount of horrendous abuse; he's apparently trained his minions well.) When I've finished boasting, he mutters, 'Well done – and can I have any quotes you don't need?' in a pleading tone. I tell him I'd rather shit in my own mouth, which is the sort of tasteful remark I make when I've been drinking before midday. I realise I'd better get a grip before I see Fergie, in case I get a flashback and call him a tinkerbell fuckwit by accident.

As I leave, one of the pressmen who'd heard me abusing his colleague earlier snarls at me, 'We don't want your sort in the press box, laddie.' Being two feet away from the exit, I bravely retort, 'I'm a *fan*, mate – the press box is for c**ts.' Which is true, of course, and I feel very proud of myself as I run away full tilt down the corridors towards the private interview room.

The *Total Football* photographer is waiting for me and Fergie; he wants to snap Fergie on the pitch. He's a cocky bloke, used to dealing with stars and running the show for cover stories like this, so he swaggers up to Fergie briskly and breezily asks 'Alex' if he'd mind trotting down to the pitch. Mr Ferguson, as I instantly resolve to address him, glowers intensely at the preening snapper and growls quite frighteningly, 'No. I've no time for that.' Looks crap on paper, I know, but he said it in a rumbling tone that carried six kinds of threatening menace. The snapper shrinks and starts to say 'But . . .' before Fergie repeats himself at an even lower pitch in machine-gun staccato. The hapless bloke crumbles, blushing furiously and exiting as fast as he can; never before have I seen a six-footer reduced to three in two seconds flat. I have to scrunch my bollox to stop myself laughing out loud. This Fergiepower is fucking fantastic! And then I realise I am alone with him. Shit. Instant sobriety. And dump the opening gambit about Jim Leighton.

In the end, it went quite well. At least I didn't get growled at and I managed not to let slip any mentions of Paul Ince or five-at-the-back. Unfortunately, he saw all my pathetically sly attempts to entrap him into saying something indiscreet a mile off too, teaching me I'm not half the smart arse I thought I was. More importantly, I learned where Fergiepower comes from – it's built on real self-knowledge and a breadth of life experience that no contemporary can match. This is a man who knows not only his own strengths and weaknesses but also those of every conceivable type of human character, an understanding built up over fifty years of a battling life. Knowledge is power, after all, and he knows how to use it. The cowards flinch and traitors sneer because they cannot match him. And we gadflies who carp about his selection and transfers, deep down, know it too.

## *The Gaffer Tapes: Alex Ferguson Interviewed*

(From *Total Football*)

Alex Ferguson meets us during a hectic afternoon's welcome pause, one that is pregnant with possibilities. United have just returned victorious from Kosice and we are awaiting the might of Juventus; the European mission has at least avoided early termination but we all know the true test is yet to come. Ferguson's team fills up the weekends in between Euro clashes by tootling around at the top of the league, playing well below both potential and the fans' minimum entertainment threshold. But as the points still come in threes, and as we wait to see how good both Sheringham and probable challengers Arsenal are going to be this season, judgement is reserved. The much-hyped 1997–98 has still got all her glitzy clothes on: we'll need to wait until Christmas to see how appealing she's really going to be in the flesh. So maybe it's more appropriate to ditch the red-hot current affairs and instead talk to Fergie about history, European destiny and the psychology of greatness.

As I wonder whether he's noticed the Slovakian beer stain on my jacket, it seems fitting to start with the European Cup. The press love to intone doomily about Fergie's European Cup 'obsession', making United's campaigns sound like *Moby Dick* on grass – but isn't it the case that all he's doing is reflecting what United supporters feel? Why be embarrassed about it? Let's be honest: Reds are endlessly poring over travel plans to Turin and Rotterdam, not to Barnsley and Bolton. Or is he purposely trying to lighten the burden of hope and expectation for the players?

'No. In fact, I don't see it as a pressure upon the players at all. And it's never been an obsession for me either.'

What? Maybe 'obsession' was too loaded a word to use, but every media message from him has signified to Fergologists the centrality of European success to everything United do. At least, being such a keen student of the game's culture and past, he must surely see this as his historic mission, his chance to take a place on the top table with Busby and Stein?

'Well, yes, it's important in my overall profile or CV as a football manager. It's more important for the players because this is how they can be judged properly. But the most important thing is to win it from the club's overall point of view. It has to be. You see, the supporters are the barometer of success at this club. For forty years, they've given us the biggest support in the country, no matter what was happening on the field. So, it's really most important for them. Once we do it, that will never leave them. What happened at Munich, and what happened in 1968, has held this club together. Winning the cup now will make us bigger and take us onto another stage.'

See? Inevitably, he frames his task within the big historical picture. So who can help but talk about 'mission', 'destiny' and, yes, 'obsession'? Surely there must be at least a small element here of emulating 1968? He and the players must be aware that without victory in Europe, they'll always have to settle for second place on the podium of the United heroes' pantheon. Certainly, ''60s versus '90s' is a popular pub debate for fans after a few Manchester brews – and even for Peter Schmeichel . . .

'Yes, they do feel it, because the older fans are saying to the younger, "Ah, you'll never know what it was like in the old days." And until the team does it in Europe, that'll always be there. And it's true that, especially before we won the league in 1993, some players would say, "All we hear about are the teams that won the leagues" – especially the '60s team of Denis Law and all that. But having won the league a few times, it's taken away all that.'

For the manager personally, there's also the legacy of Busby to consider and, at times, to wrestle with; Fergie's predecessors often seemed to find the achievements and influence of the man who inspired the modern United too much to handle. As a proud man, surely Fergie must have had his secret moments where he would compare himself to the man regarded up here as a saint – and perhaps been driven to try even harder in order to measure up? The comparison has defeated other big men, after all.

'No. It's never been part of my agenda. When I first came to the club, I looked around – and I'm not saying this as a criticism of past managers – and I said to myself, "How can anyone make a statement such as every manager 'suffered' under Sir Matt?" I'm just sad that I didn't get to know him when I was younger. I was unlucky, because I came here during the tail-end of his life, but he was really helpful to me. And I just think it needed [past] managers to come to him and seek his help. I've asked a lot of people here about this; I don't think he actually interfered a lot at all. OK, maybe it was a wee bit different for me because I'd already achieved a lot at Aberdeen. You know, I never came here thinking I had to "prove myself" – I felt I'd already proved myself at Aberdeen. Rather, I came here to develop myself and reach a pinnacle of my career. And I just couldn't understand why this great big beast of a club hadn't won the European, er, European . . . er, League Championship . . .'

Ah hah! A telling slip, Dr Freud. Perhaps the allure of that massive, glittering trophy always lurked at the back of the mind, right from the start in 1986? The last of the great traditional Scottish tyros seeking to emulate the achievements of the first? If he did harbour such desires, he could never have said so; such was the disrepair at Old Trafford in the autumn of '86 that he'd have inspired more press-room guffawing than all Ron Atkinson's witticisms combined. First things first: a league title, last glimpsed twenty years before, an ancient memory replayed in black and white. Could it really be so hard to achieve, so soul-destroying a mission that it could have brought five predecessors' careers to a shuddering halt?

'In a way, it should've been a piece of cake, with the resources and tradition. But then, after a while, when you've hit a few problems, you hit a brick wall. Then that's the testing, proving time. You ask yourself, "Well, what am I going to do with this?" That's when I said to myself, "Well, bugger it. I'm going to produce my own teams, with people who will accept challenges, and get younger people in who will take a longer-term view of things." Because a lot of the players I had then were getting to the end of their careers. And I think that as players get older, their faith and optimism get diluted as each year passes, quicker than would be the case with a younger player. I could only see Bryan Robson as someone who'd be able to maintain that great drive and impetus amongst those United players of the time. They'd have highs and lows, do well in some cups ties and big games but not so well in others – which is no use at this club. So you had to get youngsters in with drive and resolution who'd be prepared to accept and sustain the challenges you set them.'

A team in his own image, then, for Fergie has a brutal but effective lack of sentimentality about success: 'The moment of victory is fleeting – then the job goes on.' He loves to talk about a will to win, even so titling his latest book, but he refuses to wallow in triumph. He wants the next challenge as soon as the champagne bubbles begin to subside. Isn't this quite a unique psychological and/or genetic quirk? Isn't it natural for an ageing player or manager to experience the 'dilution of desire' against which Fergie rails? Where does this compulsion come from, and where can we buy some?

'I think it does come firstly from my background, in particular what my parents instilled in me. But then there are those moments, those "triggers" in your life, which also help make you the way you are today. There's an inherent part there which you take all through your life but then there are those key experiences when you're young which really make you what you are. That's what gives you your true individuality, when you become your own person. And you see that in those people who are nothing at all like their parents – I mean, as far as I'm aware, there's no great statistical basis for the idea that we're all basically our parents! So although in my case I do mirror much of what makes my parents, my brother is completely different to me. He was always a placid, good-natured boy!'

We're in Cantona-speak territory here – the eternal struggle between genetic determinism and environmentalism. Funnily enough, Fergie agrees with his erstwhile favourite son, who came to exactly the same conclusions about himself (although Eric expressed it, to the Francophobe press's amusement, in terms of the dialectic between Rousseau and Sartre). Whatever. At least in Fergie's case the putative biographer should linger long and hard on what his parents bequeathed to him, whether genetically or by example, should they wish to know what makes him tick.

'Yes, I think most of it can be found there. And as a result, above all, I grew up feeling that I had to win at everything I did. That desire became an integral part of me; that energy and desire to "do something" made me what I am. It then becomes very difficult to change the beast! And when I think about how my brother was so different, I think that although I would have appreciated having some of his qualities, I think perhaps he might have appreciated some of mine even more. Because he was a good player too . . .'

I detect a brief note of sadness in his voice, a lament for a fraternal potential unfulfilled. Yer tabloid pop-shrink merchant would doubtless see in this a contributory factor in Fergie's determination to bring through young talent and make sure it is fully nurtured and maximised. But what about Fergie's own mental health? He's made this job a seven-day-weeker, even watching four or five games on his days off, mainlining on football without pausing to replenish his veins. Yet they say he's actually getting calmer, when you'd expect him to be close to breakdown. That horrendous, tragic image of Jock Stein's last match flashes through my mind – another old-school Scot who lived every moment for the game. How is Fergie avoiding something similar, be it caused by mental or physical stress?

'There was a period after I came down here when I couldn't even go out at night. I couldn't face it. That went on for about five or six months at least. Even when we got a break and we won something [the FA Cup in 1990], everything just got even bigger. That's how it is at a club like this: now you can't go back. You know what it's like? Like when you leave the ground at the end of a match – imagine trying to get back into the ground. You can't go back – if you try, you're dead, done for. You're carried along and there's nothing you can do but carry on and go forward in the job. So at that point you then have to find a way of surviving. It's then all about assessing who you are. I couldn't go on the way I used to at Aberdeen. Equally, I couldn't go on the way I had, say, in my first games down here. If I had done, I'd have been dead. I'd really have suffered, no doubt about it. So I had to find a way of withdrawing into myself, into a cocoon, somewhere I could think. And now I can do that. I might be looking right at you but I'm not really there – and I'm not taking it in. Because I can't afford to take everything in. I've got to concentrate on the essentials. It's obvious that the essentials are more important than the peripherals – and this club is full of the peripherals. There's always somebody on to you wanting a part of your life, so you have to make sure that what you're doing is a priority. And, to me, my priorities in the job are simple. It's being at the training ground in the mornings – I love that part of it. The afternoons, well, they can be hard sometimes. But by withdrawing into myself, I find I can think clearly, concentrate, plan, always have the big picture in mind. Always. Sometimes I'm in the house and the wife'll say, "You're away in a trance, aren't you? You're in another world." And it's probably true, but it helps me survive.'

Perhaps the Natural Law Party has missed a potential supporter here? Sounds like something close to transcendental meditation to me.

'Well, I can only speak for myself, but that's the way I have to do it. Because I tell you, Richard, these later years of my life are going to have some quality in them. Because I have been through it, y'know. When I was younger, I was trying to run a pub and a football team at the same time. Making dinners for a hundred and twenty in the pub, going off halfway through to watch Clydebank play Cowdenbeath in a cup tie, coming back, washing up, doing the wages, off to my bed at 2 a.m., then back at the desk for first light . . . I can't live like that anymore! Mind you, I'm still here at 6.30 every morning . . .'

So if he's found a way to extend the normal working life, why all the retirement speculation? The angriest outburst in his new book concerned the wretched *Manchester Evening News*'s wholly erroneous 'Fergie to Quit' story last season.

'Well, the chairman mentioned to David Meek that he thinks I should retire in three years' time; of course, that creates a "situation" . . . [Paul Hince injected 'Quit' angle into a Fergie *News* interview.] I don't think anyone else should decide when you retire – you're the only one who can decide.'

Whilst wondering suspiciously what Martin Edwards was up to, I tell Fergie that I always understood he'd never leave United, that an 'upstairs' role would be his for the rest of his working life.

'Well, that's my thinking too. But we are a plc, don't forget – and, of course, you never know here . . .'

A distinctly frosty pronunciation of the phrase 'plc' gives me the green light to jump in and try to entice some indiscretion about the tight-fistedness of United's directors; after all, even in his own official book, there's a not-very-well-coded aside about the lack of transfer and wage resources.

'Yeah, it is difficult to operate within a plc. But in a way that sets me a challenge. And it's not stopped me from being successful, has it? Inadvertently, it's made this club into what it should be about anyway – about young players and their development. And it's through them that you get the true spirit of the club. If you overload with old foreigners, we cannot be Manchester United. The Nevilles, Butts, Scholes, Beckhams – they create what this club's about. That, along with the club traditions and our supporters. But it's the young players who create the spirit of United – and that'll always be the case here.'

All very true, and an excellent answer, although I'm sure he knows I'm not fooled enough to think that he's satisfied with the expenditure resources at his disposal. Sure, the plc constraints haven't stopped him being successful yet – but they still might deny him future European success. Nevertheless, I remark that it's good to end on a youthful note, for in a sense we've come full circle, back to what Sir Matt was saying in the early '50s about what kind of teams should represent Manchester United.

'Yes, that's it. There's nothing too difficult to understand here, really, as long as you remember what the agenda is. You only make it difficult for yourself if you go down the wrong road of forgetting how you got here. And part of that is about keeping your feet on the ground. That's definitely part of my job, at least on the football side of things. Sure, you get a few who may get carried away elsewhere, but that's not going to be allowed to interfere with the football side, I can assure you.'

As I leave the ground via the Main Stand concourse, adverts for United's official magazine – an Old Trafford *Pravda* for teeny-boppers – beam down from the walls, the airbrushed features of Giggs and Beckham prominent. If Fergie had these two in mind with his last comment, then he was making no empty assurance, for days later the duo tear apart Europe's greatest team. Apparently, no amount of ad shoots and/or celeb-shagging has jaded their appetites just yet. Or maybe it'd be fairer to say that the players must know the limits by now and have adjusted accordingly. They're never going to put one over on Fergie, who's learned his lessons well from the battles he fought in the Whiteside/McGrath/Sharpe eras. For at 6.30 every morning, an hour when some daring players might just be emerging from Mancunian niteries, Fergie's at his desk gathering intelligence, planning his next move and meditating over the big picture of the European Cup that, surely, rarely leaves his mind. And though he might talk about 'ignoring the peripherals', he still hears everything that squeaks within ten miles of Old Trafford – you can guarantee that players who let themselves float away on the hot air of media babble will never be overlooked as 'peripheral'. If you want to get yourself into Fergie's Big Picture – preferably a team shot with Euro Cup aloft – then you have to play it his way and behave. For, in the wake of King Eric's departure, there is now only one real superstar at Old Trafford – and it's the manager. He has stamped his imprint on the team, of course, but also upon much of the fabric of the club itself. The plc wallahs may think they own Manchester United Football Club but, after seeing the intent in his eyes, I have no doubt as to where the real power will reside for many, many years to come.

*(The autumn and winter brought endless further speculation about a takeover, this time with a twist: that it might be a TV company [specifically, at that time, Granada] who'd buy us, then create a special MUTV channel to maximise synergy. Even if we weren't taken over, some sort of United telly station seemed inevitable. We put together a perfect United-on-Granada schedule, which would introduce United players and topics into your favourite local ITV fare . . .)*

## Daily Spurt What's On: MUTV Tonight

6.00 *Home and Away*
Everybody's down at the beach for a barbie in their titchy bikinis and the girls are on the pull after drinking too many tinnies. Young Ryan is happy to oblige and whips out his pink, stiff . . . surfboard. He is beaten to a pulp on Bondi for having girly curls and no one cares because hunky Becks has turned up and pulled all the tastiest sheilas. Ryan is left with the tarts and strippers.

6.30 *Wheel of Fortune*
Nicky Campbell introduces live coverage of the away-ticket ballot. The 8,000 unlucky contestants go on to the next programme . . .

7.00 *The Price Is Right*
Fans try to guess what ridiculous prices they'll have to pay for away tickets which the *Wheel of Fortune* winners have just flogged off to Mister Moss Side.

7.30 *Coronation Street*
Sally Webster's getting bored with Kev, who's always out watching County, so big Eric goes round and gives her one. Trish is being a silly slag again so Irish Roy beats her up a bit. Mike Baldwin loses a council clothing contract to sharp Fartin' Martin, who's bribed Alf Roberts with some dodgy pies.

8.30 *World in Action*
Special in-depth report that reveals Louis Edwards was a saint, that his meat trade was 100% legit and that the Edwards family are loved by the whole world.

9.00 *In Suspicious Circumstances*
Edward Woodward introduces another mysterious case from the

archives. Tonight: how did wee Choccy McClair wangle *another* contract out of Big Boss Fergie? Was blackmail involved? Or buggery?

**10.00** *News at Ten*
Same headlines every night, brought to you by the Official *Man U Mag* team. Everything's tickety-boo, ticket prices are just right, people who swear at matches are naughty and Edward Freeman is the son of God.

**10.40** *Mark Radcliffe's NWA*
The regional arts show visits the players at home to test their artistic merit. Eric knocks up a fabulous abstract, Schmikes mimes a reworking of Edvard Munch's 'The Scream' and Maysie tries to complete page two of his 'Postman Pat' dot-to-dot book.

**11.10** *Taggart*
Obvious, really.

**12.10** *Strange but True*
Michael Aspel introduces more unbelievable encounters from the paranormal world. Tonight: the day Andy Cole scored five – did it really happen? And an expert risks ridicule with his theory that United might win in Europe one day.

*(More moaning and groaning from the author's half-term report in the* Sunday Tribune, *and for once it didn't involve Teddy Sheringham.)*

## Unhappy New Year?

(From the *Sunday Tribune*)

You would think that Manchester United fans, above all, would have nothing to complain about as they wish each other a happy new year. A full trophy cabinet, massive profits, and a Monégasque March to look forward to – surely we couldn't be better off? But as many a bloke grumbling over a pint could tell you, all the success in the world won't be much consolation if you're getting grief at home. And for many hardcore Reds, that's exactly what they're getting at their Old Trafford home on a matchday.

United's stadium, once a byword for fevered atmospherics and working-class solidarity, could now be more accurately dubbed the Theatre of Nightmares. An increasingly bourgeois 'family values' constituency of newcomers dominates three of its four stands, where they cower in respectful semi-silence as if watching some middlebrow drama at a provincial playhouse. There's your 'Theatre'; the Nightmares, however, take place in the East Stand heartlands, where lads who've followed the Reds home and away since the day they graduated into long trousers now face expulsion, arrest or lifetime bans for the heinous crime of . . . standing up to sing in support of their team. Of the myriad controversies that have attended the development of football's Brave New World, it is the confrontation over so-called 'persistent standing' that is threatening to wreck the uneasy ceasefire between those who run the game and those who finance it through their devoted support.

The deal New Football offered New Britain was supposed to run thus: 'fans' are now all 'customers', to whom clubs should cater as if they were Marks and Sparks. Every 'market segment', whether it consists of families, women, the disabled, the well-heeled or the corporate, is now able to find a niche in football stadia tailored to its needs – just as when, say, choosing a holiday destination. But what of the biggest and most loyal 'segment', the core customers who kept football alive in its '80s Dark Age and upon whom the industry's future still relies? Mainly male, working-class, traditional and vocal, these are the only customers who don't seem to have their own check-out till. And what they desire is not what New Football wants to offer: a return of small-scale terracing or, failing that, designated stadium areas where they can behave as they and their forefathers always have done, where they can sing together, dance about, jump up and down with the ebb and flow of the glorious game – in short, provide the live-event atmosphere and popular passion without which football matches might as well be viewed on the small screen.

Yet at MUFC since 1995, the club and the East Stand have been locked in a constant struggle as chairman Edwards and co. continue to refuse to discuss the hardcore's demands. The fans in turn have taken to standing up anyway, the very act itself seen as emblematic protest against the way supporters' interests in general are mishandled. The chant 'Stand Up for the Champions' has become our own rebel song. Organisations such as IMUSA and Action 135 spearhead resistance on the ground, in the media and, as United will soon discover, in the courts. For scores of fans have been ejected and banned, some allegedly being removed by stadium security using excessively oppressive force, amidst accusations of breach of contract, unlawful search procedures and victimisation.

It's a mess, but fittingly so, for the fundamental cause of the trouble is mired in confusion. The relevant legislation and licensing regulations are all so vague that no one seems able to define the technical legal status of persistent standing in an all-seater stadium, nor can anyone offer a workable definition of 'persistent standing'. Still, we can at least suggest that the sight on Boxing Day of one young East-Stander kid being plucked at random from within a block of three hundred standing fans, to be violently hauled off by hired goons and banned for life, was disgusting and obscene. But sadly not unique.

The suspicion has always been that United don't like our breed of fan; we're an impediment to the drive upmarket, as well as a damn nuisance with our bellyaching about exploitation and over-commercialisation, not to mention the odd naughty ditty about Martin Edwards's gross remuneration. Sometimes, however, they need us, such as on those special European Cup nights when Alex Ferguson called upon us to 'stand up and raise the roof'. We did so, and United triumphed. Come the following Saturday, however, and we were being slapped back down into our seats. Later, a United official would claim that 'a good atmosphere makes no difference to the team's performance' as he attempted to defend the no-singing, no-standing domestic Dead Trafford. Clearly, Fergie didn't believe that – and neither do we. The fight for the soul of Old Trafford will go on . . .

*(Grim days for the East End hardcore. Still, as ever, we could rely on the Geordie maggots to keep us amused as the memory of their FA Cup embarrassments lingered on . . .)*

## Daily Spurt News

'UNITED COULD BE ANOTHER STEVENAGE'
SAYS GEORDIE COWARD

Newcastle are to complain to the FA about being forced to play at Manchester's 'entirely inadequate' Old Trafford in a forthcoming league fixture. 'We believe the fixture should be switched,' whined a pathetic, Scots-accented club source, 'or, better still, cancelled altogether.'

Newcastle have sent safety officers to inspect United's ground and have submitted a report citing the following potential dangers:

- We shit ourselves playing in front of K-Stand, which could cause nasty slippage
- The hammerings we usually get at United severely aggravate our fans' tearducts
- Local savages hit us in the face without provocation just because we march down Warwick Road in barcodes chanting 'Die, Munich bastards'
- Erm, the pitch has a slight curve on it which could cause our players to fall over
- Our manager is not paranoid but he thinks Fergie's out to get him and that United clone their own referees
- Um, we think thieves pick on us there cos we seem to lose our bottle every time we go

Although the club's initial approach to the FA has been rebuffed, the manager is determined to press the issue. 'Having witnessed so much carnage at football grounds in my time,' cried Dogface, 'I have no wish to see United slaughtering one of my teams yet again.'

Dogface concluded, 'I'll have to get back to you later because I need to make my One-to-One phone calls to all the Toons who still love me. It'll take about five minutes.'

*STOP PRESS – Latest score: Stevenage 3 Newcastle 0 (A. Shearer, broken leg)*

*(And we've always got the Blues on permanent chuckle-duty too . . .)*

## Daily Spurt News

NEW CITY RESCUE PLAN TAKES LEE TO CHICAGO

Francis Lee has announced his latest, low-cost plan to safeguard Maine Road's future. Speaking from a laboratory at Chicago University, Lee introduced the notorious Dr Seed, who recently stunned the world with his plans for human cloning. Beamed Lee, 'We will clone the City stars of the future from the legends of the past! It costs next to nothing, so our God and only faith Gio will not have to be sold.' As journalists expressed their admiration for Lee's boldness by laughing hysterically and calling for medics, Lee went on, 'I have brought with me the samples we need for cloning – Denis Law's back heel bone, a Bert Trautmann neck vertebra, director Tueart's last remaining hair and, of course, my own contribution – a globule of pure Franny bullshit.'

Local mental health officials at first refused to commit Lee, accepting Dr Seed's argument that cloning was, indeed, a theoretical possibility. However, the strait-jackets came out when Lee went on to claim that City had 200,000 supporters and could get promoted next season.

*STOP PRESS – Latest score: City 2 West Ham 4 (pitch invasion in progress)*

*(And* Red Issue *will even squeeze a black smile out of the resident OT jackboots . . .)*

## Daily Spurt News

SPS APOLOGISE FOR 'WRONGFUL EJECTION'

Shamefaced security and club officials expressed their regret today when they admitted that they had thrown out 'an entirely guilty supporter' from the East Stand. In an amazing blunder, the suits grabbed a violent racist thug who'd been threatening fellow fans and threw him out of the ground. 'I've no idea how this happened,' said spokesman Ken Ferret, 'but I can assure you we'll get straight back to picking on young innocent kids as soon as possible.'

*(The Dave 'n' Posh phenomenon exploded during the winter, adding yet another layer of showbiz tack to an Old Trafford which was beginning to resemble a northern Chelsea. And what of the northern Crystal Palace?)*

## Blue-Paper

**THE OFFICIAL MANCHESTER CITY MAGAZINE, FEB 1998: 'ANYTHING UNITED CAN DO, WE CAN DO BETTER'**

HEL'S WEDDING BELLS

Yes, Manchester United may have filled the front pages with their Spice Girl glamour engagement, but we at City have our own showbiz romance which is bound to fill even more pages. Chairman Francis Lee today announced to a throng of three newsmen outside his toilet that he is to wed the musical sensation Helen, the old bird with the bell behind the goal.

Helen, who's thrilled the Blue masses with her top hits 'Come On City', 'Swales Out' and 'We're Shit and We're Sick of It', will break off from her city-wide tour of pub vaults to wed millionaire mogul

Lee next month. The beaming couple, following Spice and Beckham's lead with *Hello*, have already sold exclusive media coverage rights to the *Moss Side Free Argus* (circ. forty-eight and a dog). Smiling for the cameras (had any been there), Helen flashed the ring made out of concentrated medicated toilet paper which Lee gave her last night and claimed to be very happy. 'And unlike some strumpets I could mention,' she added, 'I do not take it up the arse.'

BROTHER BEYOND

Franny Lee's plan to out-trump United's new sponsorship deal ran into a few minor problems last week but we are assured we will soon be able to announce much, much bigger figures than United. At a press conference, Lee unveiled a new £20 million deal with Brother. 'There was stiff competition from another potential sponsor,' smiled Lee, 'but we're delighted to be sticking with our old friends at Brother. And we think it's very reasonable that we only have to pay them £20 million over ten years to be allowed to wear the proud name of Brother's sewing machines, despite the risk that we have so often embarrassed them on the field.'

When it was pointed out that this was not what was expected of a sponsorship deal, the chairman became angry and accused the media of mounting a witch hunt against City. 'You're always looking to do down this club. And let me make it clear for the hundredth time that I am not resigning,' he added, as he closed up his suitcase marked 'BA 201 to Rio'.

GUINNESS, PLEASE

It's been another great month for City's record-breaking boys as once again we set new marks in the record books that no Reds can match! Just take a glance at the Manchester firsts we've achieved in January:

- Most weeks spent in bottom five of Second Division
- Most minutes of failing to score against ten men
- Highest number of current players seeking transfers
- Most catcalls ever recorded at both half- and full-time – a great double of our own!
- Lowest credit rating of any urban club ever

Beat that if you can, United!

**CITY: ALWAYS MAKING NEWS, ALWAYS A BIG CLUB**

*(News reached us that Busby Babe Dennis Viollet, in his sixties, was in the States fighting the after-effects of a brain-tumour operation and a stroke – yet, like many an exiled Red, one of his greatest concerns remained how to tune in to United match commentaries! The US Reds and IMUSA worked together to give Dennis a bit of support, which included rigging him up to the Net so he could hear UK radio and getting stuck into the medical bills. He died in March 1999, having made many new Red friends in the last 18 months of his life.)*

## Redheads: Dennis Viollet

There aren't many Red legends whose story begins with, 'Grew up in the shadow of Maine Road as a committed Manchester City fanatic . . .' Typical of Dennis, extraordinary and unusual as both player and man, to buck the rule about Blues making poor Reds. A genuine five-star original Babe, Viollet was to convince many who saw him at his peak that there could never be a greater inside-left. First sight? Surely this rather frail, even wan-looking Manc kid wouldn't be able to cut it on rough pitches against hard-clogging brutes? But few footballers of his era were as prodigiously gifted, ample compensation for his slight build. He was a superb passer, outrageously fast, a visionary and had a shot of uncanny precision and timing. That he was also able to develop a seemingly telepathic understanding with Tommy Taylor should have sealed a permanent England place alongside his mate; inexplicably, he had to make do with being a permanent fixture in the classic '55–'58 team. Again, not a bad compensation . . .

Mentions of his name cascade across United's record books, of course. Most goals in a season, fourth top scorer of all time, one of the best goals-per-game averages in United history, four goals on a European debut . . . it could never be said that he was an unsung hero, despite the failure of England's selectors to give him his due. Yet, like many stars of the pre-'63 era, his massive achievements were never reflected in his pay packet. Dennis never made his fortune in football, despite being the kind of smooth and exciting talent who'd be a multi-millionaire today. In fact, he strikes a remarkably contemporary image – Dennis could have shown some of today's *nouveau riche* players what real class is all about. For he was a proper red devil off the pitch, a bit of a smoothie, pretty damn sophisticated and with cultivated tastes for the best clubs and the coolest kittens. No prizes for guessing who dominated the judging of the first Miss

Manchester United contest at the Chorlton Palais in '58: Dennis knew feminine quality when he saw it, from experience. And he was never simply 'just one of the lads'. Dennis was a bit different, incredibly popular in the dressing-room yet also an individualist who'd do his own thing, who'd seek out the better places and cut a lone path. Cantonesque, perhaps? Whatever, milkshakes at the skating rink wasn't his bag. Silky women and sultry jazz at The Continental? That'd be more like it.

On 6 February 1958, Dennis regained consciousness to see Bobby lying next to him in an icy, muddy pool of water that was reflecting the flames of disaster. In many ways, he made a miraculous recovery, being fit enough to play at Wembley and going on to score many more goals for both United and Stoke. Indeed, the one-time 'frail ghost of a player' eventually starred at centre-forward for us, which few who saw his debut back in '53 would have predicted. But the time came when Herd and Law were Matt's preferred options and Dennis was eventually sold to Stoke in 1962. Jimmy Murphy did once wonder whether Munich had damaged Dennis more than anyone realised, whether in fact he'd suffered some kind of delayed reaction. Yet, irrepressibly, he top-scored at Stoke under the great Tony Waddington and led them back to Division One; he also picked up an Irish Cup medal at Linfield before emigrating to the States. But there was never a need to wonder what might have been. By the age of twenty-five, he'd established his name forever as one of the brightest Busby Babes. No footballer in history can enjoy a greater privilege, however many caps and medals he may acquire.

*(Following the springtime revelations in the* News of the World *about Newcastle directors caught being naughty on video, other papers were supposedly ready to produce their own exposés of other leading clubs' directors. Can you identify in which club boardrooms each of the following extracts was recorded?)*

## You've Been Framed Special

**From *The Mirror*:**

MR X: 'I mean, gentlemen, we really do have to do something about this. I walked into the dressing-room and there he was, his own cock wedged up the youth-team's centre-back and our winger's todger in his mush. His glasses were so steamed up he didn't even notice I was there.'
MR Y: 'And how did those bastards on the Internet find out? By the

way, anybody know where I can flog some spares for the Monaco–United match?'

**From *The People*:**
MR X: 'Right, so that's 2,000 tickets off to our Emerald Isle friends; make sure we get the kickbacks from the hotels and travel firms and tell them to include the CENSORED-Store on the tour.'
MR Y: 'Mr Chairman, the manager would like to sign a great international player who's free but wants £1,000 a week more than our wage structure allows.'
MR X: 'Tell him to piss off. There's already enough players earning more than I do. But think of an excuse – I don't want this episode cropping up in his fucking memoirs.'

**From *The Sun*:**
MR X: 'Jesus Christ. What have I done? What the fuck have I done? Have you seen these books? Just what kind of cretins have been running this place? Oh my God. Just kill me now.'
MR Y: 'Don't worry, Mr Chairman, Mr Po**ock has just arrived and he's told the *Evening News* he's going to save us. Hurrah!'
MR X: 'Why, has he got thirty million quid and ten points in his kitbag, you silly c**t?'
MR Y: 'Erm . . . we're a big club, you know.'

**From *The Star*:**
VISITOR: 'Delivery for you, la': twenty bags of "rock" and a kilo of "sherbet".'
MR X: 'Erm, I think you want the home dressing-room, second door down.'

**And not forgetting the *Daily Sport*:**
VISITOR: 'Baa. Baa. Baaa. SQUEAL!!! BAAAAAA!'
MR X: 'By 'eck, shut tha trap, you know you love it.'

A final thought. So the Geordie directors announce to the world that:
a) Geordie bints are dogs
b) Shearer's pure Julie Andrews
c) Rich ugly blokes shag tarts and snort candy
d) Geordies are barcoded mugs and morons.

And we're supposed to think that's *news*?

Next week – *News of the World* claims the Pope is a Catholic and bears shit in woods . . .

*(There was a highly unusual build-up to this season's United–Liverpool fixture as the media talk centred on Jesus Christ and Catholic ritual instead of groin injuries and form. United had fixed kick-off time for the alleged moment of Christ's crucifixion and thus set off one hell of a brouhaha. Which got the author into contemplative mood on the nature of the United faith . . .)*

## Hallowed Be Our Name

The recent religious rumpus over United's Good Friday fixture was, in one respect, hugely entertaining. I never tire of seeing Ken Ramsden humiliated in public, and he swung desperately from one untenable position to another until final surrender to the forces of Rome. But the episode struck deeper chords too, for it got me thinking about the nature of the club and of our supporters' position in the world. Now I'm a militant atheist and generally fairly hostile to all forms of organised religion. One of the greatest experiences of my life was to shag a Spanish fifteen-year-old on the steps of her local church – sacrilegitastic, mate. But I was nevertheless appalled at United's original decision to play at 3 p.m., the time attributed to Christ's death, because it seemed that United were shitting on their own history, tradition and beliefs. Money, convenience and TV all mattered more and Ken Ramsden's spin-doctoring over the following two weeks just made the perceived insensitivity worse. It spoke of a club which no longer cared about its heritage, only about its Mammon-worshipping future. It was the offence to those who feel the club's tradition in their blood that bothered me. As I'll opine, the blasphemy was against the *United* religion as well as the Catholic.

The episode did at least demonstrate the continuing power of the RC establishment, prompting some observers to wonder whether IMUSA should be targeting bishops in their campaigns rather than MPs. Thirty years ago, when the Main Stand was thick with clerical cloth and the faint whiff of incense, the Roman domination was taken for granted. If the Church of England was the Tory Party at prayer, then Man United was the Catholic Church at play. Much of United's early support was, of course, built upon Catholic Celtic immigrants – indeed, Newton Heath almost became Manchester

Celtic in 1902. But over the past couple of decades, that influence was supposed to have disappeared. And where once the confidants of the club hierarchy included a mass of leading Fathers and Mother Superiors, now the cronies are all bread-head businessmen and wide boys. So it was kind of comforting for traditionalists to realise that the old ways haven't quite disappeared yet. It's perverse, but even an anti-cleric like me felt pleased that the God Squad could still pull a few strings and outflank the hard-faced capitalists who now shape our club's nature.

What the modern plc exec. wants is this: a brand name that doesn't actually represent anything *per se*, a non-ideological body that anybody across the world, no matter their age or location or class, can adhere to and worship. Its only value will be success; everything else should be jettisoned lest it narrow the brand's appeal. United would be football's New Labour, a meaningless construct that nonetheless always wins and can thus draw the support of all those hordes who like to be on a winning bandwagon. Don't remind anybody of what United was for 80 years of its existence – a predominantly working-class, male, Catholic and local organisation whose business was football, not the 'leisure industry'. No corporate entrepreneur can build a £500 million concern on such a limited credo. And whilst no one could object to opening up the appeal – and anyway, it's not as if female, bourgeois, out-of-town Protestants were *barred* from Old Trafford – surely the utter destruction of the nature of United, replacing it with a characterless Everyman conglomeration, should be a matter of concern? Ramsden argued that because we have so many fans of every faith, we couldn't start postponing every other game because it clashed with some religious festival. That would have been a fair point if you accept that the club should no longer have any particular definition to its essential nature. But United have not yet been fully rebranded. We're not quite at Year Zero yet, judging by the reaction of many older, traditional fans to the 3 p.m. kick-off proposal.

After I became a young Red in 1975, from a mixed Catholic/Protestant family, I soon realised I wasn't joining an amorphous catch-all organisation but a club largely built by certain kinds of people within a particular tradition. My neighbours were working-class, second-generation Irish immigrant Catholics and told me they were delighted I'd joined 'their' club. I in turn felt it right to respect the traditions and ways built up over the decades – to be aware of the rights and sensibilities of the 'host community', if you like. (So

I knew that the song my Prod classmates sang about the Pope's wedding tackle would clearly be inappropriate at OT.)

It's no big deal, of course, this Catholic/Protestant stuff: Manchester isn't Glasgow and the issue has only become pertinent two or three times in my twenty years as a Red. Most Reds under thirty don't give a toss about this anyway. But, in principle, I do not believe it is right that newcomers should be able to come into a pre-existing community and demand that it sacrifices everything it has built up over a century. It's like the invasion of the middle-class families into a working-class audience over the '90s – how dare they come in and start shouting the odds over fans' behaviour and so on when the hosts' families have maintained that club through generations past? It would be different had United been a bigoted, unwelcoming community; then the hosts would've deserved to have been culturally assaulted in such a way, just as the white trash Leeds scum deserved their kickings from the police and club in the 1980s. But United have always welcomed everybody – it's just that it always used to ask that its core traditions be respected. So Ramsden was wrong to put Good Friday down as just another religious day amongst many. If United's spirit still has a literally religious nature, it is surely still one coloured by Catholicism more than by any other faith. For the decades of sustenance local churches and their communicants gave United, especially in financially troubled pre-Busby times, surely some special dispensation for one day only was justifiable reward? Or, to personalise the issue, what do you think Sir Matt's opinion would've been? Exactly. And we'd surely all take his advice over Ken Ramsden's every time.

We have to cling on to our traditions because they matter; history makes United what it is. There's so little left now; even that enduring faith in carefree, attacking football being as important as success is under threat these days. Hugh McIlvanney, Fergie's biographer and number-one press mouthpiece, wrote last week that we should all stop moaning about performances like United's in Monaco. He cited our defeat in Lisbon in '64 as a classic example of how United used to let themselves get over-excited away from home when following the Busby creed and claimed that Govan-grim 0–0s are much better. Well, thank fuck George Best didn't think that way in Lisbon two years later. Or the lads of '65 going to Dortmund for a tricky one and roasting them 6–1. Or the blessed Babes themselves, getting three tie-winning away goals when losing to Bilbao in '57. Sure, you might fuck up in Gothenberg or Barca, but sometimes you succeed gloriously too. And it's glory, not mere victory, that you'll remember when you're old and grey. (To be frank, half the victories this season will be forgotten by June, actually.)

Knowing and celebrating our history is massively important, and respecting the way immigrants, Catholics and outsider rebels aggregated at United to shape our history and nature must surely be part of that. So of course you don't have to be a good Catholic to be a good Red – but going out of your way to be offensive to an important tradition within United's support is rather unecumenical, to say the least.

Ironically, given that the number of practising RCs at OT is at an all-time low, never have United's multicultural, multinational supporters more resembled persecuted Catholics from the bad old pre-emancipation days. Look at us, spread across the world, gathering at our secret meeting rooms in every conurbation, treated as the enemy within by the locals, tending our faith as best we can in between pilgrimages to our Vatican, Old Trafford. Talking to a Red from East Yorkshire in Monaco the other day, and thinking about this Catholic issue, I couldn't help noticing the similarities. He was telling me about the grief he gets from Leeds-supporting locals for following an alien team, as if he were a seventeenth-century Papist lambasted by Protestants for his treacherous devotion to a foreign despot. Nothing gets ABUs going like their locals who choose to follow the one true faith from afar; the intensity of the hatred parallels that of Reformation England. A Stuart era Protestant courtier once wrote about his incomprehension when witnessing native Englishmen worshipping at a Catholic church; he could understand the residents of Rome following the Vatican, but what possessed the Londoner or Norfolk man to look so far afield? Sound familiar? We're a persecuted, despised minority everywhere but Manchester's Holy See, yet as a brotherhood united we're the biggest force in the world. Such a diverse denomination can and should show a little respect to all its members – because no one outside our faith is ever going to give us any, are they?

## *Daily Spurt News*

THE 1998 PREMIER LEAGUE FANS' SURVEY: THE UNPUBLISHED FINDINGS

- Of the 50% of Liverpool fans who claimed to be born within five miles of Anfield, two thirds gave HMP Walton as their most permanent address.

- 32% of Arsenal fans had noticed a big increase in the number of pretty young boys going to Highbury recently.

- 19% of Leeds fans seemed to misunderstand the section asking for suggestions to improve crowd control, with replies like 'give the police the day off', 'supply home fans with white hoods and knives' and 'play air-crash sound effects over the tannoy'.

- When asked what they'd like to see *less* of at football matches, 64% of Liverpool fans said 'DSS Inspectors', 42% of Arsenal's replied 'Revenue Inspectors' and 31% of Blackburn's answered 'them darkies'.

- 28% of Chelsea and West Ham fans answered the 'what occupation?' question too indistinctly to register, replies varying from 'bit o' this, bit o' that' to 'duckin' and divin', me old china' and 'wossit to you, are you Old Bill?'.

- Although Wimbledon can claim to have the best-educated fans, with 33% holding a degree of some sort, the two girls in question have not yet passed the practical part of their B.Tech in cookery.

- Of the 46% of Newcastle fans who said the club was the most important thing in their lives, 0.3% have owned a season ticket for more than a year.

- 24% of Man U fans think the Old Trafford atmosphere is 'jolly super' or 'spiffing fun'.

- 0.06% of Chelsea fans think the best way to travel to a game is by helicopter.

*(Although, like most Reds, the author couldn't give a toss about England's national team, the World Cup did offer the opportunity to spread the Scholes gospel, in this case to the* Sunday Tribune *the day before Paul's France '98 debut.)*

## Redheads: Paul Scholes

(From the *Sunday Tribune*)

Manchester United fans' biggest surprise this past England-hype fortnight wasn't the exclusion from the squad of Nicky Butt and Phil Neville or even the unmasking of Teddy Sheringham as a Gazza-wannabe. No, the real jaw-dropper was to be presented one morning with half a dozen press interviews featuring Paul Scholes. Not only had the Howard Hughes of Old Trafford's Fledglings spoken in public, he'd even posed for photographs. Reds might marvel at Glenn Hoddle's motivational skills, for it has long been assumed that Scholesy can only be corralled within fifty yards of a press mike or camera at the point of a gun. That he said nothing of any interest at all, making even the notoriously tedious Shearer seem fascinating in comparison, did at least reassure us Reds that the fundamentals remain secure: Paul Scholes does not want to be a celeb personality. He just wants to play football, for Manchester United and England – end of story.

Only two groups of people will ever know what he really thinks about himself and the glorious game: family 'n' friends, and his professional colleagues. To him, the Fourth Estate and its associates inhabit a foreign, alien land, and he's happy keeping it that way. Sponsors and commercial interests will have to make do with the tartier end of MUFC, yer Giggsys and Becksys and Coleys; so far, there's been one sighting of Paul on the back of a cereal box and that's about it for Mammon. United pay him well enough, he reasons, so why make himself more of a public target? It's the oldest cliché in the book, but he prefers to let his feet do the talking on the pitch. And what a conversation when it includes Scholes! Supremely intelligent, canny, at times visionary, endlessly inventive – Scholes is the connoisseur's choice of Fergie Fledgling, a compact-mini version of a footballing model popularised by Dalglish and Cantona. Now that Gazza has exited stage left, blubbing into his kebab, Paul Scholes finds himself under the World Cup spotlight, ready to prove the maxim that it's the quiet ones you have to watch.

They used to say this about all the United Fledglings, admittedly: they're just modest, good lads who prefer to be tucked up in bed with their cocoa at ten o'clock, a perfectly balanced collection of level-headed model pros. Informed sources now know that this analysis was always overly simplistic and some senior players at United have been muttering this season that a couple of the kids have been getting a little too cocky and self-possessed for their own good. And David Beckham is a separate phenomenon, surrounded by as much concern and pessimism as exhilarated admirers. One name you'll never hear mentioned within such brow-furrowed discussion is Scholes. Dig all you want around his home town of Middleton, or within the black propaganda departments at Old

Trafford, and no one will have a word said against him. Doubters despair, hearing the same lines: 'he's completely without pretension or side', 'he's just a good, quiet, honest boy', 'he'll never desert his roots, his family and his Manchester mates'.

An eavesdropping Fergie would purr with approval, yet for a couple of years Reds did wonder whether the manager was reciprocating the respect Scholes clearly has for the Ferguson lifestyle ideology. Of all the kids, Scholes seemed to be getting the fewest breaks in the team and transfer speculation began to mount during 1996–97. Ferguson himself told supporters that winter that he didn't think it possible to play both Scholes and Cantona in the same XI and that he'd have a job keeping Scholes busy until the time came for Eric to quit. The Scholes Fan Club, massively represented in Old Trafford's East Stand heartland, grumbled at this; the unwanted circumstances of the conundrum's resolution, when Eric stunningly departed months later, rather dampened our joy that Scholes would now be able to take his place in the sun. But our own ginger spice is there now, happily freckling under the heat, and few Reds would resile from my opinion that Scholes's unique temperament, ability and crucial adaptability set him up to be a potential star of Mondial '98. That, in some Reds' opinion, is not a prospect wholly to be savoured, for the inevitable result will be hordes of European clubs swarming around Middleton offering multi-million-dollar deals; fortunately, as implied above, Scholes is perhaps the last player at United to be susceptible to such blandishments.

So what is Scholes going to offer Hoddle and the ungrateful Red-hating nation this month? Anyone who saw him run rings around Juventus last October knows that we can take skill and application against top opposition for granted, but he has extra qualities that should have given him the edge over Gascoigne in any event. His genius in a tight corner is unique in the squad; he's actually happier in the thick of a centre-field mêlée than he is out in wide space. The archetypal Scholes image is of him surrounded by hostile forces on the apex of the penalty 'D', somehow conjuring a lofted pass or a precision lay-off when there barely seems room to breathe. No other England player can use the ball under pressure as he can; indeed, England's greatest weakness is that Scholes's possible creative rivals, Anderton and McManaman, are useless when given a bit of a battering by good Continental markers. Scholes will thrive on the challenge. And if he does get the space to step back and see the full vision, he will deliver as reliably as Beckham, suggesting that Hoddle can afford to play Beckham wide and thus benefit from the Cockney's crossing ability. Put Paul in the box as a midfielder breaking forward and England will reap the rewards from a player whose on-target ratio is better than all but Shearer's. And if England are on the back foot, as they surely will be if they ever see round two, he has a priceless and unusual gift for an offensive player – he is also superb in front of the backline, where his tackle-and-immediate-lay-off routine has been honed to perfection during many tough United matches this season. In tournament play, where general versatility and emergency adaptability are at a premium, Scholes is Hoddle's joker. He'd prefer supplying killer through balls to Shearer – or scoring himself, of course – but he'll play anywhere without complaint or diminution of contribution. In a squad overly populated with one-trick ponies (and donkeys), he's a godsend.

Before you rush out to place a tenner on him winning the most man-of-the-match awards, two caveats must be entered. Bobby Charlton has been quoted correctly judging that United's players were all 'shattered' by the end of May, and we saw some of the effects culminate in the exclusion of Butt and Neville. Scholes, form-wise, was quieter this spring than at any time since he debuted for United and it remains to be seen whether the World Cup elixir will give him a sufficient boost. He can be injury-prone, too, and remains an asthmatic under treatment. That said, the potential is thrilling. The recently vacated title of England's Favourite Ginger is his for the taking.

*(The next day, he scored a brilliant match-winning goal in England's World Cup opener. And for about a fortnight, United's England players were actually – gulp – getting popular. Thank God for David Beckham.)*

# 1998–99

## *Mystic Red '98*

(From *Total Football*)

So *Total Football* readers delight in my prediction from last August coming true – United are currently pot-less, and looking distinctly dowdy-first-wife in comparison to glam new sweethearts Arsenal. The more *nouveau riche* kind of Red will have spent the summer agonising over this empty trophy cabinet but the hardcore aren't as arsed as you might imagine. Monaco hurt, undeniably, but many will tell you we got what we deserved for being so negative in the first leg. What happened to the United buccaneer spirit of '66 and '68? Or, indeed, that of '94? The whispered truth is that we're becoming boring – and no true Red can accept that, whatever the silver prize. The replacement of the celestial Cantona by the resolutely earthbound Sheringham turns out to have spoken volumes.

By the time you read this, you'll know if United have splashed out on more than just yet another hugely expensive foreign centre-back – and, consequently, if Martin Edwards was telling the truth when he claimed the plc was now ready to invest big-style to win in Europe. (Now that we've even been caught domestically, you might suggest that this declaration came about four years too late.) Fergie is a fifty-something in a hurry, and one expects he'll be holding the club to their word. Reds, though, will probably forgive another failure as long as the entertainment picks up; recently, bored K-Standers were finding it more fun to batter visitors on the OT forecourt than watch Cole and company's baleful predictability . . .

*(In the weeks before the Sky takeover bid was announced – something, incidentally, the author had been predicting in* Red Issue *for over a year – the imminent prospect of a pay-per-view deal was concentrating early-season minds in both the City and at United. We expected, any day, to get a letter from the Kens along the following lines. We still might within*

*the next few months, of course. As it happened, we all got a rather different letter from chums Martin and Mark within the month . . .)*

## 'Dear Member . . .'

MUFC AND SKY OFFER YOU THE OPPORTUNITY OF THE SEASON!
Yes, pay-per-view is coming and your club has collaborated with your favourite broadcaster to offer you, the loyal United fan, the chance to support the team from your comfy armchair.

In accordance with MUFC policy, these individually tailored packages will be available to you depending on your position as a supporter.

**Family Edition** (Family Stand, North Tier 3, etc.)

- Minimum four viewers per household broadcast, £100 all-inclusive. (Except sound. And colour's extra too.)
- On-screen interactive link to the Megastore mail-order department so you can order goods via your remote control.
- Specially adapted commentary channel will digitally alter crowd noise so that no swearing chants will be heard over your speakers.
- Family Channel dedicated cameras at the ground will transmit censored pictures to you so that you are not offended by the sight of fans standing, Choccy blowing his nose or the opposition scoring and making your brats cry.

**Members' Edition** (rest of North Stand etc.)

- £12 to apply for broadcasts (not guaranteed); £15 per broadcast.
- Collect 'proof of purchase' that you have watched other programmes on MUTV cable to be considered; we will debit your account for every programme you sign up to watch.
- Choose from such exciting cable PPV offerings as *United Reserves Live!*, *The Reserves Replayed*, *Cooking with Pally: Fried Mars Bar Special* and *Choccy's DIY Hour.* (Please note that you will have to watch every programme around the clock to be assured of a Premiership match broadcast.)
- NB: Norwegian viewers will receive all broadcasts as long as they continue to pay their bribes to our approved local middle-men.

**Super-Exec Edition**

- The TV set and satellite equipment will be delivered by chauffeur, installed and then dismantled for every game you apply for so that your mansion will not be spoiled by tatty working-class-style permanent dishes.

- Interactive remote controls will allow you to fire rays at the screen and have any fan at the match whose face you don't like arrested and/or beaten up.
- Your personal match usherette will remain by the side of your set throughout the broadcast and will see to your nourishment and oral sex needs.

**Economy Edition** (East Stand, West Stand Lower, etc.)
This has been withdrawn because we need you to attend the game to provide atmosphere for the viewers. Please come. Nobody will pay to watch boring football on TV inside a mausoleum. We're sorry we used to make you feel so unwelcome. Oh, go on, we'll let you stand, and fight SPS. Be your best friend?

**The Small Print**
You may apply now for your PPV package by sending a cheque for the full amount for THREE YEARS in advance, together with ORIGINAL birth certificate, three s.a.e.s with 85p stamps and the last FIVE seasons' voucher-sheets. No credit card or cash payments; no telephone enquiries; no guarantee if we cash your cheque that you'll be switched on in time for the first match. This offer is controlled by a separate company called MUSKYPPV, which has no connection to MUFC except that they give us all the profits, so don't come crying to us if the whole scheme's a disaster.

## *Daily Spurt News*

AYE, MINISTER

The recent reports that Prime Minister Tony Blair has asked Alex Ferguson for tips and advice in dealing with management issues seem to be borne out by a leaked document that has fallen into our hands.

The paper, which experts claim is in the United manager's handwriting, offers a series of instructions to Blair to tighten up his Number Ten operation in Old Trafford style. A note initialled by Blair in the margin reads, 'Better not show Mandelson this.' The tips include:

- Reshuffle your Cabinet posts every fortnight, however settled and successful your ministers are. Experiment with apparent mismatches, e.g. make Robin Cook Minister for Women's Rights.

- Keep your star performer minister Gordon Brown out of the central powerhouse Treasury role and stick him on the edges of the action – Agriculture, for example. Or Ambassador to Argentina. Keep him away from pop stars.
- At European summits, be as low-key and cautious as possible; do not propose, say or do anything unless absolutely necessary. You will be very successful and the toast of Europe. (*PM – Are we sure this is logical?*)
- Maintaining Position: Change Prescott's job description – *never* let anyone be recognised as your Deputy. Pretend you're going to retire to the House of Lords from time to time, then angrily deny it.
- Media Management: Keep Humphreys and Naughtie off balance by taking stopwatch into interviews on *Today* programme; shout 'Oi, I make it another three minutes yet' when they try to interrupt your answers. Intimidate the BBC by slagging them off all the time; try saying 'They're all Tory supporters with Tory supporters' club scarves' and declare you'll only appear in future on sycophantic ITV shows.
- Sack Press Officer Alastair Campbell. I can supply you with a great replacement called Ken. You can have him for as long as you want. Actually, if you want a new Chancellor, I could throw in Martin too.

Meanwhile, reports that Blair has offered Mo Mowlam's services to mediate between Sheringham and Yorke are being discounted.

GRASSY KNOLL

BBC researchers seeking to supply lynch-mob fuel (*Erm, surely 'background info'? – Ed.*) for Radio Five's various phone-in shows have discovered the dark truth behind David Beckham.

'Not only did he lose us the World Cup we would have surely won,' said Hugo Isuc-Littlejohn last night, 'but we have evidence of many almost equally awful crimes.'

The research team cite 'reports on the Internet' that Beckham personally caused the Russian rouble to crash by refusing to endorse a Moscow factory's new boots (the VodkaMulePredator), that the geophysical effects of the nation's tears during France '98 have caused Britain's poor summer, and that it was worries about

Beckham's lifestyle that caused Henri Paul to crash. ('He wasn't from Manchester, was he, so he must have been a United fan.')

Mystic Slut of the *Daily Spurt* believes Beckham to be the reincarnation of Martin Boormann ('They both have blond hair and two ears') and a survey of fanzine editors this morning revealed that 99% want to see Beckham publicly executed on the next anniversary of the St Etienne match. 'Failing that,' said Gary Fatracistfuck of fanzine *Hammers Über Alles*, 'he certainly must never play for England again, lest he cause us to blow another championship challenge, and his child must be born outside England to protect future generations.'

*LATE NEWS: Crunch Euro Qualifier: England 3 Germany 0 (Beckham hat-trick, Owen sent off)*

BIG CLUB TICKET NEWS

Readers may have noticed that last month's pitiful Man City–Notts County attendance of 10,060 was made to look even worse by the revelation that 500 local schoolkids were given free tickets for the game and that some ticket-buyers didn't actually attend. Further investigation has revealed the following business report for that night's match, leaked from City's ticket office:

- Free tickets to scouts promising to buy unwanted City pros – 600 (actual turnout: seven)
- Free tickets to, um, local non-police law enforcement officials – 1,300 (turnout: eight Doddies, three Goochies)
- Free tickets for Junior Blues 'Bring a Buddy to City' scheme – 3,000 (turnout: twelve Reds there for the grin)
- Free tickets to councillors considering Eastlands plan – 400 (turnout: two; the rest were at United reserves)
- Free tickets to youth players City hope to turn pro – 800 (turnout: eleven, City's own youth team, left at half-time)
- Free tickets to Joe Royle Fan Club members – three (turnout: three, all on bench, on-duty)
- Free tickets to entire population of Georgian town (part of Kinky deal) – 4,000 (turnout: one Ukrainian debt-collector at wrong ground looking for former Manchester resident)
- Actual tickets sold on the night – three. One to the Ukrainian for his companion (large Uzi and tripod), two for confused old man and his dog looking for 'a place to do whoopsies'. Latter customer very pleased with Maine Road facilities. Dog appeared to recognise contents of Oasisburgers in the FrannyLeeBar.

*(The takeover bid was duly announced, and an extraordinary public battle between hostile supporters and Sky/United began, with the wavering position of a large block of undecided or ignorant fans a great cause for concern. The author spent some autumn time on the Côte d'Azur, happy to be hundreds of miles away from Murdoch's evil kingdoms, on the way to see Eric play beach football with Prince Albert. I spent the day in a French village about five miles north of Monaco, whose story of some fifty years ago is typical of that country's communities, and the modern parallels suddenly struck me like the proverbial thunderbolt. If you recognise contemporaries in this, you're meant to. It seemed to strike a chord with the rebel leaders at IMUSA, who immediately slapped the piece up onto their website.)*

## 'The Pride of All Europe?'

When France and Germany fell into war in 1939, the village's inhabitants ran around like headless chickens, as if it were the most unexpected event since Napoleon escaped from Elba to march on Paris. No matter that the country had been on war alert for a year: somehow the nation had convinced itself that an invasion would never happen. 'A takeover by the Boche? We'd been allies and partners for years. We ran businesses and corporations together. We didn't want to take them over, and we assumed they didn't want to take us over either.' Yes, there'd been a bit of a scare the year before, but the men in charge had laid the threat to rest at Munich, hadn't they? France carried on as before, oblivious to the threat, busying itself making money and paying scant attention to its defences. A few voices in the wilderness continued to cry 'Attention!', but what did that fool Churchill know?

As the real war broke out, and a woefully underprepared France became overrun with invaders seemingly overnight, the true nature of the village and the country became evident. A people who'd always paid lip-service to the idea of being united – and perhaps even believed it – realised no such unity existed. Even the one basic tenet they thought they shared – that they were all supporters of France, true red-white-and-blues – proved to be baseless, for their response to the takeover of their home proved only that they all had wildly different ideas as to what the words 'France', 'patriot' and 'supporter' actually meant. As one villager put it, the worst experience was not the invasion itself, but the realisation that those you thought were your true comrades were often no such thing. The effects of that lasted long after the takeover was finally repelled.

When the blitzkrieg was unleashed, France staggered hurriedly to the front, pulling up its pants on the way. Its opponents had been plotting for six months; France had to improvise on the spot. To be fair, the French rallied to the call that morning, the gut instinct that their home was being invaded overcoming all doubts and hesitations. Only about one in twenty of the villagers actually refused to fight from the beginning, and they were the kind of extremist collaborators who'd made no secret of looking forward to such a takeover. What the villagers didn't know then was that their government was riddled with German sympathisers, would-be collaborators and capitalist tycoons who saw profitable opportunities in submitting to powerful foreign domination. In any event, collapse at the front lines would make the task of those politicians intent on selling out much easier. For of the 96% that responded to the invasion, a majority soon proved to have no real stomach for the fight. Whole regiments virtually gave up at the sight of the enemy's firepower. If it wasn't quite desertion, then it was certainly resigned defeatism. 'What could we do? They were stronger than we were. They were bound to win in the end. We'd fought for so many causes in the past and this was just one fight too far. Whatever you do to them, Germany just gets stronger and stronger; what is the point of fighting the inevitable?'

The government settled the matter by surrendering and ordering the populace to cease resistance. Indeed, they encouraged co-operation and immediately began to talk of this new foreign presence as allies, friends and partners. Some in Paris had actually been looking forward to this day and exulted in their 'triumph'. Marshal Pétain, a fixture at the head of France for thirty-three years, remained in power – under Nazi control, of course – and accepted a seat on the German Board of Control. He knew how France worked, and he could help the Germans make the most of it. He spoke to the supporters of France via the media and promised that he would look after French interests. He said he believed he'd done the right thing and that France would benefit from being under German parental control: 'Germany wants for France what you want for France – stability, prosperity, an ever-increasing influence throughout the world.' (Perhaps Goebbels would have made it snappier: 'We and you want the same thing. *We* want to be number one; *you* want to be number one. *We* want to win an empire; *you* want to win an empire.')

In the village, as the troops returned, a fierce internal debate raged. The numbers of pro-Nazi collaborators and sympathisers swelled to about one in five. An equal number pledged outright opposition to the death and went off to form what became famous as the French Resistance. Nowadays, of course, every other old villager claims he was a Resistance fighter. But it is far more likely that he formed part of the silent majority, those who still claimed to be patriots and supporters of the colours but who weren't prepared to fight the takeover. Indeed, as time went on, many would enjoy the easy life, quietly grateful they weren't at a battlefront or running around on exhausting missions with the Resistance. They would continue to find pleasure in life as they always knew it, watching the Sunday afternoon boules tournaments, drinking too much Côtes de Rhône in the bar at lunchtime, going off to Italy, Spain or Germany with their sports clubs. Resistance appeals to their pride and soul went unheeded: yes, they had lost their independence; yes, France no longer stood for the values they were brought up on – but they had found they could live with it.

Indeed, far more seductive was the propaganda of the collaborators. They speculated grandly on the glorious future for the French under the Nazis, how this stronger power would lift France up and above their trading rivals, how the riches of the pan-European Nazi Empire would flow into France and make her more successful than she could ever have been on her own. 'France will dominate the world once more with our German brothers at our side,' ran one article in the village newspaper; meanwhile, stories about the ill-fated experiences of previous Nazi conquests in Europe were suppressed. Around the village, the acquiescent were everywhere, often outsiders who'd never been particularly welcome in the first place, or small businessmen and shareholder types, more alive to the quick franc and to the cheap thrill of easy superiority over the rest of the world than to the values of the village and the French Revolution. More painful was the sight of once-trusted comrades getting stuck in a mire of equivocation and fence-sitting, like the local dignitaries who were socialists before the war but now had to choose between what they'd thought were their principles and their well-paid government jobs. Or the local paper editor who'd run editorials condemning the Nazis for years but who now counselled a 'wait and see' approach. As someone once said, evil triumphs not so much because of what evil men do, but because fundamentally good men fail to do anything to stop them.

The Resistance was right, of course. Germany did not raise France to new heights but exploited her mercilessly, just as it had done with every other conquest. Germany cared only for Germany, as should have been obvious merely by looking at her record around the continent. Sure, for a couple of years Frenchmen who signed up to the Nazi's Waffen SS won military triumphs all around the globe, as did Vichy Army French forces under Axis control. But these were increasingly recognised first and foremost as triumphs for Nazism and Germany, not for France, and then as actions of which they should be ashamed. 'Success' and 'victory' are easily achieved on someone else's back but they are only *worth* something when they are yours alone, won in the name of your own values and beliefs. And that essential loss of independence in 1940 came to be seen as the crux of the matter: as most Frenchmen now accept, France did not really exist between 1940 and 1944, except in the person of General de Gaulle in his London exile. Takeover almost ruined France forever; the white knights' rescue came just in the nick of time. However you dress it up, surrender and defeat mean obliteration. A country can exist as people and territory but without its independent soul it cannot be a *nation*. The same analogy applies to a football club. Because, of course, the name of this village should be Vieux Tra'fourd.

## Daily Spurt News

PHEW, WHAT A SCORCHER!!
TAKEOVER FEVER HITS ENGLAND

In the wake of the Sky/United deal, corporate raiders all over the world have rushed to the UK to bid for English football clubs. Direct from the Stock Exchange, we have the latest link-ups that have excited City analysts.

**Manchester City** are welcoming an agreed bid from Viagra. Chairman David Berntfingers said last night, 'Our new owners will keep us big – a big, bigger club, getting stronger and harder until we see something silver. And I assure fans that with Viagra on board, the club will have no trouble staying up this season.'

City's share price remained unchanged, however, as unimpressed brokers doubted whether a miracle drug would ever be invented that could cure City's ills.

**Liverpool**, meanwhile, are as usual denying anything's going on and that it's nothing to do with them but are in fact deep in talks with the Mirror Group Pension Funds (Offshore Division) with a view to a merger. Fund Group spokesman Bobby Maxwell said today, 'It's a perfect synergy of skills and interest – both Liverpudlians and MGPF are brand leaders in robbing pensioners and ruining their lives. And then claiming in court, "It wasn't us, la'."'

**Arsenal**, the most attractive target in the capital, are already at the centre of a bidding war as companies fight to gain control. Arsenal's world-famous playing and managerial personalities are attracting bidders who see possible advertising and endorsement spin-offs to help their core products. Interested so far are Hard Rider Inc., San Francisco (manufacturers of triple-strength 'Backdoor Boy' condoms), Mothercare and the Group 4 Private Prison company.

**Newcastle** have angrily rejected an offer from Sorny Pictures to act as a tax write-off for the next three years. Sighed a Sorny spokesman, 'We need to dump £60 million a year into a legitimate business for tax reasons; buying ridiculously overpriced players for Newcastle and letting their incompetent management ruin them whilst failing to win any trophies whatsoever would have fitted the bill perfectly.' Sorny will now put their money into assured disasters *Godzilla Returns* (introducing cute sidekick 'Scrappy-zilla') and a series of Willis/Schwarzenegger sensitive dramas.

Other rumoured links yet to be confirmed: **Leeds** are receiving unusual proposals from pharmaceutical industries researching how the hell BSE transferred *from* humans *into* sheep; **West Ham**'s supporter database attracts the German-financed Fourth Reich Construction consortium, based in an obscure Paraguayan village; whilst Vatican sources suggest the Church is considering buying out and asset-stripping **Glasgow Rangers** 'just for a laugh'.

## *The Dark Side of the Moon: The Man U Museum*

THE MINISTRY OF TRUTH?

They'd announced my football club was going to be sold – not just sold, mind you, but stripped of its independence and tarted off naked to a fiscal lecher whom I'd always held responsible for the destruction of British decency. So, naturally, I wander off to Old

Trafford, half-expecting to see riot police battling Reds on the forecourt, and find . . . well, nothing. In fact, the Red Café contains literally nothing: it is utterly deserted, apparently its normal state, save for half a dozen bored waitresses earning dosh for nowt. (A common sight at OT, hey Jordi?) My attention is drawn to the museum next door – never been before, might as well give it a whirl. Today's soundbite, courtesy of the master phrase-*meister* Walshie, is that United has just sold its heart and soul and knows the price of everything but the value of nothing. (All right, Walshie owes Oscar for this, but good effort all the same.) Perhaps here, of all locations at Old Trafford, one might find some residue of that heart and soul in the mementoes of heroes and legends past; it felt like it could just be the right place to be, today of all days. Potentially limitless value, for the price of £4.50.

Barely through the door, I bump into Melissa Moore, who's all over the papers that morning after being active with her spraycan on the forecourt. It's her first time here too and I instantly know she's here for the same reason as me – it doesn't need to be said. We schlepp around the displays together, muttering *sotto voce* insults at the day-trippers who mooch past, glaze-eyed, clearly understanding little of what they're seeing. I put my 'serious historian' hat on and get stuck into the display cases, hoping these treasures from the seasons of our forefathers will lift my spirits. Instead, by the end of our tour, I'm seething. Even here, in what should be a kind of blessed sanctuary – a museum, like a library, is a centre of true civilisation – the beast that is the modern United squats centre-stage, pissing and shitting over everything it touches. King Midas in reverse indeed, as a local band once sung.

I remember the hype when this museum was relaunched. It would be a proper, almost serious temple for true Reds, run independently by a respected historian and archivist. Appeals went out for material – not just the usual old boots and caps, but political, controversial stuff too. I was expecting warts 'n' all, the Full Monty; instead, like the last frame of the film, you get no such thing. The last frame of this tour was a beauty, though. But first things first.

The museum is, I soon realised, a fantastically accurate parallel of the modern club. So well did this image fit, I wondered if a very sophisticated hoax was being carried out. At first glance, it looks marvellous, state of the art. The display rooms gleam and glisten, there's a pleasing sense of modernity, space and clever design; it's like looking at the inside of the stadium. Yet after a few minutes the sterility of it begins to overcome you. It reeks of man-made materials, it feels oppressively false, and the fucking Muzak warbling through the speakers drives you demented. Suddenly, you're flashing back to a bad day in North Tier 3, being blasted by Fane and wondering how the concrete and PVC box you're squeezed into connects to the Old Trafford you used to know. A plastic stand for plastic people, some might say. The museum feels about as solid and permanent as the corner stands at City, actually; it's more like a travelling circus exhibition that's stopped off here and could be carted off by some spiv at any moment – just like the club, it now transpires.

Looking more closely at the displays, I realise that there's quality gear in there but it's treated so cack-handedly as to make it seem worthless. Items are crammed into cases *en masse*, with maybe a two-line caption on the case, and they are placed too far away from the punter. Look, but don't touch; see, but don't understand. In a proper museum, every item is fully sourced and explained; here, they're just dumped in front of you and left to fend for themselves. Many items, especially letters and contracts, might as well be invisible. Speaking as someone who's spent a lot of time in archives and historical centres, it's perhaps the most abysmal waste of material I've ever seen. 'Never mind the quality – check out the quantity' seems to be the credo.

At times, this policy is utterly aggravating. You enter one room and in an unlit, neglected alcove, unshielded by glass, is a mass of scarf bales. A scrappy notice says 'please don't touch these'. Now you and I know what these are – the scarves left for Sir Matt – but many visitors won't have a clue and there's nothing there to explain them. Indeed, the state they're in makes them seem unwanted, contemptible, even – what a mess we bloody supporters left, hey? I remember the emotion invested in the gestures that threw these scarves into their original positions and feel like screaming at the museum staff – except that there's none around. Proper museums have guides on hand to elucidate and educate. Here, they just don't give a fuck.

I suppose this attraction works on very plc principles. Ex-players and fans have contributed with immense generosity, for no financial reward but merely for the satisfaction of adding to a United cause. The museum then treats these gifts cavalierly and charges fellow Reds an extortionate £4.50 for a tour that deserves about half an hour of your time. The Munich Room is a particular disappointment – poorly resourced, appallingly lit (I think they're going for a funereal effect but it just looks like they're too cheap to buy hundred-watt bulbs) and badly positioned. Look very carefully and you'll find an unbearably poignant little podium bearing Eddie Colman's passport and watch, rescued from the scene and intensely redolent of 3.04 p.m. that February day. It has to take its place in a giant case with loads of other stuff, of course, and you can't see inside the passport, yet at that moment all you want to do is see Eddie's unharmed young face on page four. Move along there, people, we gotta increase the footfall . . .

Perhaps that is the reason why everything is so inaccessible – they just don't want you in there too long. Because stay long enough and you'll start finding Orwellian holes all over the show. Perhaps, behind one of the many doors marked 'Private', you might find some little Winstonian figure, dropping 'doubleplusungood' bits of United history into a tube for burning. Michael Knighton, a central figure in recent United history and the guy who conceived the new museum concept, can only be found as an *en passant* mention on someone else's display. Hooliganism gets five date marks on a tiny time-line; that's it. Club politics? One HOSTAGE leaflet and one 'StandUpK' flyer amidst a display stuffed with pieces, the latter not actually mentioning the dread letters IMUSA at all. That's all, folks, move along, nothing to see here, everything's hunkydory at this club. And that's official, sonny; it's in the museum, innit? The laughable Supporters Room (two good items, both patched '70s denim jackets) has one whole wall full of pictures of United books, fanzines, mags, records, etc. Everyone is up there, just about. But guess who's been airbrushed out of history? Your friendly soaraway *Red Issue.* We're the only fanzine not on the wall, just as I'm the only well-known United author not there and music correspondent Peter Boyle is the only Red recording artist not featured. Paranoid? Us? Well, can you blame us? The museum tells visitors we don't exist. Now, lads, that was hardly likely to get you a good review in itself, was it?

The worst, Room 101 if you like, is fittingly in the basement, the room where history's dark censorship is always performed. Here, in a massive chamber, dozens of interactive screens flicker, promising you access to the 'Official United History'™. Every game, every player, every personality, every event: they're all there for you to read about at the touch of the screen, from the legendary to the most obscure. Except for two people, whose biographies the screens refuse to link you to and who 'Official United Fans'™ are not allowed to know anything about. Step forward Martin and Louis Edwards. On the very day that Martin was boasting about the thirty-three years these two butchers have run our club, and how that gave him the divine right to sell us all out, it seems that this proud record of stewardship must be denied to the club's patrons. I wonder why? What could it be about the Edwards family tale that the children must not know? Cos what's a little Revenue-cheating, insider-dealing, director-shafting, fan-exploiting (Louis), bimbo-fucking, club-selling (Martin), shit-eating c*ntery between friends, hey? HEY?

And no, they don't show the *World in Action* programme on their umpteen video screens either. But they do have 'Physio with David Fevre' on a loop. (Crutches available at the exit gate – MU brand, naturally, £39.99 . . .) Oh, and there's both heart and soul on sale too: 625 mill the pair, I believe. Just hope the museum doesn't get hold of 'em – they might end up stuck underneath a bale of scarves . . .

### The Red Issue Unofficial Museum

Welcome to the *Red Issue* Unofficial Museum, which you can visit at Jethro's maisonette in Salford for two Bensons. Our new consignment of exhibits has arrived, and we are proud to showcase the following items, which we are sure you'll agree offer a better representation of United than the Official's efforts.

- A collection of ladies' *faux*-silk undergarments, donated by Miss Debbie and Miss Lynette, in tribute to our chairman. See the exciting original stain-work on these items, which DNA testing will undoubtedly reveal to be the work of an Edwards family member (and/or Bill Clinton).

- A rare original preview copy of a Granada TV programme on videocassette entitled *World in Action: The Man Who Bought United*, dated 1980. This item also bears unusual stain-work containing Edwards DNA, although in this case we believe the material emanated from Louis's anus whilst viewing said programme.

- A remarkable agglomeration of weaponry confiscated from Scoreboard End United infiltrators in 1976; includes rare example of full battle-axe of a type last used in anger in Britain in 1470. Appears to be graffitied with legend 'Sheep-killer'.

- Victims cabinet: new items include Mike England's 1974 teeth, donated by Mrs Holton, and blood-stained boots belonging to R. Keane (FA Cup semi 1995), E. Cantona (Swindon 1994) and M. Buchan (City 1975).

- Behind-the-scenes display: typical contents of a player's dressing-room locker, here showing what was in Bryan Robson's circa 1986 [massive pile of empties].

- Only copy of 1984 offer document for United from Robert Maxwell to Martin Edwards. [*PIECE OF PAPER SAYING, 'I HEREBY OFFER YOU 200 QUID TO TAKE THE BURDEN OF UNITED OFF YOUR HANDS, SIGNED FAT BOB.' UNDERNEATH MARTIN ADDS, 'GREAT DEAL! I'M A FINANCIAL GENIUS! PAY IT INTO MY SWISS ACCOUNT, BOB.'*]

- Selection of season tickets confiscated from East Stand ejectees, 1997 (kindly donated by SPS Enterprises). Some appear to have been in the same name since 1922.

- Chamber of horrors: new batch of realistic waxwork severed heads, featuring Jordi Cruyff, Rupert Murdoch and a new Paddy Roche to replace the last one, which had been repeatedly attacked by museum visitors.

- Balaclava unearthed at archaeological dig in Upton Park. Thought to have been worn by Mad Bob from Carlisle. About a hundred other similar items known to be in existence appear to remain in private hands.

- JUST IN: Manchester United's heart and soul, found in a bin bag outside a large media building in Isleworth, September 1998. Carbon dating reveals it to be 120 years old. Apparently now worth about £650 million; previously thought to be priceless.

*(The outing of Peter Mandelson, the man who was to decide our Sky bid fate, encouraged us to be pro-active in our lobbying. Sadly, he didn't stay in his job long enough for us to receive his response . . .)*

### *Red Issue Open Offer to Peter Mandelson*

Dear Mandy,
After this week's events, we think we understand you better and would like to appeal to you once again to reject the Sky bid for United. In the spirit of friendship (and in no way meant as a bribe, or a house loan), we invite you to join us as an honorary member of the Red Army. We offer for your enjoyment:

- Long, hot, sweaty coach journeys in the company of eighty or so fit young lads
- Massed visits to the urinals at half-time
- Front seat at Peter Boyle pub performances (nudity guaranteed)
- The opportunity to jib in and share tight little seats with strange men
- The chance to kip six to a room on Euroaways
- Lots of 'frottage' physical contact when United score

This offer expires 12 March.

PS: Obviously, if you try shagging anyone you'll be beaten to a pulp, but we trust these sorts of activities will keep you going until you can get to Clapham Common.

*(Our excellent comrade fanzine* Red News, *put together by some of Britain's greatest drinkers, took a break from Murdoch-bashing to run a special autumn issue in praise of great United songs and songsters and it proved to be a runaway best-seller. The author contributed this piece about our infamous streaker.)*

### Redheads: Peter Boyle

(From *Red News: Special Edition*)

Blessed are those Reds who were lucky enough to be introduced to the United experience in the mid-'70s. Today's youngsters may be sick of hearing us old farts reminiscing about the good old days after the fourth pint, but what, after all, are 'good old days' for, if not to serve as a reminder of what 'United' really means? Chucking a kid into the maelstrom of, say, 1974–75 could affect him in any of three ways. For the footballing purist soul, it would be the sight of dual-winger 4–2–4, flailing madly at the opposition and battering them senseless into defeat: once witnessed, that was your footballing ideology sorted for life. The sight of another kind of battering would attract the more physically inclined, the results of which you can still see today on various forecourts (or in Eccles pubs). For the likes of Peter Boyle, Burnage's second most famous Red after Bonehead, there was a third inspiration: the vision and, above all, sonic explosion created by the Stretford End. Boylie was taken to Villa at home, one of that season's classics, and never looked back. Indeed, for a while he never looked forward either – his dad had to keep turning Pete's head towards the pitch, so bewitched was Boylie by the fervour on the terraces behind him. Even today, when you glance across at J Lower, you can still see the four-year-old in the Boyle as he jiggles about impatiently, imploring face turned towards those above him as he tries to get another chant going. (He also still wets his bed, but that's another story.)

It wasn't until he was fourteen that he embarked upon one of the classic young Red's rites of passage – the other two being first beer vomit and first forecourt punch – namely, the attempt to start his own chant. 'We were playing Charlton, mid-'80s, and not one fucker joined in,' recalls Pete with a shudder. Some never revisit such a scenario of humiliation and will settle instead for becoming one of life's joiners-in, but Pete remained determined – however much of a twat he felt that day, he was going to be a leader. If not, as he once dreamt, of a top ten indie-pop group, then at least of his own little corner of OT, becoming a legend in his own (veggie) lunchtime. And he had some key attributes: a foghorn voice that could trample all over even the likes of Tony Hadley or Cher; a magpie way with words and nicked tunes, as is common in Burnage (hello, Noel); and the priceless asset of performers down the ages: no sense of shame whatsoever. A man who willingly gets his squirrel out in front of 30,000 at Selhurst Park isn't going to be fazed by standing on a pub table for a pre-match singsong, is he?

Boyle hates Chelsea FC with a vengeance. Ironic, then, that it'd be during footballing combat with the rentboys that his key performing moments would arrive: in 1992, when he first managed to take a whole section of the crowd with him (singing 'Dizzy'); in 1993, when he premiered 'Eric the King' and received his first, head-spinning, mass applause; and in 1994, when it was clear at Wembley that he was beginning to become a minor celeb. I could see it happening at the semi that year, behind the goal Hughesy immortalised, as a straggly Boyle exhorted the strangely silent Reds on the benches to vocal action. Sure, some punters were asking 'who's that fucking nutter?' and suggesting he needed both a haircut and a diet, but others were knowledgeably explaining to them that this was The Boyle, semi-legendary creator of chants and self-promoter *extraordinaire.* Four 'Bathtub' albums, one 'Cantona' CD and two chart singles later, there's not many left who don't know who he is and what he's done or are unable to tell a 'Boylie in Drunken Nudist Shame' story from some Euroaway.

As someone who's observed his career closely, and, admittedly, participated on one or two occasions, I have my own Boylie 'magic moment': Port Vale away, '94–'95. The youth team played for us that night and won, later graduating to do the double double, so it was a significant footballing signpost. But I have to confess that far more memorable was the experience in our terraced end. Amidst a classic night of singing, the zenith saw Boylie perched on a post, somehow reducing the entire end to silence so that he could sing the verses of 'Eric the King', before leading the thousands into enormous choruses. The home fans couldn't believe what they were seeing; it was such an extraordinary and dramatic sight, as if staged for a movie's key set-piece. That was a remarkable, often painful but ultimately exhilarating season, in which unity and terrace song were touchstones. 'Eric the King' in particular became a political manifesto after January; not surprisingly, it's Boylie's own favourite composition.

That night on one of the official coaches back to Manchester, I overheard a young knobhead about halfway back grumbling, 'Who does that idiot Boyle think he is?' I turned to say something but realised that I'd seen this kid on the terrace just in front of me, trying to start his own chant and failing miserably, about five minutes before Boylie took centre-stage. It was hard to suppress a smirk.

But there are other, less puerile critics of Boyle-ism, usually from within the Armani brigade who think it's cooler to sit in silence and compare clothing purchases. I've heard them call Boyle and his kind 'embarrassing muppets'; their ideal seems to be to scowl at the pitch, then go out and carve up a casual or two before scooting off with not a hair or button out of place. Each to his own – OT has room for all sorts, after all. But such types seem to be in the minority. Personally, I think the role of the singer and the song has never been more important. The Sky bid has made us all consider what 'United' actually means. Is it the stadium, the players, the club, the supporters, or what? I've always argued that it's none of these things but a spiritual feeling, something intangible. It comes out through the actions and ideals of certain people from time to time, say, in a Cantona through ball or an Andy Walsh diatribe. You know it when you see it, but it's hard to describe and, fortunately, impossible to sell. Every spiritual movement since the dawn of time has chosen to express itself in song; indeed, the songs usually age better than the sacred texts. To me, nothing feels more purely United than to be at an away ground amongst three thousand Reds, every man jack of 'em singing with all their passion and commitment a new United song that's spread like wildfire. That's United: supporting the team like no others can, buzzing off something together and *en masse*, and keeping both football and life fresh and innovative. At least six times out of ten, it'll have been Boylie who invented the song, or popularised it, or started the swelling chorus. That deserves a doff of the ski-hat, I reckon . . .

*(Have you felt offended/cross/outraged during this book? Then you might want to use a variation on the following, which we produced after an upsurge of hostile letters from tossers, women and City fans . . .)*

## The Red Issue Do-It-Yourself Complaints Letter

(delete where applicable)

Dear Sir,

As a: mother of three innocent kiddies
season-ticket holder of forty years' standing
committed Red who watches United on satellite
tosser with nothing better to do

I would like to register my:
outrage
utter disbelief
complete contempt
single-figure IQ

and protest at your appalling abuse of:
our tremendously successful chairman

our heroic sharpshooter Teddy Sheringham
the so-called 'day-trippers'
the spunktastic Miss Zoë Ball

I only looked at your publication thinking it was:
the programme
the official magazine
*United We Stand*
*Big 'Uns Monthly*

and would immediately cancel my subscription, if I had one.

I have also written in complaint to:
my local MP
Mr Ken Ramsden
Mary Whitehouse
Whitehouse Monthly

Yours: disgusted of Knightsbridge
appalled of Wilmslow
outraged of Hong Kong
erect of Todmorden

Signed:

*(Eric came back for his farewell match to benefit the Munich players at which the season's record for black-market ticket prices was set – yep, more than the top Euro games. Still wasn't enough for the author, who refuses to let it go . . .)*

## King Chronicles: King of the (Sand)Castle

Eric's return for the Munich match seemed to do the trick for most Reds. 'Closure', I think the Yanks call it, that last act which finally, neatly, sweetly, puts a relationship to bed for good. It wasn't enough for me, though – greedily, and a bit pathetically, perhaps, I've always liked to think of myself as a bigger Cantomaniac than the next man. I was already fascinated by him long before he came to England in '91 and I suspect this fascination is going to endure long after the Munich videotape has worn away. As United teeter on the edge of the Murdoch abyss, more than ever Eric seems to represent the last grand United hurrah, the final years of unalloyed pleasure before the name United becomes irredeemably corrupted (unless Walshie and co. can stop it all, of course). He could well go down in history as the last true United hero – that is to say, the last whose deeds served only the football club and its supporters, rather than some heartless multinational conspiracy.

There's been talk that Eric's planning to make some sort of footballing comeback, but I hope not. I don't want the purity of the legend tarnished. The minute a player becomes a manager, coach or something 'administrative', he enters a political arena where – *pace* Sir Matt – blind hero worship isn't really sustainable. And that was half the joy of being Eric's subject – in these knowing and cynical times, here, shockingly, was a hero to love unconditionally, unironically, with no room for doubt.

So I planned a trip to Monaco last month to watch Eric and his pals play beach football, just to add a little personal PS to the heavily scripted mass performance at OT a fortnight before. You hear some say that it's a bit demeaning to see a King buggering about on a beach when, by rights, he should still be leading us at OT. They said the same of Best in the States in '76; there's something about replacing grass with astroturf or sand that just ain't right. But Eric always did what he enjoyed, and fuck what anyone else thinks. And at least he's keeping fit and active in between film shoots, just in case (*Roy of the Rovers* fantasy-alert) there's a listeria epidemic at OT and he has to be recalled to score the winning goal in the European Cup final. (I really did dream that. What a sad bastard!)

Over two thousand punters had crammed into the *mini-stade* north of Monaco's port for what was officially dubbed the Second International Tournament of Beach Football. There was some serious business (relatively speaking) of a six-nation competition, but most had come to see Brazil play a Prince Albert Selection, consisting of Eric and his mates – Bossis, Ettori, brother Joel, Michel, Albuquerque, Bellone, Hansi Muller et al. And I have to say Eric looked happier on a pitch than I'd seen him since late '96, and why not? Just him and his best pals, messing about in the sunshine, showing off the ball skills none of them had lost and picking up a nice wedge at full-time. For I hadn't realised that in some parts of the world, this beach bollocks is getting to be a big deal. Eurosport were transmitting the games, sure, but it was the gigantic TV Globo who dominated, beaming live pictures back to South America, where six countries were taking them. An earnest

Brazilian explained, 'For us, this is our equivalent of you Europeans playing in the park with your coats as goalposts. This is what day-to-day football is to the average Brazilian – skills and sand. Or dirt, if you live in the *barrios*.' He claimed crowds of 20,000 watched the tournaments live in Brazil, the matches often pulling in more than 'proper' league games in the national championship; 25 million were watching this friendly on telly back in South America. It's big business already, one which could make Eric a second fortune, and doubtless NewsCorp are busy planning their first acquisition. Americans are keen too because of the number of goals and the amount of skill on display, so much more preferable to heavy-duty tactics and 0–0 draws. If Eric thought he was escaping the money game, he was wrong.

Brazil, the beach football world champions, beat Eric's lads 14–9. The Frenchman looked a few pounds overweight, naturally, but the technique on the ball was unmistakably vintage Cantona. He scored his side's first goal and playfully whooped up the celebrations; as the first half went on, he amused his team-mates and the crowd with toreador impressions and Don Quixote poses. It was as different from those furrowed-brow days of spring 1997 as you can imagine. I was glad to see him genuinely happy at last, and kind of relieved he isn't at Old Trafford now to be drenched in the shower of shit Sky have cascaded upon us, to be witness to the divisions that now exist between us all. Us and Canto, we knew each other at our best: United and passionate. The affair ended at the right moment, for sure.

Of course, where there's Cantona, there's controversy. After the tournament's closing ceremony, press and sponsors stomped furiously around the car parks like thwarted lovers – Eric had refused point blank to speak to anyone about anything, not even about his films. Had I judged his mood wrongly? Perhaps he wasn't feeling as laid-back and at ease with himself as I'd thought? Around a corner on the way to the station came the reassuring answer. There was Eric, surrounded by kids, not a hack or moneyman in sight, chatting and laughing away, signing as many autographs as possible and applauding as the children showed him their own ball skills. Apparently he was there for an hour, just him and his private audience, shooting the breeze and basking in the sunset. The twilight of his football career is almost over; a cinematic season dawns. Good luck, Eric; you'll always be the King of *this* castle . . .

*(We knew Alex Ferguson loved MUTV and is always contributing programme ideas, but it looks as though they don't always get broadcast; we at* Red Issue *found this script in MUTV's dustbin, marked 'I don't think prudish Rupert would appreciate this one'. This was, of course, the month that Fergie's notorious comments about Dion Dublin's shlong were reported nationally . . .)*

## 'Cockwatching' with Alex Ferguson

'First of all, I thank MUTV for this opportunity to discuss one of my favourite subjects; I jus' couldna resist. Mind you, I tell youse now, none of this squad matches up to old **Dion**. What a boy! When we sold him, it was 500K for the player, the rest for his length . . .

'Anyhows, we start my report on the team with young **Ryan Giggs**. Lovely tapered dick on him, a real beauty. Used to have terrible trouble like President Clinton – it bent way too far to the left. Made me wonder about the state of young Davinia's tunnel. We sorted it out with electrodes and constant psychological nagging – now it's dead straight and central. Just doesn't produce anything anymore, unfortunately. **Gary Neville**'s another with a fine-looking weapon, lovely and firm but just a bit wee for me – needs to be another two inches to be a classic tube. Still, I hear he does very well with it, so perhaps what the missus says about size not being important is right. **Paul Scholes**, well, youse all have seen his popping out of his trews in those pictures. Don't be fooled by the apparent wee-ness of it – you put the boy in the position he likes, just in the hole, and he'll expand to fill it, no problem. And looking at the size of his lady friend, and imagining her torpedo bay dimensions, he needs to!

'**Teddy Sheringham**'s has disappointed me and I rarely even bother looking at it these days. Looks like a dried-out dead turkey and nothing rouses it from its furry nest, although I've seen it stir when Teddy sees Glenda on the telly. **Jordi Cruyff**'s a funny one – whenever I take a wee peek, it's very exciting, bright purple and throbbing for action. But the minute I turn my back and tell someone else to come have a look, it's gone all shrivelled and pathetic. Mark my words, one day that boy will amaze everyone by spurting all over the place. A bit like young **Andy Cole**, who's got a tremendous lunchbox on him but tends to go off at the most unfortunate moments and in embarrassing directions. I've talked to him about self-control and he's getting much better, especially now his new friend **Dwight** has arrived. Now there's my kind of boy, with a smile on his face and a willy he's not ashamed to show to me or the cameras or any passing goalkeepers. I canna resist spending big money for that kind of action. But I was wrong about **Henning Berg.** His looks the business, the biggest and thickest I've seen, but can he do anything with it? It just hangs there like a wet saveloy and would be useless in someone's box. Very disappointing.

'Anyways, I hope youse all enjoyed this look behind the scenes. I'm off to meet that MUTV regular **Peter Boyle**. I'm told he's just the kind of fan I like.'

*(The disappointments were coming thick and fast throughout the autumn: the Sky bid, then Schmikes's shock decision to quit, soon to be followed by Kiddo's sensational walkout. There seemed to be little 'side' to the Peter decision, making the occasion purely one for homage – but the Kidd Affair would require a more cynical approach . . .)*

### *Redheads: Peter Schmeichel*

The famous and much-ridiculed nose, I suppose, actually says it all in a symbolic way. Big, throbbingly red, dominant, unmissable, unique . . . Owner Peter Schmeichel takes his *adieus* as an OT hero, and we're not quite accustomed to the fact that he's irreplaceable. We all balefully flick through the credentials of his would-be successors and pronounce them inadequate. Bosnich, Wright, Van Der Saar, Baardsen, Barthez . . . all mere Sheringhams to Peter's Cantona, we conclude. It is alongside the Frenchman on the tripartite podium of key '90s heroes that Peter belongs – a tad ahead of Roy, perhaps; a notch or two below his friend and King. Within eighteen months of his arrival, he had proved to even the most sceptical the truth of two current orthodoxies: one, ancient, that Championship teams require Championship keepers; two, modern, that Europe now produces better keepers than Britain. He ran United's defence as though it were his own private totalitarian state and on that ironclad foundation everything else was built. Too right United have allowed him a free transfer for services rendered; he must surely be the greatest United keeper of all time.

And to have secured him for that laughably low fee of £625,000! Not that the fee looked so funny when he first arrived: both he and we were aghast as Wimbledon forwards ploughed into him early doors, making Peter in particular wonder what the hell nightmarish perversion of football he'd got himself into. Hard to believe now, after years of watching Peter impose his sheer presence and courage on all and sundry, that his first reaction to this horrible mêlée of penalty-box assaults was to shout 'Run away!'. Unlike Eric, he hadn't swaggered right into this gaff asking 'Are you big enough for me?'. But such was the speed of his growth as a team personality and as a player that eventually only Eric had greater claim to truly gigantic status. If you think about it, how bizarre that any player should, for example, habitually call everyone in front of him 'F*ck**g c**ts' at ninety decibels throughout a match, or harangue 10,000 hardcore lads behind him for not supporting sufficiently loudly, or lecture the entire club in the media for not worshipping Eric enough (!) – but, because it was Peter, it just seemed natural, barely worth remarking upon. Larger than life, too big for the frame, eleven on the dial; in retrospect, it's obvious only United were capable of containing his girth.

The measure of the player is that you can pick out matches at random in the record books and be virtually assured he played a pivotal role. As someone said last week, he didn't make a reputation on showboat saves at 4–0 up – he made the astounding stops at 0–0, when the pressure was on and the odds against. His 1995–96 season remains especially overpowering in the memory; his double act with Eric carried the faithful through half that campaign, match after match witnessing Peter producing salvation, then Eric deliverance. The archetypal display at St James' Park could fill a chapter of any autobiography in itself, so frightening was his immensity in goal, so stunning was Eric's capitalisation. The first double owes so much to him too, when he often became the opening gambit of attack only seconds after performing his last-line-of-defence duties. Football looked on, open-mouthed, at this virtuosity: he was unstoppable. For some reason, I'll always remember him at Goodison that year, performing his full array of tricks including the celebrated 'starfish'; Everton forwards were visibly wilting in his presence. I could have sworn he was deliberately taking the piss, so outrageously confident were some of his interventions. He appeared to be about eight foot tall that night – and I knew we were probably seeing the best we'd ever see in green (or yellow, or black, or purple . . .)

Nothing is sadder than watching a hero decline and I'm glad Peter's going to spare us the full extent of that, just as his mate Eric did. There have been signs – though none which warrant some of the stick the shabbier end of the press have meted out – that he's losing some edge, and it's typical of a self-confessed manic perfectionist that he spotted this long before the media's wiseacres. We hear he's bought a house near Nice after falling in love with the south of France when based there with Denmark. Not surprisingly, with noises in France suggesting Fabian Barthez is going to Olympique, he's being linked with AS Monaco, where life would be easier, warmer and perhaps richer. He's done Fergie a final favour by giving United plenty of time to find a replacement; typically, he's stuck his oar in to nominate Barthez or Sorensen. Whomever we go for, we need to face it now – there's no replacing Peter. Welcome the new arrival with open arms and take away the burden of Peter's ghost, for even £20 million is not going to buy us an equivalent. As the cliché goes, they broke the mould with Peter – in fact, it was probably he himself who did it, chucking it at Gary Neville. Let us just hope that before he leaves he receives the one medal left to complete his collection . . .

## 'The Life of Brian'

*(A Judean People's Front Production* AD *1998)*

SCENE: Pythonesque. The role of Brother Martin is played by John Cleese . . .

MARTIN: 'Right, brother directors, I think here's an item we can all agree on. Let us express our total, complete and totally complete opposition to the demands of brother Brian, who appears to want extra money and some sort of guarantee that he'll be in line for the top job when our commander in the field retires. I mean, what has Brian ever really done for us, hey?'

(*General murmuring. A lone voice pipes up.*)

'Um, well, most of our people seem to think he's been one of the keys to our recent success, actually. Although I take nothing away from the glory of our commander, naturally.'

(*General muttering of agreement.*)

MARTIN: 'Yes, yes, that's all very well – but to promise to make him the next commander and pay him a king's ransom in the meantime?

What's he got that we should be interested in, hey? I mean, what experience could he offer?'

(*Mutter, mutter, mumble.*)

'Erm, how about the fact that, as a warrior, he conquered Europe at the age of just nineteen and fought at the top level all his career, coping with a wide variety of tactics, positions, leaders and colleagues and thus now knows all about battle from the playing side as few others can?'

MARTIN: 'Yes, yes, yes, but that's ancient history now, brothers. The modern leader needs to know the modern world. Come now, let us move on.'

'Well, he has been instrumental in developing our fighting tactics so that we're on the brink of European victory, as well as creating the most advanced training regime in Britain, not to mention having travelled the world in search of new methods, gaining the respect of fellow leaders in every country.'

MARTIN: 'Oh. Well, yes. Granted, that may be true. But where's his judgement and his grasp of man-management? That's what's really needed here, you know.'

'Actually, most of the young warriors who've come through here have been either discovered or guided to the peak of their careers by brother Brian. He also knows more about other fighters across Europe than almost anyone else and is personally probably the most loved trainer in Britain, whose skills at dealing with different personalities are legendary.'

MARTIN (exasperatedly): 'All right, all right, we're getting off the point here. Granted, he has some attributes, but we can't be held to ransom like this – do you know how much he's asking for? A bloody fortune! We have responsibilities to our members, brothers. Think of the little old ladies who've given us their life savings.'

'Erm, isn't it true that until very recently brother Teddy was earning more in a month than Brian was in a year? And that the current commander earns five times what Brian does, even though they're virtually equal partners at work? And that you, dear leader, have often made more money in ten seconds than Brian will make in his lifetime? And that any other leader in the country would pay up without hesitation?'

MARTIN (glowering): 'Yes, thank you for that contribution, brother Andy. The fact remains that by raising the question of the succession, brother Brian is destabilising the organisation. What do you want me to do – give our commander the push to accommodate this upstart's ambition?'

'Uh, I think you'll find that he just wants to know very roughly when his chance will come and if he's in with a shout. Y'know, before he reaches retirement age, that's all.'

MARTIN (thumping desk): 'Right, I've had enough of this. Let's get this straight. One of you try and tell me this: apart from his enormous experience and achievements as both a warrior and trainer, his tactical expertise, his superb coaching methods, his personal contacts across the world, his modest wage demands, his lovable personality, his commendable patience and the fact that he's a fighting Red through and through, *what can brother Brian really do for us?*'

'Um, win loads of trophies?'

MARTIN: 'Oh, fuck off!'

[Exit Brian to the land of Ewood and Martin to the Temple of the Money Changers with eighty million sovereigns]

*(Christmas arrives; United may be one short around the turkey but a Milanese Easter resurrection beckons. Meanwhile, the* Spurt *proclaims seasonal goodwill to all men. Er, except for Scousers, of course. And Bitters, and Sheep, and . . .)*

## Daily Spurt News

'NO DISASTERS' DISASTER HITS MURKEYDIVE

The economy and morale of this once-proud city of Liverpool are taking another savage beating this year which promises a miserable

Crimbo all round. A complete lack of tragedies, disasters or excuses for lynch mobs has left locals even more penniless than usual and, worse, without hope too.

'Worra we gonna do?' wailed Sharon Jism, who, with common-law husband Bazza, was loitering outside the Toxteth benefits office. 'Once upon a time, we could look forward to filling our days with grieving for the cameras, stealing flowers from graves to sell or joining the mobs outside courts. But now there's nothing,' howled Miss Jism, peeling a large onion.

Bazza, who hasn't worked for over a year, explained sorrowfully, 'There was so much here once, la'. You could earn a few quid doing rentamob duty for the Sky cameras when the latest killers came past in the Marias. Or there was good money doing photocopies of disaster piccies and selling them in Bootle as charity souvenir specials. But it's all gone. Now me and the family have to make do every week on our combined benefits, which only come to £355. Crime is our only alternative now, innit?' said Bazza, who has ten years' worth of robbery convictions.

The scenes were worse outside the Florists' Association annual meeting in Aigburth, where a spokesman claimed many members had been forced out of business. 'I've hardly sold a rose since Diana's funeral. We're just not getting the turnover of self-pitiable incidents we used to enjoy.'

Local council officials are seriously concerned by the lack of florally appropriate catastrophes. Said trade circle chief, 'Florists drove this local economy, providing spin-offs for the whole community. Queues outside used to need servicing and whole rows of shops would depend on them, supplying drinks, ciggies and Social Fund application forms as they waited and grieved for days on end. Now it's all gone.'

Hoped-for bonanzas never materialised either. 'We were looking forward to some serious weeping and wailing when Roy Evans got the sack,' explained one Anfield florist, 'but it turned out everyone was delighted to see the fucker go. The only one crying was Roy.'

There is, however, a dawning realisation that resourceful Scousers might yet turn the situation to their advantage. 'We are thinking of declaring the lack of disasters as a disaster in itself,' explained a local official, 'thus bringing back into work the thousands of laid-off floral workers, grief counsellors and associated specialists. Otherwise, we'll have to resort to the council emergency plan and ask Michael Owen to sacrifice himself for the good of the community.'

*ON OTHER PAGES IN YOUR ECHO TONIGHT:*
PC SHOCKS CITY: 'I'M NOT ON DRUGS'
HOULLIER WARNS: 'THE OVERRATED PRIMA DONNAS WILL BE SOLD'
CITY CELEBRATES AS FAMILY CHOOSES TO MOVE INTO MERSEYSIDE
AIRPORT ANNOUNCES TOP NEW ROUTE: LIVERPOOL TO WALTON
STOP PRESS: LIVERPOOL FC PLACE TWENTY-THREE ON TRANSFER LIST

## *Daily Spurt Christmas Classified Ads*

GAMES FOR ALL THE FAMILY'S FOOTIE FANS!

**Connect 4** – Liverpool version. All you have to do is make four players connect up together to make a solid backline and you win. It looks so simple but young Roy (not pictured) spent years trying to crack it! (Caution: pieces easily broken. No money-back guarantee.) RRP £75 (six pence to wholesalers).

**Cluedo** – United brand. A much-loved little Kidd is done away with. Whodunnit? Colonel Plums with the lead pipe in the changing-rooms? Miss Scarlett with the revolver at The Cliff? Or Mister Stupid Greedy C**t with a backstabbing dagger in the boardroom? A game of no mystery whatsoever.

**Buckaroo** – Sky blue finish. The world's favourite bucking bronco game! How long can you stay in the hot seat before you're tossed into the air? A game of no skill and impatience as you pile debt upon debt onto the figure in the seat until the horse named Kippax can't take no more. Comes with realistic angry cowboy posse accessory figures and replica reverend-with-megaphone. Ride 'em, Big Joe!

**Buccaneer** – Long Rupe Silver edition. The great pirate game for the whole family. Sail the seven seas raiding as much cash as possible from every country you visit before retiring in triumph to Treasure Island, having bled everyone else dry. (Note: pay-per-play game box can't be opened until you insert £9.99.)

**Diplomacy** – the classic game of alliances, deals and backstabbing. Sadly, available in every club's colours.

**Chinese Chequers** – Comes in Crystal Palace colours. Marvel as all the counters, money and board disappear. Endorsed, and probably invented, by Terry Venables.

**Manchester City Games Compendium**
Features all the classics – Downfall, Going for Broke, Trivial Pursuit, Snakes and Ladders, Scrabble.

**Hungry Hungry Hippos** – Hilarious fun for all Geordie kiddies! Can you keep fatties Hall and Shepherd fed with enough cash, tarts and nosepowder? Not suitable for over-eighteens lest they burst into tears.

**Mastermind** – Alex Ferguson special edition. Can you guess which pieces he's going to put in which position? Hours, nay, years of bewildering fun. (STOP PRESS: Withdrawn from sale for being out of date. May be back on shelves come spring, though.)

### *Daily Spurt Christmas Charity News*

The following celebrities have generously donated their time this Christmas to collect society's unwanted . . .

NSPCC – Two current London managers have volunteered. 'Any lost little girls or boys? Or boys? Any boys? Send them to us and we'll provide a warm Christmas plum pudding and pull some crackers.'

RSPCA – Leeds United FC. 'Any unwanted pets for Christmas? Send them to Elland Road, where they'll be treated as one of the family. Animals with pliant rectums preferred.'

**Lifeline** – Three generous Liverpudlians who'd rather remain anonymous will remove those tempting piles of smack and coke to help you quit (sniff sniff).

And don't forget to support this year's Blue Peter appeal in aid of Moss Side's deprived, who just need 3,008 people to turn up at their home so that they don't embarrass the fuck out of themselves again . . .

### *Daily Spurt Christmas Charity Appeal*

This Christmas, have a care for the troubled and unfortunate, for those who just can't take it anymore, who've had enough of the woes of modern life, who can no longer find humour and consolation in their existence. Their minds become unbalanced, they might begin to act strangely – and when they come together, terrible mass psychosis can result.

We have all heard of the collective madness recently witnessed in Moss Side, when the sight of one piss-taking newspaper photo was enough to send thousands into frenzy, attacking journalists and howling at the (blue) moon. For the people of Manchester City have broken through to the other side and reached the dark abyss where souls and hope perish. Despair, Destruction and Division Three are but one step away.

**So support the MANCAP charity . . .**

. . . and instead of taking the piss when you see a young Bertie in the street, have pity. He's probably completely off his trolley.

Don't shout '5–0' or sing Boylie's 'Division Two' tune. Give him the number of a good shrink or the Samaritans. Offer him your belt so that he might put himself in a strait-jacket.

If he looks like he's about to run amok berserkly, tell him he supports a big club, that you can't get relegated three times in a row and that the spiky monsters under his bed who keep screaming 'Franny, Franny, Franny' in the wee small hours aren't really coming to get him.

Have pity. Bitterness hurts. A pat on the back instead of a smack in the face should be your present to a Blue this Christmas. Maybe share your turkey with him. JUST DON'T LET HIM NEAR THE FUCKING CARVING KNIFE, THE MAD BASTARD!

*(A bizarre story blew up over Christmas in which John Gregory was accused of being 'football's Alf Garnett' for his alleged Little Englander attitude to foreign players. Managers as sitcom stars? Yeah, why not? How about these?)*

## Daily Spurt What's On: Christmas Comedy TV

*Rising Damp*

*Starring Joe Royle as Rigsby*

It's a miserable Christmas for Rigsby, almost alone in his dilapidated house that no one wants to visit (bar 3,008 rats). His main tenant Alan can't score to save his life, there's no money in the kitty, that flash bastard Philip across the way pulls all the birds – and taunting him about his non-local origins doesn't seem to help. His cat Vienna, named after his only triumph in life thirty years before, is his only friend. Deep down, it's a dreadfully sad show, but everyone laughs until they piss all the same.

***The Odd Couple***
*Starring Roy and Gerard as Felix and Oscar*
Chaos and confusion reign in this flatshare comedy of mismatches. Roy's so tidy but Gerard's a scruff; Roy's careful with money and Gerard's a spendthrift. *And Roy's a c**ting Scouse twat failure whom we all hate and who's pathetically unemployed like the rest of the scum and whose grave we'll dance on* whilst, er, Gerard's not too bad really. (Series cancelled, October.)

***Steptoe and Son***
*Starring Alex Ferguson and Brian Kidd as Albert and Harold*
Grumpy mean old man keeps a tight grip on the family business, thwarting poor Harold's every youthful ambition. When willing tarts like Misses SkyBlue and Goodison come to tea offering possible escape to Harold, Albert sits farting in his armchair shouting, 'He's got crabs, y'know,' and wailing, ''Arold, don't leave me, 'arold . . .'

(Spin-off feature film was made in which they go to Europe and suffer a series of hilarious cockups and disasters.)

*(The Hoddle Affair, uniquely fascinating for being both hilarious yet also a tragic reflection on Britain's pathetic public morality post-Diana, put The Manager back at centre-stage. We continued to count our blessings with Alex; thank God no one listened to us back in December '89 . . .)*

## Daily Spurt News

NEW FA CRISIS: IS WILKO 'DOING A HOD'?
Only days after sacking Glenda Hoddle for being a barmpot religious cripple-kicker, the FA faces a new storm tonight over successor Howard Wilkinson.

Just as dozy hacks missed last May's Radio 5 interview in which Hod claimed, 'All spads got what was coming to 'em, mate,' so too have they failed to notice the dark period in Wilkinson's life when he fell amongst a pagan sect in Yorkshire.

But now the lynchmob (*surely 'concerned citizens'? – Ed.*) have been furnished with evidence by *The Sun* that Wilkinson did indeed serve time at the grisly cult HQ known as Elland Road, which the paper says proves he should be immediately strung up. And the details certainly aren't pretty:

- Sect adherents are expected to strip semi-naked in freezing conditions and chant monotonously like old hippies used to. Observers report a mass hysteria which seems to convince the chanters they can fly.
- Arcane 'healing' rituals involving farmyard animals are said to be popular; they consist of 'the laying-on of the penis', 'feeling the cosmic aura of the anus' and 'getting in touch with the inner rectum'.
- Other faiths' followers are treated as mortal dangers: visitors to Elland are pursued by foam-mouthed packs of crazed zealots who attempt to stone 'infidels' to death.
- And, in a vile escalation from the Hoddle case, the pagans not only seem to hate the disabled but also anyone who's not white, has not lived in Leeds slums all their lives and can talk in a normal, intelligible accent.

Prime Minister Tony Blair denounced Wilko's 'sick, twisted past' today during his appearance on *The Jerry Springer Show* and called for him to be sacked and deported, which 'President' Al Campbell didn't bother to deny.

Wilkinson has apologised to the nation and asked for further offences to be taken into consideration, namely once managing the inbreds at Hillsborough and being a Yorkshire git in general.

*(Mind you, pre-Barca, of course, some wondered whether we were all going a bit far in our adulation of Alex as his jaw-dropping testimonial details were announced . . .)*

## Daily Spurt Testimonial News

THOSE FERGIE TESTIMONIAL DETAILS IN FULL

*By your Gold Trafford correspondent, David Piss-Weak*

THE CONCERT

The Maracana Stadium, Brazil, will welcome 200,000 grateful punters (who will pay £500 per ticket) for an all-star gig hosted by Mick Hucknall. The Simply Red star will commence proceedings by offering Alex a blowjob (declined) before launching into a two-hour a cappella medley of old 1950s hits. Artists will include the fully reformed supergroups The Rolling Stones, The Who and – top of the bill – The Beatles, with coffins of departed members specially disinterred for the gig. A hologram of John Lennon will announce, 'Alex, you're gear, man,' before two million butterflies sprayed with gold leaf are released into the sky.

THE DAY AT THE RACES

Every racetrack in Europe will be holding Fergie Steeplechase events, which punters can watch at home as a pay-per-view event for £25 if they can't afford the £1,000 Platinum Club paddock tickets. The entire royal family will attend at Haydock, where they will defer to the boss by letting him occupy the royal box alone whilst they hang about the car park. Willie Carson will then allow Fergie to ride him to exhaustion around the course, with a dozen naked handmaidens waiting at the finishing post to mop Fergie's brow when he arrives.

THE GOLF EVENT

The 2001 Ryder Cup will be brought forward and played on Fergie's birthday, when he will be given the chance to sink the final putt. All the world's leading golfers will be handing over their year's earnings to the testimonial pot and they will together present Fergie with a gold-threaded 'Masters' jacket, hand-stitched by Arnold Palmer on his deathbed.

THE DINNERS

A 15-course banquet will be held in every country of the world that has an MUSC and Fergie will be flown to each in Concorde, paid for by Jack Cunningham and Gordon Brown Taxpayer Travel Services. Royal Swan, Beluga caviar and Château Lafitte '35 will be mandatory at every meal. Diners may join in for a fee of £800.

Yes, a great calendar of events, welcomed today by Martin Edwards, who commented, 'Isn't it great that the fans will be paying for what we were too tight to give Alex in his contract?'

Please note: anyone suggesting that this testimonial is a bit over the top, that Sir Matt got nothing like it and that Kenny Dalglish donated all his proceeds to charity will be taken care of by Testimonial Usher Services (prop. Ned Kelly).

*(As United waited for spring – and Europe – to return, life at OT was a tad dull and the football merely functional. Luckily, the Blues and Dirties are always there to entertain us . . .)*

## Daily Spurt News

NEW 'FAKES FOOL VIEWERS' SCANDAL!!

Just as the recent Vanessa/Kilroy affair was beginning to die down, Manchester has been rocked by the shocking revelation that the city's punters have been repeatedly hoodwinked by fake performers. Said one appalled viewer yesterday, 'I've been paying for years to watch what I thought was the real thing – now it turns out we've all been conned. It's a disgrace.'

Shamefaced bosses at Maine Road launched an inquiry today after admitting that several of their managers and players in recent years have been impostors, frauds and incompetents looking to make a quick buck.

'I blame the agents involved,' squeaked director David Berntfingers. 'We asked them to find us top-grade bosses and strikers and we hired them all in good faith to entertain our spectators. But it turns out they were all hopeless amateurs.'

Particular attention has focused on a forward imported from the south who was supposed to be a proven scorer but was later unmasked as a worthless journeyman from army surplus stores. Several other 'top foreign stars' turned out to be chancers looking for visas who were laughed off stage. Worst of all, the club was targeted by a notorious 'repeat offender' who has made a habit of fooling viewers all over the country. The so-called manager, who cannot be named, had pulled the same trick in the Midlands and the south and earned thousands of pounds before audiences wised up and booed him off. The club were even conned by a would-be rich saviour who turned out to have nothing to offer but toilet paper and some grotty two-colour shirts.

One of the agents involved mounted a robust defence of the scam yesterday, claiming that Maine Road deserved all they got: 'After all, they've been pretending to be a big club for 30 years – how fake can you get?'

CITY DEMAND 30 YEARS' WORTH OF REPLAYS

Maine Road bosses were quick to act today in the light of the Arsenal/Sheffield United affair, claiming that the precedent set at

Highbury should immediately lead to several replays of historic City matches. Amongst many others, directors have lodged the following incidents with FIFA and the FA:

- 1995–96: Roy Keane was a bad sport in accepting that FA Cup match penalty. Match should have finished 1–1, and we now demand a replay at Maine Road (which we expect to win on the way to Wembley glory).
- 1994–95: United were bad sports when they ran poor Terry Phelan ragged; he was clearly carrying a knock. Restart the match at 0–0 (and let's see them try and score five this time).
- 1993–94: When we were 2–0 up, one of our players had to stop to blow some snot out. United took advantage by playing on and scored several moves later. Restart match at half-time.
- 1976–77: In our 3–1 defeat which cost us the title, United advanced a throw-in five yards further down the line and scored 30 minutes later. Match should be awarded to us by default, making us 1977 champs and, of course, 1978 European Cup winners, probably.
- 1968–69: Euro Cup preliminary round. One of our lads had a gippy tummy in Turkey; we demand replay vs. Fenerbahce so that we can have another chance of playing in the *actual* European Cup.

Alex Ferguson has surprisingly offered to play any rematches, remarking that his Under-18s could do with the shooting practice.

GET TO WORK, YOU LAZY TWATS

The Government's recent announcement that, as part of the New Deal, free tattoo removal will be offered to jobseekers will not apply in Merseyside. Although it is expected that thousands of otherwise respectable and presentable people elsewhere in Britain will benefit from having tattoos removed, research has shown that Liverpudlians need rather more help than the State can afford. A No.10 spokesman explained, 'Businesses we surveyed said that they'd only employ Scousers if: (1) they could be rehoused outside Merseyside; (2) they were weaned off their various drug habits; (3) they could be trained to lose their hideous accents; (4) their genetic make-up was surgically altered to remove inbred criminality. When we added up the potential bills from surgeons, elocution teachers, rehab clinics and housing costs, it came to more than the lazy fuckers would ever earn in their lifetimes.'

Government policy on Merseyside is now, unofficially, 'to give them lots of dole and skag and let them get on with destroying themselves'. So, no change there then.

INSIDE YOUR NEWS TONIGHT

- Houllier's latest excuse: 'GM foods have turned my players into vegetables.'
- Kinky's Ajax nightmare: 'I've fallen so low, I'd actually consider re-signing for City.'
- Chelsea sensation: Wise completes 90 minutes on pitch (but kills minicab driver on way home).

*(And then there's always the self-proclaimed geniuses in MU's Commercial Department to make us smile/gag with their latest tacky wheezes . . .)*

## Red Issue's Unofficial United Hotel

If the much-hyped new United 'quality hotel' down the road isn't quite your cup of tea, *Red Issue* is proud to announce its new alternative B&B in glamorous Ordsall.

- We'll be offering packages including tickets (strange-looking stubs from season books, often numbered 13) and passes which'll get you served in the Dog within 30 minutes.
- Nightly cabaret in the lounge features Pete Boyle and the Low Cs plus a stripper (Pete Boyle).
- Peruse our unique selection of memorabilia in the foyer (includes new exhibits, 'CS Canisters We Have Loved' and our collection of robbed police helmets from across Europe).
- Watch our special selection of films in the TV room, from the *Debbie Does Denton* series to our exclusive documentary featuring police CCTV footage of United's firm running amok, *You've Been Caned.*

Then settle down for the evening in our newly opened Whiteside Memorial Bar.

- Constantly flowing pumps, including spirits on draught
- Drinks served in five-pint kegs

- Reclining couches for overnight sessions
- Tasteful selection of puke-buckets

Choose any one of our themed rooms for the night:

THE ROBSON SUITE
- Widescreen TV tuned to Sky Sports
- Maxi mini-bar (can hold 50 pints)
- Assortment of sex aids including vibro-crutch
- Wife-detector alarm fitted to door

THE BLACKMORE BOUDOIR
- Flashing disco-ball lighting
- Black satin sheets, furry wall-to-wall shagpile
- Radio tuned automatically to Mega FM (Barry White, Isaac Hayes, etc.)
- Condom dispenser
- Set of ready-to-sign sexual consent forms

THE YORKE ROOM
- Gigantic ghetto-blaster
- Eight video cameras and screen
- Free tart supplied for threesomes
- Wardrobe with full range of skirts, stockings, etc.
- Extra cot for sidekick Andy

THE SHARPE SUITE
- Hotline phone direct to Moss Side Supplies Ltd
- Rizla dispenser
- Mini-bar restocked with munchies after midnight
- Set of 'Parlo Italiano' language tapes
- Nice view of girls'-school entrance

And if you need to hire a car during your stay, we're proud to recommend our local partners, Ged's While-U-Wait Hotwire Service, which will deliver any model you specify within about 20 minutes.

(Caution: paint may still be wet. Numberplates not included. Do not ask for credit, or a receipt, as a smack in the mouth often offends.)

*(Liverpool then made an impressive grasp for our headlines, largely via the efforts of Robert Fowler Esq., who should surely be knighted for services to public morale.)*

## Daily Spurt News

POLICE PREJUDICE: NEW SHOCK FINDINGS

Only weeks after police were sent reeling by the damning conclusions of the Lawrence Report, a new blow has been struck by an inquiry mounted by Liverpool College.

'There is no doubt,' said Professor S. Fingers, 'that police in Britain are institutionally Scouseist.'

The findings result from a thorough survey of the Liverpool public conducted wherever Scousers gather in numbers (DSS offices, twenty-four northern jails, drug dens all over the region) and were sent to Parliament and the police yesterday.

'It's true, la',' said one contributor, a Mr B. Sinbad. 'They just hear our accents, or take one look at our skin colour, and they assume we're criminals and vandals straight off. We're scapegoats, like.'

The report highlights statistics that appear to show national arrest-counts are higher for the following categories of people: those with blotchy, pus-strewn skin tones, those with whiney, skrikey accents that grate, those with postcodes beginning with 'L', those in ill-fitting market-bought shell-suits made by obscure brands such as 'Nuke', 'Adidarse' and 'Reefbok'.

'These categories just happen to match the characteristics of Scousers,' said Prof. Fingers, 'which demonstrates that the police are singling out Scousers for arrest and persecution.'

The report has been received with urgent indifference at Westminster, where Met. chief Paul Condom wearily pointed out that the figures were no surprise, given that 90% of all crime since 1970 had been committed by Liverpudlians.

When asked if his officers were guilty, perhaps, of 'unwitting Scouseism', he replied, 'There's nothing "unwitting" about it, mate.'

Mr Sinbad was unavailable for further comment on this reaction as he was busy making off down Bootle High Street with our wallets.

LE SAUX–FOWLER FALL-OUT: A NEW TWIST

A Manchester District League game descended into a near riot after a mass punch-up sparked by an incident that echoed last month's

Fowler–Le Saux bust-up. Deeply upset player Tommy Wright was sent off for headbutting an opponent but claimed his reaction was completely justified after the other player had 'outrageously and viciously taunted me with personal slurs'.

Eyewitnesses report that the player had enraged Wright, a happily married resident of Manchester, by calling him 'a raving Scouser' throughout the match and challenging him with, 'Come on, then, where's your granny-stabbing Stanley?'

Wright continued, 'The last straw came when the player bent over in front of me, wiggled his arse and pointed to his back pocket, saying, "Go on, there's my bulging wallet – have it away, you thieving twat." I had no option but to bust his face open.'

Team-mates explained that Wright, too upset to speak further, had been born in Chester and that the opponent had disgracefully tried to use this to imply he might be some kind of Scouser. 'Can you imagine any allegation more hurtful than that?' wondered his team captain.

The local FA are expected to rescind the red card on the basis that the retaliation was entirely justified. 'Players must expect to be taunted as poofs or nonces or whatever,' explained an official, 'but accusations of Scousery have no place in the game.'

ROBBIE FOWLER'S FOOTIE-FORM GUIDE

Exclusive to this paper, Robbie previews the weekend's action by examining the top players and giving us his verdict.

**Tony Adams** – 'He's started reading, hasn't he? Isn't he getting into poetry or summat? Must be a PUFF.'

**Andy Cole** – 'Always going on about his friend Dwight and how lovely and matey they are, inhe? Wears an ear-ring. Obviously BENT.'

**Steve McManaman** – 'Caught him listening to a dago language tape yesterday. Talking foreign! And reads the la-di-dah *Times.* What a WUFFTER.'

**Vinny Jones and Eric Cantona** – 'Now they've been disappointing. Were men's men, but started acting, didn't they? Everyone knows actors are all BENDERS.'

**David Beckham** – 'Dyes his hair. Likes to give it up the arse, so they say. Always mooning over kids. Clearly a NONCE.'

**David Ginola** – 'Look at his fucking hair. What a girl. Says he uses shampoo AND conditioner. Sounds French – and they're all perverts, aren't they? Total QUEEN.'

**Marc Overmars** – 'Now there's a player. Clean cut, short hair, proper sportsman and a gent. Don't mind sharing a shower with him anytime. He's a top GEEZER.'

*(Finally, European competition returned and Fergie successfully got us past the Milanese, though not without running foul of UEFA. Few disagreed with our verdict that the fine was worth every penny . . .)*

## Fergie's Quarter-Final Euro-Cuisine Guide

**Italy:** Well, obviously, the first thing you do is check under the sauce to see if it's actually pasta or not. I mean, they might tell you it is, but you gotta be sure. It could be poison or something – I remember 'The Borgias'. Fucking Italians, with their diving and cheating – God knows what they get up to in their kitchens when no one's watching them. Where were they at Anzio? Eh? Eh?

**Germany:** I've been to Munich and Dortmund so I know all about this. Check under the sausage is my advice. It could be sauerkraut. And send it back if it is. Sour kraut, see? 'Bitter German', see? Bitter about the war. I worked it all out. God knows what it might be. You can never be too careful, what with Germans and their track record with ovens.

**Spain:** Take a damn good look in that paella, it's a bloody minefield. You know it could be baby donkey's testicles in there. Which they cut off in front of the parents at Christmastime. Or so I've heard. Fucking Spics, never trusted them since that UEFA Cup match in '82 with Aberdeen when we were denied a blatant throw-in after 32 minutes. Spanish ref, of course. Say no more.

**Ukraine:** Well, there could be all sorts hidden inside a lump of black bread, couldn't there? Uranium, mebbe. It's all made by the Mafia, y'know, Andrei told me. Where's fucking Ukrainia anyway? That's not

Europe, surely? Is this one of those Israel-in-Eurovision deals? We're taking our own food anyway. Let's face it, these Europeans are just too suspect. I mean, what have we ever said to offend them anyway?

*(The boss might recognise a few of the following too . . .)*

## The Red Issue Guide to Gaffer-speak

WHAT THEY SAY VS. WHAT THEY MEAN

'It was sorted out behind closed doors' = We've had an enormous punch-up over it
'It's in the club's best interests' = It's in my best interests
'We respect our opponents' = We hate them
'They'll be tough opposition' = We should walk it
'We're fully committed to this competition' = So, have you seen our reserves yet this season?
'We're taking it one game at a time' = We can't wait to get all this league shit out of the way and play the cup match
'This is off the record' = Take this down carefully and print it big
'And you can quote me on that' = Unless I deny I said it
'We had full and frank discussions' = I've told him he's a c**t
'You'll have to ask the chairman about this' = It's that c**t's fault
'The fans might not understand this but . . .' = They're going to string me up, aren't they?
'We'll be saying no more about it' = He's never gonna hear the end of this
'I've asked him to stay and fight for his place' = He'll be in the reserves from now 'til doomsday
'He's an invaluable member of our squad' = We want three mill for him
'No, we've made no approach for the player' = We're very interested in him
'We might be interested in him' = He should be signing tomorrow
'We're going to bid for him' = We've no chance of getting him
'Now is not the time to go into that' = Wait until my diary/memoirs come out next month

And those player adjectives in full:

*Yeah, our boy is . . .*
'committed' = a psychopath
'a born leader' = an arrogant loudmouth

'full of flair' = a lazy ponce
'hard-working' = skill-free
'one for the future' = on the transfer list
'always making the right runs into the box' = crap at shooting
'working on his crossing' = never going to be allowed down the left again
'full of jokes and fun' = a complete pain in the arse
'a good trainer' = shit on matchdays
'a keen student of the game' = getting ideas above his station
'one of the lads' = an alcoholic
'a quiet family man' = an unpopular loner
'keen to help the less fortunate' = a serial offender: always on community service
'one who lets his feet do the talking' = one who can't string three words together
'my kind of player' = a fucking creep
'for sale, as soon as we find a mug to buy him' = David May

*(April was spectacularly defying the poet's maxim: if this was cruelty, then whip us harder, master. Qualification for Barcelona and victory over Murdoch – as Andy Walsh remarked, now we were going for the quadruple . . .)*

## Invoice to MUFC from Takeover Facilities Ltd

RE: EXPENSES INCURRED IN HELPING FURTHER BSKYB'S BID FOR MUFC PLC

To: 569 press releases – £5,690
*(It's not our fault no journalist has believed any of them since October)*

To: Dirty-tricks operation against IMUSA personnel – £25,000
*(Total result of six months' surveillance: one officer may have had dodgy League Cup token. Case unproven)*

To: Phone calls to Ms Wendy Deng's bedroom in New York – £975.43
*(Remember: RMs 'not involved', so don't put this through books)*

To: Parliamentary Lobbying – £50,000
*(i.e. Contents of brown paper envelopes for selected MPs)*

To: Big party set-up costs to celebrate OFT approval in October – £10,000
*(Cancelled)*

To: Large office dartboard with pix of Messrs Walsh and Crick affixed – £15
*(For staff motivational purposes)*

To: Supply of *Big Boys Monthly* as 'present' to former DTI boss – £700
*(Returned, slightly spoiled)*

To: Knocking up those silly over-complex financial-offer docs – £100,000

To: Our own 1,037 staff hours charged @ £1,000 per hour – £1,037,000

To: Our 'profit-bonus-double-option-reward-extra-treat' – £470,619.57
*(It's the same kind of scheme you like, Mr Edwards)*

**Grand Total: £1,700,000** (rising to £2.23 million by year end)

NOTE TO CLIENT: We have calculated that a 14% rise in the Old Trafford admission charges will precisely cover this invoiced amount without you having to cut dividends.

Yours in sport and exploitation,
Takeover Facilities Ltd

*(Sir Robbie, however, was continuing to exert himself in his one-man mission to keep the Scousers ahead of United in the news . . .)*

## *Daily Spurt News*

FOWLER IN NEW DRUGS SENSATION

In the wake of the amazing revelation that a Berwick Rangers player spent his entire career on hard drugs, Robbie Fowler has stepped forward to stun the public with further admissions. 'I'm afraid it's true,' sobbed Fowler last night. 'I've spent my entire career completely free of all drugs.'

Experts and fans alike are reeling with shock, having long taken it for granted that Fowler was an idiot druggie whose bizarre and pathetic behaviour could be entirely explained by his nasal intake. But Fowler's shameful admission changes all that.

As Liverpool University's Professor Sealing noted, 'This means that Robbie is not a helpless victim but just a fucking twat, pure and simple. Let all Scousers form a lynchmob and kick him to pieces.'

FOWLER ASSAULT: ARRESTS MADE

Two large mustachioed body-builders, lifted in the wake of Robbie Fowler's misfortune in a local hotel, have spoken of the events in the toilet that night. 'It's all a mistake, really,' explained a Mr Bandit from west London. 'This young lad walked in, started talking dirty to us about being Cockney wankers and so forth, then he bent over, rubbed his arse and said "Come on, then, yer all arse, do you want some?" So we gave him several inches' worth – who could resist such tempting behaviour?'

DYKE REVEALS PLANS FOR UNITED

Greg Dyke has unveiled some of his ideas for United should the ex-*TVAM* supremo and chairman of Channel 5 succeed Roland Smith: Keith Fane and Fred the Red to be sacked and replaced by Roland Rat; entire team to sport Schmike-style facial hair; late-night MUTV line-up to include *Night Calls With Dwight, Debbie Does K-Stand, Mega's Compromising Situations*, etc; new shirt logo 'Ha! – Fuck You, Rupe'. IMUSA's concerns have been laid to rest after Dyke promised to appoint new Fan Liaison Officer (Ms M. Messenger).

MUSIC NEWS: THAT ARSENAL SEMI-FINAL SONG SHEET (AMENDED VERSION)

'Que sera sera,
Whatever will be will be,
We're going to Wembley,
(Er, in August, as league runners-up . . .)'

'We'll see you all outside
(That'll be us, legging it to the station)'

'You're gonna get your fuckin' 'eads kicked in
(But not you, Mr Tony sir, nor your 700 mates)'

'Will we do the double double? Will we fuck . . .'

*(Poor Robbie: we at* Red Ish *helpfully knocked this up for him under the assumption he'd probably be needing it further . . .)*

## Anfield Printing Supplies

*(Est. 1972. Specialities forging fake DSS books, bail chits, etc.)*

PREPRINTED APOLOGY PRESS RELEASE FOR R. FOWLER ESQ.
(delete where applicable)

To whom it my concern,

My solicitor/manager/mother and I would like to unreservedly/unequivocally/tearfully apologise for the latest incident/scandal/matter under police consideration.

I now realise that my missing training/taunting opponents/sniffing goal-lines/toilet fight/any other stupid fuck-up has severely damaged the reputation of not only myself but, more importantly, that of the club/my family/Scousers everywhere/the entire British nation.

In future I will try to conduct myself in a manner more befitting my profession/club/proud Liverpudlian heritage.

However, I would like to add that other parties have not helped in this matter by seeming to make things worse than they are, such as the meejah/those southern puffs/racist anti-Scousers/dem Chelsea, like.

So in conclusion I would like to remind you that I have been properly misunderstood/stitched up/scapegoated/picked on by outsiders/persecuted and that underneath all this I remain just a sensitive/lovable/cheeky/mirth-making/salt-of-the-earth Scouse fuckwit.

Thanks, la'.

Luv Robbie
(sniff sniff) (broken nose, right?)

*(And yes, we DID know there was a war going on . . .)*

## Daily Spurt News

REFUGEE CRISIS LATEST

They are everywhere these days, dressed in rags, begging for a bit of money, food, anything; yet so few seem to want to help them.

They are the poorest people in their region, originally from a wretched land that no one ever wants to visit, but their plight brings little pity from their neighbours. Why? Can it be true, as some mutter, that their years of supposed drug-dealing, thievery and general misbehaviour have weighed heavily upon their reputation?

Now, at last, Britain stirs itself to offer these unwanted masses aid, opening up institutions across the nation to give them shelter. 'Yes,' said the governor of HMP Wymot last night, 'we'll open our doors to them. We've done so before and we can do so again.'

The Scousers were reported to be delighted.

WORLD CUP 2006 UPDATE

The Nigerian FA, flush from the 'success' of the World Youth Championships, have unveiled their programme for their 2006 World Cup bid to FIFA.

**2 p.m.** Opening Ceremony
**3 p.m.** Opening match kick-off, sponsored by Shell Oil Exploration (Death Squad division)
**3.15 p.m., 3.30 p.m., 4.20 p.m.** Breaks for power cuts, floods, diarrhoea
**4.50 p.m.** The Paying-Out-of-Bookies'-Bribes ceremony
**6 p.m.** Disorganised display of general civil war and formation looting
**7 p.m.** Execution of the day's crowd arrests
**8 p.m.** Kick-off of Nigeria's first match
(preceded at **7.50 p.m.** by the instruction of the referee by His Excellency General Obungo and ten large men with machine guns)
**8.45 p.m.** Half-time. Exhibition five-a-side – Biafrans vs. some hungry lions
**9.45 p.m.** Full-time. Pitch invasion. Military coup.

FIFA boss Mr Blotto, commenting on the plans, said, 'Fifty grand? That'll do nicely.'

BANKS FIRES BACK AT SOUTH AFRICA
After fresh controversy surrounding new accusations from the SAFA that England's bid is tainted by hooliganism, Tony Banks has responded angrily. 'The scenes at Middlesbrough were nothing to do with hooliganism – it was simply a joyous explosion of emotion from happy supporters, just like at Villa Park.' He went on to suggest that the trouble in Kosovo was 'a bit of boisterousness amongst lads' and that the Holocaust was probably 'just an accident with the gas mark settings'.

*(And so to a triple-edged end-game that would defy description. On the morning of the Championship decider, I wrote this preview for the* Sunday Tribune. *I don't know who had the task of doing the review two weeks later but I pity him, for once again sport would laugh in the face of those of us who attempt to put it into words . . .)*

## 'Barman, Make Mine a . . .'

(From the *Sunday Tribune*)

Beginning this afternoon, Manchester United face three games to win all three top trophies available to an English football team. Has there ever been an eleven-day Red prospect like it? Grasp the enormity of what United are on the brink of achieving: a feat that has only previously been seriously attempted three times in over forty years of competition.

Understandably, it is being said by some that success would confer upon this United team the title of Old Trafford's All-Time Greatest. That would be untrue: the vintages of 1957, 1967 and 1994 all probably still have the edge. But a treble would undoubtedly make these players Red Immortals, names that fans in a hundred years' time will still be able to recite. Furthermore – and do not underestimate the appeal of this in Manchester – we will have achieved something that those Scouse gits never managed during the twenty long and tedious years they bored their way around Europe. In the tribal battles we love to fight, we'd have a double double AND a treble to cite in response to the Kop's taunts about four Euro Cups and eighteen titles. (Yes, even as we hit these heights of international sophistication and historic achievement, we still cannot resist the parochial temptation to rub the neighbours' faces right in it . . .)

But I suspect that a failure to complete the domestic double's portion of the treble would have about as much of a dampening effect on our Barca-bound hordes' sense of euphoric expectation the next morning as it did on Liverpool's twenty-two years ago: next to none. Why?

Ambling lazily down Manchester's Market Street yesterday, I kept hearing one word repeated like a mantra as I eavesdropped on the soundbites of passers-by: 'Barca'. Indeed, since late April, few Red Manc conversations have progressed far without mention of the Catalan city, usually in the context of questions such as 'how we gonna get there?', 'what's the score on tickets?' and 'are we gonna do Bayern, or what?'. (Conventional wisdom, incidentally, suggests the answers are 'we'll walk if necessary', '£300 a pop and rising' and 'only if Butty plays the game of his life'.)

The point of this observation? That, yes, there is an unprecedented treble on for Manchester United but let no one be in any doubt as to which element of that triptych rises effortlessly above the others, at least as far as the Reds in the stands are concerned. Fergie can talk all he likes, as he has done this week, of the league being the pot that matters or that the team will not be playing it cool in the FA Cup final; we merely smirk knowingly and put it down to his dressing-room psychological tactics.

Admittedly, for about twenty-four hours in the aftermath of the semi-final's euphoria, there was much blather in Turin bars about being happy enough with the achievement of reaching the 26 May final, about enjoying the extraordinary party which will take place in the Ramblas that night no matter what the result. But once we'd grown accustomed to the sensation of qualification, resolve hardened – Manchester wants this European Cup. Badly. We've never needed Billy Bremner to tell us you get nowt for coming second.

A thirty-year wait to emulate 1968's heroes has a lot to do with this overwhelming desire; all we twenty- and thirty-somethings are fed up of hearing the old-timers tease us with their extravagantly glorious memories of Bernabeu and Wembley. And there's the almost genetically inherited understanding amongst this generation of supporters of what European competition has contributed to the legendary qualities of United; the list is headed by 1958 and '68 but there's been so much more to it than that. This unyielding hunger for the trophy surely infects the team and its management just as severely – Alex in particular must know that he's never going to step up on to the pantheon alongside Sir Matt unless he gets his hands on that elusive pot. A 'mere' third domestic double will still not be quite enough.

We're also a club in a hurry. This is the last European Cup which will be able to claim any real lineage and pedigree, and even then it's a stretch. From next season, and doubtless increasingly so with every season that passes, the competition will degenerate into a workaday Euro-league, populated by teams finishing third or even fourth in their domestic leagues. Even as things stand now, we do feel slightly queasy that we're in the competition as '98's second-best outfit – much of the satisfaction which would be gained from a league victory today derives from the realisation that our legions would at least enter Barca on the 26th as the current champions of England. Moreover, the threat of takeover continues to swing doomily over Old Trafford; thus here is the chance to win OUR Cup for US, before the team and its triumphs fall into outsiders' hands.

So if the worst were to happen this afternoon or next Saturday, don't expect the shameless Sky TV cameras to find too many Reds crying in the stands. If the oyster hors d'oeuvres are off, we've still got the fillet mignon to come, haven't we? To be consumed with several thousand bottles of San Miguel . . .

*(Well, I got that wrong: make it several million. I'm not going to bore you with yet another futile attempt to sum up the emotions of the Red Planet that night. I do believe some subjects simply cannot be encapsulated in words: the seconds before you touch a new lover for the first time, the harmonies on 'Pet Sounds', the sight of 600 United 'boys' steaming through a cordon . . . and now you can add Solskjaer's Goal. One thing's for sure – it marked Journey's End for thousands of us. And there's no better moment to bring this book to a close. All together now: 'Who put the ball in the Germans' net? . . .')*